REY

BEHIND THE MASK

REY MYSTERIO

BEHIND THE MASK

Rey Mysterio
with Jeremy Roberts

World
Wrestling
Entertainment®
BOOKS

SIMON &
SCHUSTER

London · New York · Sydney · Toronto

A CBS COMPANY

SIMON &
SCHUSTER

London · New York · Sydney · Toronto
A CBS COMPANY

This book is a publication of Simon & Schuster UK Ltd under exclusive license from World Wrestling Entertainment, Inc.

Photos on pages 4, 12, 17, 20, 24, 44, 80, 96–97, 102 Courtesy of Rey Mysterio.
Photos on pages 84, 90–91, 108 Courtesy of *Pro Wrestling Illustrated*.

This Simon & Schuster paperback edition November 2010

Designed by Richard Oriolo

Printed and bound by CPI Group (UK) Ltd, Croydon, CR0 4YY

10   9   8   7   6   5   4   3   2   1

ISBN 978-1-84983-389-9

A CIP catalogue record is available from the British Library

This book is dedicated to my wife, Angie,

my son, Dom, and my princess, Alilis, for their support,

To my parents and all my family members for their love,

And to my uncle Rey Misterio for training the hell out of me.

While I was working on this book,

my uncle suffered an injury that left him paralyzed from the waist down.

My hopes and prayers are that he gets better.

CONTENTS

ABOUT MY NAME

MOST FANS TODAY know me as Rey Mysterio. At different points in my career, however, I have been called Rey Misterio Jr. and Rey Mysterio Jr.

Except where it makes an important distinction, I've used Rey Mysterio throughout this book for simplicity.

One other thing: Because of the mystery of the mask, I have not used the real names of Mexican wrestlers if they have not been publicly unmasked at the time of this writing.

While we're on the subject of names, during its long history, World Wrestling Entertainment, or WWE, has also had several names, most notably World Wrestling Federation. To avoid confusion, I'll generally call it WWE or, for variety when appropriate, the company. While the name and corporate structure may have changed during the period of time I'm writing about, the organization has been essentially the same from the point of view of both the fans and the wrestlers.

Prologue: Creating the Tornado

There's a time in the afternoon before a big wrestling match when the arena starts to empty out. The TV crews have set up their gear. Most of the wrestlers have had a look at the ring, gotten themselves ready for the show, and taken off for a bit of rest or maybe dinner.

That's a time I love. I sit in the seats, maybe near ringside, maybe farther up, and stare at the ropes.

My mind moves down to the ring. I visualize myself moving, flying through the arena. I start on the top rope with a moonsault, then a flip that turns into a spin. The move transforms into something different, something impossible to describe except with my body—something no one, not even I, have seen before.

Visualizing moves is something I've done for years and years, practically since I was alive. Years before I became a professional wrestler, I would sit down in the bleachers in a tiny gym, waiting to take lessons from my uncle. In my mind I was already in the ring. I'd fling myself around, imagining things my body wasn't capable of.

It's still trying to catch up.

After all these years, you'd think I'd have worn out the possibilities. But the opposite is true. I feel as if I have a lot more left to explore. I have a long list of moves I haven't found the right moment to reveal. The partner, the event, the time, have yet to come.

Wrestling is a constant challenge. You push your body every night. It hurts—it hurts beyond words. But the mind wants to soar, and the body must follow.

I love it.

I DON'T REMEMBER
WHOSE WEDDING
THIS IS, BUT DAMN,
I LOOK GOOD.

Beginnings

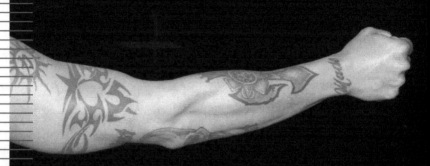

I come from a family of hard workers, Mexicans as far back as I know. Both of my parents were Mexican, but like a lot of others they have held jobs and lived on both sides of the border throughout their lives. My father, Roberto Gutierrez, grew up very poor. He never really went to school—he went to work instead. When he was eight, his job was picking up waste to feed the pigs. He learned things on his own, getting his education in the streets. He found bigger and better jobs and finally got to the point where he ran a factory warehouse for a picture-frame manufacturer. It took years and a lot of effort on his part, getting up before dawn and coming home well after sunset, but he made it work. As kids, we were well cared for. Not rich, but never hungry.

My mother, Maria del Rosario, divided her time between work and raising us. I have three brothers: Rojelio, Roberto Jr., and Luis, all older. She cleaned houses and had other jobs, making money to help support the family.

I was born December 11, 1974, in Chula Vista, at Scripps Memorial Hospital. That happens to be the same hospital where my son and daughter were born. While it's changed a bit over the years, I still felt an attachment when my children were born there. I thought it was pretty fitting that they started life where I started.

Being born in the United States made me a citizen—the first one in the family. Then as now, America represented a better life for the next generation, with the promise of education and freedom.

My parents named me Oscar. That's an unusual name for a Mexican-American, but there's no elaborate history or romance attached to it. The name popped into my father's head one day. He liked it, and that's what he decided to call me.

To be honest, I never asked my mom where that name came from until I started working on this book. It's funny, I guess: No matter how curious you are about most things, there are always a few things that you take for granted.

Soon after I was born, my father's company offered him a job in Tijuana. It was a very good job, but he didn't want to relocate the family. My parents had bought a house in San Diego, and they wanted to make sure we all finished high school there. So my father started commuting every day. Distance wise, Tijuana and San Diego are very close. But the border can add a lot of time to the commute.

It wasn't too bad in the morning: He'd leave San Diego about 5:30, cross the border, and get to work by 6:00 A.M. Coming home was a different story. He'd leave work around 4:00 P.M., but with the traffic he wouldn't get home until 6:30 or so. If he stayed later, he'd be home even later, very often well into the night. He'd get home, and soon have to go to bed so he could get up first thing in the morning.

That was just one of the sacrifices my parents made for us. It's the story of all immigrants: to work hard for the next generation.

Rey Misterio

WRESTLING HAS ALWAYS been a big part of my life. My uncle Miguel—Miguel Ángel López Díaz—was a well-known *luchador*, or wrestler, over the border in Tijuana, wrestling as Rey Misterio. He is my mother's younger brother, and she'd often take me to see his shows. For a while, he worked for a construction company and lived with us in San Diego. He would work during the week, then head down to Tijuana Friday nights to wrestle. I'd tag along, excited by the show and happy to be with my uncle.

My uncle's ring name translates as Mystery King or the King of Mystery. It's a reference to an important ingredient of *lucha libre*, or Mexican-style wrestling. With so many wrestlers using masks, mystery about the sport is a constant.

Unlike me, my uncle is a little taller than the average height for a Mexican, and he wrestled as a heavyweight, his billed weight around 220 pounds. He's a powerful man, and by the early 1980s he was well known in Tijuana and Mexico. He was also developing a reputation as a gifted and exceptional teacher, training a large number of students who would go on to superstar careers in the ring.

All I knew was that he was my favorite uncle, and I loved being around him. He was practically as close to me as my father or mother. He and his wife at the time, Lilia Lopez, used to babysit me. He was still in his twenties, without any children of his own, and he cared for me as if I were his own son. He was living on a ranch, and we'd ride horses together or drive my three-wheeler. That was the kind of family we were—very, very close.

I loved tagging along with him to TJ—what we called Tijuana—when he would teach his wrestling classes. The sessions were held in a gym next to the Tijuana Auditorium. It was there that I first had a chance to go into the ring. I was really little, no more than four or five, maybe even younger. I'd jump and play around, like any kid would do when he sees a ring. I'd imitate what I saw the wrestlers do. I'd hit the ropes, bounce off the second. I would climb the turnbuckle and jump off, land on my feet, and roll.

I remember my uncle standing on the outside of the ring as another wrestler pushed the ropes open. I'd run and dive between the first and second ropes, landing in my uncle's arms. I was sure he'd catch me, and he always did.

Going as a fan to wrestling shows with my mother and grandmother—Leonor Dias—brought me into the life at an early age. I would go into the locker room with my uncle and see all my favorite wrestlers. I'd watch them go over high spots, working different steps and moves, putting two and two together. Of course, at the time I had no clue how hard they were working. It all looked very easy. I'd imitate what they were doing later on and learn almost by chance.

Backstage, I was able to see a lot of my favorite wrestlers without masks, which was a real privilege. To meet someone without their mask is a huge honor, and a sign of respect.

Lucha Libre

IN MEXICO, PROFESSIONAL wrestling is known as *lucha libre*. The words literally mean "free wrestling," and the phrase is sometimes translated as "free-style wrestling." But the real definition of Mexican wrestling goes beyond what the words mean on their own. In fact, words themselves really can't describe it. To understand *lucha libre*, you have to experience it.

Wrestling in Mexico shares a history with wrestling in the United States, and much of what you see in the ring is similar on either side of the border. Even with that in mind, though, wrestling in Mexico tends to be higher flying, with more high spots and more acrobatic action than you see in the typical American ring.

Tag team wrestling, often with three wrestlers on each team, is more popular in Mexico than in the U.S. It's common for matches to be decided by Two-Out-of-Three-Falls rather than simply one as in the U.S. Until recently, there was less emphasis on continuing storylines and more use of comedy in Mexico compared to the U.S.

But the most obvious difference between American wrestling and *lucha libre* is the masks. They're a colorful part of the sport and, as I mentioned, they have almost a religious significance to fans and wrestlers. .

A lot of popular stories about *lucha libre* connect the masks to the ancient Aztec or Mayan cultures, where masks had a religious significance. Wrestling historians point out that the masks' history in Mexican wrestling seems only to date to the 1930s or so. But the idea of the ancient connection is a strong one, and it may be one reason masks are so important.

Not everyone wears a mask. But for those who do, putting it on is like putting on a new identity. The mask is part of who you are in the ring, your real face as a wrestler. You're still you, of course—but you're also different.

Masked wrestlers will go pretty far to avoid being identified and seen without their masks by fans. Mil Máscaras never took off his mask inside the locker room. He even wore it into the showers, choosing to shower in the end stall if he wanted to wash his hair. No one ever saw him unmasked, in the ring or backstage. El Hijo del Santo was the same way, and is to this day.

That's how intense it can be. It's very close to a religion.

I get asked all the time "Rey, do you ever take off your mask?"

Of course I do—but not in the ring; not when I'm performing, doing a show, or meeting people. The mask is part of my respect for the profession and for the people I'm entertaining.

I also had it taken off for a period of time when I was wrestling—but we'll get into that later on.

Good versus Evil

IN *LUCHA LIBRE,* a lot of the matches are seen as contests between good and evil, much more than they are in the United States. Wrestlers are divided into *técnicos* and *rudos*. The word *técnico* is said to come from an older term, *científico,* or "scientist," and it refers to wrestling that is more scientific or technical—in other words, a style that follows the rules and laws of wrestling.

Rudo means "crude" or "rough." A *rudo* is expected to use any method he can to win, and he won't be above breaking the rules to get a pin.

In the U.S., wrestling fans use the terms *babyface* and *heel* to classify wrestlers, and it's usually said that babyfaces are on the side of good and heels are evil. But the distinctions aren't as strong here as they are in Mexico. Here a heel could be very popular and even a borderline babyface, without the sense of being evil. It's usually different in Mexico.

Mexico's greatest *luchador,* El Santo, provided a model for *técnicos* to follow. Born in 1917, Santo, el Enmascarado de Plata (Saint, the Masked Man of Silver), was to Mexican wrestling what Babe Ruth was to baseball—if Babe Ruth had also been the leading actor of his time.

Santo wrestled for fifty years, never taking off his mask until only ten days before he died. He'd wrestled for years and starred in dozens of movies, but he always protected his identity.

In his movies, Santo battled countless evil creatures: vampires, mummies, and all kinds of monsters. The dark side. He had the same identity in the ring: a good guy who fought evil. Everyone who has followed has had to pay at least some respect to that model.

I think the personalities of *técnico* and *rudo* can reflect who people are in real life. I don't mean that *rudos* are bad people, or that a *técnico* is a perfect human being who never does any wrong. It's more subtle than that. If you're the aggressive type and you get your switch triggered easily, you may favor the *rudos*. In my case, I was always very humble, very spiritual, I loved to be on the good side. I loved the sport and leaned toward being a *técnico*.

Sometimes I wonder how my life would have been if I'd grown up on the other side—always getting into fights in school, eventually becoming a wrestler, but going toward the dark side.

I thought about that when we were doing the Filthy Animals. But I'm getting ahead of myself.

My (Brief) Career as a Truant

ON THE WHOLE, I was a good student in elementary school. I didn't give the teachers any problems. I liked doing my homework and I got along with most of my teachers. My dad and my mom came from very poor backgrounds, and both had very minimal educations. They're both pretty smart, my father especially (he's smarter than most college professors). But that upbringing really showed them the value of school.

Probably because of that, they wouldn't let my brothers and me take education for granted. They were always pushing us to study. Always. School and homework always came first. Later on, when I started going to wrestling school, all of my homework had to be finished or there was no wrestling that night. I had to keep my grades up or I'd be out.

I don't want to give you the wrong idea. I wasn't a truant, but I

ON MY
GRANDFATHER'S
RANCH. WE
CALLED HIM PAPA
BENNY. THE GOAT
WAS CHIVITO.

wasn't a star pupil or goody-two-shoes either. I was something of a class clown, and I could get into a little trouble that way. I tried to pick my moments as best I could, but this wasn't always possible.

I did have a *brief* career as a truant in fourth grade, but it ended poorly.

I used to love long hair, which was the style back then. Mine was long and straight, and for some reason I thought it would look better if it was a little wavy. So I begged my mom to let me get a perm.

"You're not going to like it," she told me.

"I will. I do. Please, please, please."

You know how kids are. I wore her down eventually.

I got the perm on a Sunday. I remember it clearly. When I rinsed off—I remember washing my hair two or three times—the curls were like jheri curls. They were circles, not waves.

I wasn't too sure of the look Sunday. By Monday, I was positive that I didn't like it.

I went to school on Monday, and it didn't take five seconds before they were making fun of my hair outside. I was embarrassed. REALLY embarrassed. I wanted to hide, bury my head in the ground.

I didn't even make it to the first class. I ducked out and went straight home.

My mother used to leave for work shortly after I went to school, so the house was empty. I snuck in and watched TV all day.

My mom came home later that afternoon.

"How was school?" she asked.

"Oh, it was great," I told her. "Lots of fun."

She gave me a funny look.

"And what did your friends say about your hair?"

"Oh, they liked it. They liked it a lot. They thought it was cool."

Another funny look.

"Good," she said, and she went off to cook dinner or do something else around the house.

The next day I didn't make it to school at all. I left at the normal time, but up the hill I hopped into a big ditch and hid until my mother left for work. Then I went back and watched some more television. I watched *The Flintstones, I Love Lucy, The Price Is Right* and *The Dick Van Dyke Show*.

It was great.

Around the time school was over, I found a hat and went over to a little 7-Eleven mall area where we used to hang out and play. The life of a truant suddenly seemed very appealing, even if it came with a terrible hairstyle.

I pulled this off for four days. The school probably called my house once or twice to see what was going on, but of course I wasn't about to answer the phone.

Then someone in the school office decided to try my mom at work.

Busted

I WAS WATCHING TV in my room at about 9:30 in the morning when I heard a car pull up in the driveway.

Oh shit.

I turned off the TV and hid under the bed.

The door opened.

"Oscar!" yelled my mother. "I know you're in here. So you better make this easy. Come on out. Come on out!"

The third time she yelled, I figured I better give myself up.

"Why haven't you been going to school?" she demanded when I crawled out.

"Well, I didn't like my hair . . ." I gave her the whole spiel but got very little sympathy.

In fact, I got *no* sympathy.

"I'm going to cut your hair now and take you to school," she said.

And she did. There was no arguing. In minutes my curls were gone, along with the rest of my hair. And it wasn't exactly a SuperCut look either. She just grabbed some clippers and chopped off my head.

I mean, my hair. But it felt like my head.

I was crying, but that didn't get me any sympathy either. We went over to the school. Someone in the office said that maybe I should come back the next day when I calmed down, but my mother wasn't having any of it. Her decision was final.

School was too important to miss—especially for something dumb like curly hair. Or no hair, which was now the case.

So they walked me to class. I sat there with my head down, sure that everyone was staring at me. But then, little by little, the cloud over my head seemed to lift. Things didn't seem as bad as I thought they were, and by the end of the day I'd just about forgotten the whole misadventure. I went home and made up with my mom.

I can laugh about it now—but only because I have destroyed all photographic evidence of how ridiculous I looked.

Learning to Be Tough

BY THE TIME I was eight, I knew I wanted to try wrestling as a career. I managed to convince my uncle and my parents to let me start training. It wasn't really hard: My parents were always cool about letting me do what I wanted, so long as I had school taken care of. And of course my uncle was the one running the [wrestling] school. He loved having me around.

I was the youngest kid in the class by far. The next youngest was sixteen. Everyone knew that the only reason I was there was the pull I had because of my uncle. But the other students were all pretty nice to me. The instructors treated me the same as the other students. My uncle may even have been harder on me. Despite my age, his expectations were high, and I had to work to meet them.

I don't know if they do this in the States, but in Mexico we learned how to chop or slap across the chest very early. It's a pretty basic wrestling skill. My uncle would grab me and show the class how it was done. His hand was twice the size of my chest—it was like a bulldozer taking out a doghouse. There were times when he hit me so hard my chest would start to bleed.

Yes, it really does hurt. It especially did then. In fact, it hurt so badly that a few times tears came to my eyes and I walked out of the ring, ready to quit.

He would ignore me and continue on with the class.

It usually took me about fifteen minutes to realize I really wanted to go back inside and learn. My uncle would ignore me until after the class. Then he'd make me understand, again, that he was treating me just the same as everyone else. Even at eight years old, I learned I had to man up.

Still, it was hard to take at times.

"You know what, this is the way we train," he'd tell me. "If you're going to stick around, you're going to have to take it. There's no backing out. No easy way. If you think I'm hitting you hard, that's the way we hit. Hit me twice as hard."

It was part of my education, learning how to be tough.

The Class

THE GYM WHERE we trained was next to the Tijuana Auditorium, the major arena for professionals in the city. The gym was—let me be kind by calling it old school. With a lot of emphasis on "old."

The ring itself was an old boxing ring that had been adapted for wrestling. The ropes were made out of wire covered with hose. It was hard to get a bounce off them. Some of the corners had the hose torn off, with wire sticking out. They were hard when you hit them. The bottom of the mat was stiff. There was no spring in the center, and the top was torn.

Wrestling rings in Mexico are built a little differently than the ones in the U.S., but this was stiff even for Mexico. It was wood, with maybe two inches of some sort of foam. A leather mat sat on top of the foam. The mat was as rough as an unpolished stone—I think the cow who gave up the hide for it must have been through a war. And the surface was torn and patched. All of this made the ring uncomfortably hard.

And don't let me forget to mention the hole in the roof over the mat. When it rained, water would leak in. We would work around the wet spots—and the buckets that were there to catch the rain.

But here's how hardcore we were: We didn't care. Hard mat, rain puddles—we ignored them as best we could. We just wanted to be in the ring.

The first classes focused on the basics. We would jog around the gym, warming up and building endurance. From there we would do

duck squats—where you squat, grab your ankles, and walk like a duck. There were push-ups, Hindu squats, and sit-ups. No weights, just exercises.

All of that took thirty to forty-five minutes. Then we would get into the ring for another forty-five minutes to an hour. The work varied, but usually we would do tumbling: forward rolls, back rolls. We learned how to take bumps, how to run the ropes. We learned the basics of mat wrestling, how to lock up, how to put on holds, how to get out of holds.

At that point the class separated. Beginners would go by themselves, still working on basic moves. The more advanced people would work together. We'd get individual instruction, slowly learning the profession.

I still remember some of my trainers, including Cavellero 2000, La Gacela, and Super Astro. I still have some of the bruises they inflicted as well.

Good bruises, all good.

Super Astro worked us especially hard. When he was coming, we knew a few of us were going to be on hospital report the next day. He'd start us out with five hundred squats and five hundred pushups, and ramp us up from there. If you survived one of his workouts, you were tough. Of course, he was also one of my favorite superstars growing up, a very innovative and creative wrestler. He was doing an early variation of what I now call the 619. Short like me—maybe even shorter—he was a huge inspiration in my career.

Tijuana

RIGHT AFTER I finished elementary school, we moved to Tijuana. My parents decided to move because of my father's job, which had increased in responsibility—and pay. Even though they moved, I continued going to school in Chula Vista, California, commuting back and forth.

Usually my mom would take me. We would leave our house at 5:30 A.M. If traffic was good, it would take us about fifteen minutes to get across the border, and from there it was just a short drive to school. If traffic was bad, it would take about an hour, and I wouldn't get to school until close to 7:00.

Sometimes, when traffic was really bad, I would get out of the car, cross the border walking on foot, take the trolley up to Iris Avenue, and then from Iris I would either take the bus or walk to school. That was a good four- to five-mile walk.

When you're a kid all those things work out, but now when I think about doing something like that I say no way. I love to walk, but that's pushing it. Especially for school.

I'd get out of class around 2:45. If I was taking a bus home, I would get home around 3:30, and I started my homework on the way home. This was important, because I wasn't allowed to go to wrestling school unless my homework and chores were done.

We all had chores and responsibilities. I was cooking my food, washing my clothes, and cleaning my room by the age of ten. None of us were momma's boys. We were taught how to be men.

Back then my favorite thing to cook was rice and beans—every Mexican has to have his homemade beans. I still like that simple dish. There's nothing like beans and a little rice to fill you up. My real specialty was ramen noodles—add water and you're good to go. It takes skill to boil water. Maybe I'll open a restaurant when I retire.

I wasn't the only kid in the school going back and forth. If you asked any Mexican-American parent at the time where they would want their son or daughter to learn, they'd answer the States immediately. So when work took them back across the border to Mexico, they'd do their best to make sure their kids were still getting a good education, even if that meant a day's worth of commuting back and forth between the two countries.

Besides wrestling, the sport I really loved was football. We'd play during recess. I was usually a receiver. My tricky moves and speed earned me the nickname Weasel from my friends.

I loved to grab the ball in midair and just run, man, just run. I always say that if I hadn't become a wrestler, I would have been the smallest football player ever to make the NFL.

Another sport I loved was surfing. My mom's older brother, Ampelio, used to live near Rosarito Beach, about twenty-five minutes from Tijuana. He was a big surfer, very accomplished. I think I was in high school when I convinced him to take me out and teach me how to use a surfboard. He took me to a spot called K38, showed me the basics, and then got me going.

I wiped out on my first wave.

And my second.

And my third, fourth, fifth . . . I quickly lost count. Somehow I managed to keep enough salt water out of my lungs and belly to still float, and by the end of the day I got the hang of it. I still remember how happy I felt that first time I managed to stand on the surfboard for fifteen seconds—the beginning and ending weren't pretty, but the middle was fantastic.

Come to think of it, the ending was a real smash . . . into the waves, that is.

The Company and Its Stars

ABOUT THE TIME I started high school, my brother Rojelio—we called him Lalo—started managing a pizza restaurant named Godfather's Pizza. My mom began working for him at some point, setting up the salad bar and such, and eventually I got a job there too, working after school and on weekends folding pizza boxes and busing tables.

The thing I remember most about that job was the television in the back room where I took lunch. On Saturdays it would be set to wrestling shows. It was there that I first saw World Wrestling Federation, as WWE was known at the time. If I'm not mistaken, the show was a rebroadcast of *Saturday Night's Main Event*, and it would air somewhere around noon.

WHO KNEW I'D HAVE A HISTORY WITH FOOD AND MY BROTHER? HERE I AM WITH LALO AT AGE 7 EATING A TORTA.

I watched Hogan, Jake "The Snake" Roberts, the Macho Man, Ricky Steamboat, Tito Santana, and a long list of others. A lot of the matches were squash matches—very short, one-sided matches.

I remember watching Jake "The Snake." This was back in the late 1980s, before his recent tribulations. He was a wild guy even then, but in a good way.

The contests didn't stand out as much as the character: *Look at this guy coming out with a snake.*

And it was a real snake. He used it to psych out his opponents, and it was a real mind job. He'd come out to the ring with a python in a canvas bag. He called it Damien.

When Jake finished an opponent, usually with a DDT, he'd let the snake slither over the other victim's body.

Whoa . . .

Jake is generally credited with inventing the DDT, now a mainstay of wrestling. The move starts with a front facelock; the wrestler then falls backward, jamming his opponent's head against the canvas and, if things go well, getting the pin.

CMLL

BESIDES WORLD WRESTLING Federation, I used to watch CMLL—Consejo Mundial de Lucha Libre—all the time. (The name means Worldwide Wrestling Council.) CMLL is Mexico's equivalent of World Wrestling Federation, and back then it featured all the big Mexican stars.

As I grew older, joining CMLL became my goal. I was like, *Man, I want to go there. I want to make it there.*

It never came into my head that I would be able to go to World Wrestling Federation, to make it in America. My sights were set on Mexico City, which was far enough away, and the CMLL. That was the big time as far as I was concerned. It was my dream.

The Best Teachers

WORK, HOMEWORK, CHORES, and wrestling school—that was my life, though not in that order.

I would head to the gym Tuesdays, Wednesdays, and Thursdays. Classes usually ran from about seven to nine. At nine, most of the students would go home. The advanced kids would stay and work with the instructors individually. Naturally, I hung around. It was the best time to learn.

But Thursday nights were even better. With the gym right next to the Tijuana Auditorium, it was natural for the wrestlers who were going to perform there on Friday to come in and work out. They'd come into Tijuana on Thursdays, check out the auditorium, and end up working out in the gym. It was the best time to be there. Sometimes my uncle would send me into the ring with Shamu to show my stuff. Shamu was a great partner, always making me look good.

With luck, I'd get a chance to go into the ring with them. When I did, more often than not they'd teach me a move and even do a few minutes of mat wrestling with me. It was cool.

I can't remember all of the stars I met. Negro Casas was one of them. Leon Chino was another, and so were Caballero 2000, Super Astro, and La Gacela. They were huge Mexican stars, and to this day I think about them and their work—and their kindness toward me. I got a little bit of knowledge from them each night.

Beginnings of Buzz

FEW PEOPLE REALLY knew I was studying to be a wrestler in elementary school and junior high. By the time I got to high school, though, there was a bit of buzz going around that I was training. I liked it.

I remember telling a few of my friends that my uncle was Rey

Misterio and that I wanted to be a wrestler too. The reaction was almost always the same.

"Aw, come on, man, go on."

"No, no, no," I would tell them. "It's true."

"You? Be a wrestler?"

It was hard to believe, not just because wrestlers were famous, but because I was so small. I had to prove myself, even to my friends. Once they saw me working, though, they believed.

Soon after I got to high school, one or two of the school wrestling coaches came to me and asked if I'd sign up for the wrestling team. I really wanted to do it, but between my part-time job at my brother's restaurant, homework, and training, I just didn't have the time. So unlike a lot of kids and many professional wrestlers, I never had a chance to wrestle in high school.

The Hunger Grows

EIGHT YEARS OLD, nine, ten . . . eleven, twelve, thirteen—the years moved on. I trained and learned, I learned and trained. Every year, every month, every day, I got a little better.

I also grew hungrier. Not just to learn more about wrestling, but to get into the ring for real. One by one, other kids I trained with made their debuts as professionals. I wanted to make mine too. It didn't matter that they were older than me. By the time I was fourteen, I'd been training for six years and I felt like a veteran.

I didn't know if I was going to be a professional wrestler. I did know I wanted to be one.

But did I have the courage, the special spunk, the "light" that a wrestler has?

I didn't know. But I *did* know that I couldn't find out until I stepped into the ring in front of a paying crowd.

And I wanted to do that more than anything else in the world.

IN CIUDAD JUÁRES, A TOWN THAT BORDERS EL PASO IN TEXAS, ON MY FIRST TOUR AS COLIBRI. I'M 15 AND I WON THIS TROPHY.

Luchador

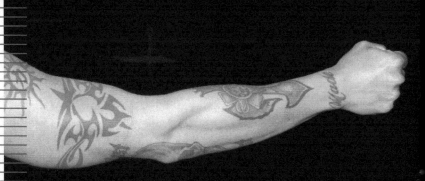

Fourteen is very young to be a professional wrestler.

Too young, in fact: Even at the time, someone who was fourteen needed his parents' permission to wrestle.

I was small—very, very small, even for a fourteen-year-old. I barely weighed a hundred pounds and stood under five feet tall. Even with my parents' permission, finding a promoter who would put me in his show wasn't going to be easy.

I remember going to my uncle when I was fourteen and telling him I wanted to get into the ring.

"Come on," I told him. "I've been training for, like, six years. I want to wrestle now, man. I want to wrestle. I'm tired of training—not of learning, but of being in the gym and not being able to wrestle. I want to wrestle in front of a crowd."

We had a really long conversation. He thought that I was ready, technically, but physically I had a long way to go.

He had a point. There was no way I looked like a wrestler. Looking back, I remember that when he would present me to other wrestlers at that age, they would say, "Get a few more pounds on him, and he'll be good to go."

But that was *not* what I wanted to hear. That was like telling me to wait forever, and I didn't want to wait, not even for ten minutes. I knew in my heart that I was ready. Maybe not to be a star—that would come later—but definitely to get into the ring and perform before a paying audience.

In wrestling, as in anything, you have to push yourself to move ahead. You have to strive for the next level, and getting into the ring was the next level. I was sure that if I really wanted to get better—and I did, I really did—then I had to get into the ring.

Even if no one else thought I was big enough.

Size Mattered . . . to Others

MY SIZE HAS always been a downfall. It's made me have to prove myself again and again.

At that point, I'd grown to about five foot. Maybe. I was very skinny. I weighed one hundred pounds. That's very small.

But you have to remember, I'd been wrestling with much larger people since I was eight years old. I'm talking about kids who were sixty pounds heavier than me at first, then anywhere from one hundred to nearly two hundred pounds heavier. I'd lived with the size difference my whole life. It was natural to me.

I guess that's why it isn't that hard for me to face big guys in the ring today. I take the size difference for granted. It limits what I can do against them. But it doesn't mean I can't beat them. Again and again I've gone into a match with a big man and managed to find a way to come out on top. Speed and technique can overcome a lot.

More important, I give the fans their money's worth. They can see my heart, even when I'm overmatched. And that's really what wrestling is all about.

Back then, though, the world hadn't seen what Rey Mysterio could do. They still knew me as little Oscar.

Even the famous wrestlers who would watch me work out in the ring weren't convinced.

Gaining Weight—or Not

GETTING YOUR BODY to grow taller is impossible, but you can put on weight. A lot of wrestlers have made up for their short size by putting on pounds of muscle. My uncle's friends were convinced that that would work for me as well.

"You gotta get some weight," they'd tell me. "Eat more."

A few used to tell me to drink beer. They seemed convinced it had some magic ingredients that would fill me out.

"I'm fourteen. I can't drink beer," I'd say.

"Come on, drink some beer."

I actually tried a few times. It didn't help.

People were *always* giving me advice about gaining weight. "Eat this, eat that," they'd say. They would give me recipes left and right.

I remember during one breakfast, I saw Leon Chino eat twelve egg whites and rice—then he said I should do the same.

Twelve egg whites?

No way. Swallow slimy globs of glue that looked like the droppings of the alien monster in *Ghostbusters*? I'd rather drink salad dressing. Besides, twelve egg whites weighed more that I did at the time.

Then Leon told me about drinking beer.

"Beer has something in it that will make you gain weight," he'd said. "You should try some. Go ahead. Come on."

"No, no."

"It has something good in it for gaining weight."

Yes, carbohydrates. That's the magic.

"Drink a beer in the morning," he advised. "One for breakfast. Then one for lunch. Then one for dinner."

Chino had really sculpted muscles, but as far as I know, modern science has not advocated the beer diet as a means for bodybuilding. Maybe it makes the training go easier; I don't know.

But seriously, my weight was always a problem. Combined with my height, it made me look too small and too young to be taken seriously.

Even the great Negro Casas told me I was too skinny.

Most of these guys didn't realize how young I was, or that my genes were just to be a small guy. There really wasn't much I was going to be able to do about it.

The Test

I KEPT PUSHING my uncle. Finally, in 1991, he said that I could take the licensing test and see how I did.

To wrestle in Mexico, you need to be licensed by a special commission that oversees the sport. It was like going through a driver's test to get your license, only harder. It lasted four or five hours, and covered basic wrestling skills and conditioning.

The judges were old-school professional wrestlers. Each tested and passed you in a different section. The first was conditioning: You had to do a certain amount of jogging, squats, Hindu squats, and other exercises. The second part consisted of taking bumps on the mat: tumbling, forward rolls, backward rolls, all that stuff.

Part three had you run the ropes and do high spots. They weren't looking for real high-flying maneuvers, just your basic wrestling moves: headlock, tackle, dropdown, hip toss, leapfrog.

Then all the judges got together and watched you for the final part: an actual match.

I passed the first three parts with flying colors. My match was a little shaky—the judges said I could use a little improvement—but I passed anyway.

Underage

MY AGE MADE passing the license a big deal. It even made the papers.

I was so young that, in order to actually get the license, my parents had to go down to the boxing and wrestling commission and sign a paper saying they would be responsible for me if anything happened in the ring. My mom was a little worried, but she went along with it because she knew how committed I was.

There's one thing about that waiver that I've never understood. Promoters in Mexico don't pay for wrestlers' injuries, no matter how old they are. If you get hurt, you have to suck it up and figure out how to get to the hospital on your own, let alone find a way to pay for your treatment. At least that's the way it was when I wrestled there. So I've never really understood the fuss: My parents were going to take care of me no matter what.

The Green Lizard

FUSS OR NOT, I was officially ready to wrestle. Now all I needed was a mask, an outfit . . . and a name.

Actually, I thought I already had a name: Rey Misterio Jr.

It's a tradition in Mexican wrestling for the son of a wrestler to take a form of his father's name as a show of respect and honor. The most famous instance was Santo's son, El Hijo del Santo, who was a superstar around the time that I was training. Many, many other wrestlers have done the same thing.

Growing up, I'd always assumed that I would be Rey Misterio Jr. My uncle didn't have any children of his own at the time, and there was no one I respected and honored more in the wrestling profession than him. It seemed natural.

So I was shocked when he told me, a few days before the match was lined up, that he had come up with a name and an idea for an outfit: The Green Lizard.

"Get a green outfit and you're set," he told me.

Green Lizard?

No way.

"I don't want to be a lizard," I said. Really, who wants to be a lizard? Lizards are slimy, sneaky—not for me.

"Green Lizard is a good name. I have a mask."

"Give me a better name," I insisted. "I want to be Rey Misterio Jr."

"No, you're not ready," said my uncle.

"Come on, Uncle."

"No, you're not ready for that."

It was an hour-long discussion, but I could have saved my breath. He wouldn't give me the name.

"One day, when I feel like you're ready, we'll go ahead and talk about it," he finally said. "But you're not ready now."

I finally accepted that it was an honor I would have to earn. And so I became The Green Lizard.

"Sure It Fits"

MY OUTFIT WAS made by Bruno Vitorio, an old-school wrestler and a friend of my uncle's. He was also a bit of a character.

Bruno and my uncle were close in the ring, where Vitorio wrestled as The Destroyer. In fact, my uncle had unmasked him in a Mask versus Mask match at one point in their careers.

By the time I met him, Bruno was head of mall security at the Plaza Patria in Tijuana. There were a lot of wrestlers on the security team there, including my uncle. It was a good way for them to earn money, and their size and wrestling skills made them pretty imposing.

The mall was four blocks from my house and my hangout spot on weekends. I would cruise the halls with the wrestlers I knew when they were on duty. I got to meet a lot of girls that they were dating. Most had girlfriends in every store.

I remember one guy. We'd go from store to store, and he'd be getting kisses and presents—shirts, jewelry, whatever—in each place. I was learning young the essence of being a wrestler: how to get stuff for free, and how to have more than one girlfriend.

Bruno made outfits on the side. I don't remember how much my first outfit cost—maybe ten or twelve dollars—but it was definitely yellow and green. And I don't mean subtle yellow and green, like you'd see in camouflage. Neon signs were dimmer than my outfit.

It was also very hard to fit into, even for skinny me. Bruno made the legs too narrow, which is saying quite a lot.

Not that he would admit that he'd made a mistake.

I was in his office when he gave it to me, and I remember trying it on. I struggled and pulled and stretched, hoping to squeeze my legs in. All the time Bruno was saying, "Yeah, yeah, man. It fits you. Come on, slide it in."

"I don't know," I told him, sweating from the effort.

"Come on, try it on."

I pushed some more.

"Hey, Bruno, I don't think—"

"No, no, it fits. Come on, come on."

Bruno was one of the guys I respected and looked up to, so I didn't want to contradict him. But the legs really were too tight.

"Slide them in, slide them in," he insisted.

I kept trying. Somehow I got the costume on.

My mask was something that my uncle had. It was metallic green with a yellow design. I looked like a salamander, and not a very tough one at that, but at least I was ready to get into the ring.

My very first match was in a Tijuana churchyard over in the El Soler section of town. I wrestled El Gatonico, and I *think* we put on a pretty good show for the hundred or so people there—I was so excited I don't remember any of it. My pre-match butterflies were the size of vultures flinging themselves around my stomach, and the match went by faster than the last day of summer vacation. But I was finally a pro.

Colibri

I WRESTLED IN churchyards and carnivals and even ranches for a few weeks, just getting my start. I didn't like the name Green Lizard, and I begged my uncle to help me come up with something new. Finally, he got an idea.

"We're going to call you Colibri. Hummingbird. You're small, you fly around. We're going to give you colors that are very kid-oriented. The blues, yellows, reds—nothing too dark or gray."

We call those "cake colors" in Mexico because they're the pastel colors you might put on a child's birthday cake. As it would turn out, they helped me attract a following among very young fans, who identified with the little guy in the ring.

It may seem like a great plan, but I didn't give that part of it much thought. All I knew was that anything was better than The Green Lizard.

Along with the new name, I needed a new costume. I had the guy who was making the outfits for my uncle, Sergio Jimenez—a great cat who became one of my friends and who used to hang with us when he got off work—make an outfit for me.

With my confidence building, a new name, and a new outfit, I was ready to graduate from the churchyard to the auditorium and a real show. The problem was, I couldn't find a promoter to take a chance on me.

Booked

THE SKINNY-LITTLE-runt syndrome was haunting me again. No one wanted to take a chance on a fourteen-year-old who looked smaller than Tinker Bell. Finally my uncle managed to hook me up with a promoter named Benjamin Mora. My uncle was Mora's biggest star and worked with him in Tijuana a lot. I'm pretty sure Mora agreed to put me on the program only as a favor to my uncle.

Even so, he wasn't easy to convince. He took one look at me and said, basically, *No way, Rey.*

"Fuck, look at him," Mora said. "What if he breaks in two?"

My uncle told him that he would be responsible.

"I don't want any problems," Mora told my uncle.

"What problems?" said my uncle. "There won't be problems."

"No, no, I don't want any problems."

"Come on. Book the kid a show. Trust me."

"No, no, no."

"Come on."

My uncle can be pretty persuasive, and finally the promoter gave in. I was booked for an early, pre-card match at the Tijuana Auditorium.

Bella Lucha

MY OPPONENT WAS Shamu, who would go on to a long career in Mexico. He was bigger than me, though not by all that much. He was chunky, though, and weighed a good deal more than me. He was an excellent mat wrestler. We'd go on to become pretty good friends.

I was very, very nervous. The knots in my stomach got tighter as I walked out of the locker room, dressed as Colibri. Some kids near the runway pressed close to high-five me. I started slapping their hands back. I was acting cool, but my stomach was churning all over the place.

I still have that same feeling before my matches: the same knots and butterflies. Championship belts, respect from the fans, applause from other wrestlers—with everything that I have proven, all that I've achieved, I still feel the nerves in my stomach when I go out there. They're not as intense, certainly, but they're still there.

I feel as if I have to prove myself all over again at every meet. And I wonder if I can.

Once I'm past the curtain, the nerves melt away. And that's what happened that first night. Slapping the kids' hands—a lot of them were taller than I was—untied the knots. The tension slipped away, and by the time I was in the ring, I was thinking, *Come on, come on, bring it on, Shamu!*

And he did. We locked up and did a little mat wrestling, checking each other out, feeling out the crowd. I remember breaking up a couple of times when we got close to the ropes.

That was where my lack of experience first showed itself. The ring size was different from what I was used to in training, and I had a little trouble locating myself in the ring. Now I'm very aware of all the little details like that, but I didn't understand the subtleties then.

Finally, we hit our first high spot. I got a dropkick, and Shamu took a bump to the floor. I raised my hand for a cheer, and wouldn't you know, I got some applause.

Wow, this feels cool, I thought.

Wow!

I remember doing a moonsault from the second rope a little later in the match. I was outside the ring and jumped from the apron to the second rope, then did a moonsault out to the ground. I think that's where I really got the fans' respect. They gave me a little bump there, a little heat. It felt—you can imagine what it felt like.

If I remember correctly, I finished that match with a frankensteiner, a move that has remained one of my favorites throughout my career. Shamu was sitting on the turnbuckle. I jumped up, hooked him, and gave him the frankensteiner. When we came down, I pinned him.

As we were getting out of the ring, a bunch of little kids came up to me yelling, "*Bella lucha, bella lucha!*" Good match.

They high-fived me and I came back into the locker room. I saw my uncle right away, and he said that I had done well. I was more than happy. I felt like I had walked into the biggest toy store in the world and they said pick whatever you want, it's free.

El Hijo del Santo

EL HIJO DEL Santo was wrestling in Tijuana the very first time I wrestled as a pro. And he made my debut even more memorable.

The name El Hijo del Santo means, literally, Son of Santo. But besides being the son of one of the most famous Mexican wrestlers of all time, he's a legend in his own right. At the time I started out, El Hijo del Santo was already one of the most popular wrestlers in

Mexico. He was in his twenties; he's become even more famous, if you can believe it, since then.

I had been training with Negro Casas, one of Santo's chief nemeses at the time. Negro comes from a wrestling family almost as extensive and storied as the Guerrero family. His brother's a wrestler, his father's a wrestler—it's a very big family, very well known in Mexico.

That night, Negro told Santo to come down and watch me. "Come on, come on, we got to go see this kid wrestle."

In those days, there were no monitors in the locker rooms. They couldn't go out into the audience to watch. So they peeked out through a small crack in the locker room door. When I got back, they both congratulated me on my moves. I couldn't believe it.

We laugh about it now. But just imagine—the most famous wrestler in the country was watching my first show. You can't dream of an honor like that, not on your best day.

Five Bucks

I WAS REALLY excited. I thanked Shamu, got my five bucks, and left.

That's what they paid me. Five dollars. I still have it.

I see the promoter, Benjamin Mora, every so often. He'll ask if I want to come around for an autograph signing or some other function.

I kid him.

"Remember when I wanted you to book me the first time and you said no? Now you want me to do an autograph signing?"

"No, no, no," he says. "I was scared that you might get hurt."

"Come on. Admit it. You didn't want me to wrestle for you. You didn't think I was any good."

"No, no, no . . ."

It took another three or four months before I started getting booked on weekend shows, which naturally drew much larger audiences.

Soon I started going to Tecate and Mexicali, cities that weren't that far away, and doing shows there. But my real base was Tijuana, at the Tijuana Auditorium, right next to the gym where I'd trained for so many years.

My matches were the first ones of the evening. They'd usually start around 7:45, a full forty-five minutes before the real card got under way. We used to call them the popcorn matches. I would be wrestling while the fans would be coming into the arena, finding their seats.

With so many distractions in the arena, it was hard to win them over, but slowly they started paying attention. The people who were there early tended to be the hardcore fans, and it was among them that I built my first following. They would see me every week. Maybe there were a hundred, a hundred and fifty people at first. My skills and energy got me over with them.

A buzz started about "this kid who's a high flier." I heard fans tell others, "Hey, you got to check this kid out. But come in early, because he usually goes on *really* early."

It's funny, but they didn't seem to care about how skinny I was. The promoters and many other wrestlers had insisted that people wouldn't take me seriously because I was so small. Yet the hardcore fans were the ones who adopted me first.

Some of my first matches as Colibri saw me wrestling against Caballero de la Muerte (Death Knight) and El Salvaje. I had trained with both of them, and I would go on to wrestle with both for many years in Mexico. Caballero de la Muerte later became better known as Fobia. And El Salvaje transformed into Psicosis, my partner and opponent throughout much of my career. Some other great partners and friends were Kid Norteño, Gatonico, Neon, Thunder Bird, and Estampa De Bruce Lee—my friend Geko.

More and more fans started coming in to check me out. Instead of eight o'clock, they'd come in around seven, get something to drink, sit down. Then I'd come on. They gave me so much energy it was unbelievable.

I think the smart fans knew that I was related to Rey Misterio.

That may have intrigued them, since my uncle was a huge star. At a minimum, it added to the mystery. They probably thought: Let's see if this kid *really* has it. Let's see if he's the future.

It was a challenge I loved.

Inventing Moves

EVEN IN THOSE early days, I was inventing moves. I'd see something and try to do my version of it. I'd add a little twist, something personal, something to make it new in the fans' eyes.

Mexican wrestling was very much different than American wrestling at the time. We were all high fliers. I tried to be the highest. I would do acrobatic dives all over the place: in the ring, onto the floor, even into the audience.

Here size was my advantage. I was barely more than a hundred pounds. I had a guy who weighed twice my size catching me. I wasn't getting hurt—I was landing on a big pillow.

I would do moonsaults from the top rope. I would springboard from the top rope and do flying DDTs. I worked on my own variation, starting with a Tornado DDT from the top rope, springing from the rope into the move.

I would do another variation where, if I was hitting the ropes and the guy bent over for a backdrop, I would bounce off the ropes, jump, hook around, spin into the DDT, and snatch him.

Wham! Very fast, very impressive.

As time went on, I started sitting down and watching tapes of other matches, either in Mexico or Japan, where the high-flying style was very popular. When I saw something I liked, I would take it, squish something into it, and make it my own.

We were hot. Every Friday night, we sold out.

I don't like to brag; I've learned that it's much better to be humble. But as Colibri I was lucky enough to win a *novato*, or rookie of the year award from the Mexican wrestling commission. And the next year I was given a most-improved award.

The awards were special to me then, and still are. I still have the plaques on my wall in my small office at home. I don't think there's a higher honor than being noticed by others in your profession.

Love at First Sight

WRESTLING WAS A big part of my life. But it wasn't the only part.

I was still going to school, of course. High school wasn't as much fun as elementary school, but I wasn't there to have a good time. A few of the teachers were especially tough. I remember I got this one reading teacher who had flunked all three of my brothers. What were the odds that I'd get her too?

Ai!

But I kept at it. My parents were insisting that I get good grades, and I worked hard to keep them up.

I didn't live those wild teenage school years a lot of kids have. I didn't have time. Aside from occasionally skipping a class here and there, I was a pretty steady student and a serious worker at my job. And a dedicated wrestler.

Which left little time for girls.

Too little.

Wrestling school was the one place I spent most of my time. There weren't many girls hanging around wrestling schools in those days, so it wasn't very surprising that I didn't meet many girls. But then the school had to close down for a while.

By coincidence, a new gym had just opened near my house, and my uncle went over and offered to hold wrestling classes there. As soon as he started teaching there, I went over as well, along with the rest of the gang.

One day while I was working out, a girl I knew came in with a friend. The girl I knew was a wrestling fan, and she came over to chat a little. She had the scoop on everything that was going on, so we liked to talk.

Right away, I noticed her friend. It may sound corny, but it was one of those things: We laid eyes on each other, and there was love at first sight. From the moment her friend introduced us, there was something between us. She smiled, and I knew she liked me, and I knew I liked her.

I think it was my hair that attracted her. I had long, blondish hair, and I'm pretty sure that that and my babyface look hooked her. When she was doing cardio and I was in the ring, I would catch her peeking at me from the corner of my eye.

Her name was Angelica Contreras Alcantar. She was my first serious girlfriend.

There were complications. Angelica—or Angie, as I call her sometimes—was a little older than me, already in her last year of high school. And she had a boyfriend.

In fact, the boyfriend was why she was at the gym in the first place. He had just gotten a call to attend a university in Mexico City, so he could study to be a doctor. He was going to be away for almost a year. So to get him off her mind, she'd decided to start working out.

I immediately offered my services to help her train.

She just wanted to do something to take her mind off her boyfriend so she wouldn't be thinking about him that much. She hadn't counted on running into me.

I was in love. She was too—but she didn't know it yet.

A few weeks later, a buddy of mine invited her friend on a date. I tagged along, and so did Angie. We went into a club—I had to sneak in with a fake driver's license—and we started having a good time. After that, we went to a movie, *Turner & Hooch*.

It's a Tom Hanks movie, with a lot of laughs. It's a good movie, but I didn't see much of it. I was looking at Angie. We cuddled a little bit, and then we had our first kiss.

It was good. So good I can still remember it. There's nothing like the first one.

Her BF

SHE WAS VERY honest about having a boyfriend the whole time. I said that wasn't a problem, we were just friends and all.

My heart said something else, but what are you going to do?

There was no denying the attraction between us. It was a very flirtatious friendship. She was still dating a doctor-to-be, but she saw more and more of me. I was her workout buddy. After the sessions, we would walk home—not hard, since her house was literally in front of mine, only a few short steps away.

How had I missed seeing her all these years?

There were a few times when my competition came up from Mexico City. I was usually pretty cool about things, making myself scarce, but when it came time for her high-school graduation party, I insisted on going.

"You don't understand," she said. "My boyfriend is going to be there."

"I don't care. I want to go."

"But—"

"I want to be there. I'll be cool."

"You can't—"

"I won't do anything."

She finally gave in and said okay.

Her family already knew me. Her mom, Maria Contreras Alcantar, was very strict, very hardheaded, very old school. Now that I have kids, I understand exactly what she was thinking, but when you're a kid . . .

Anyway, I went to her graduation party, myself and one of my friends. We chilled. In fact, I was sitting at the table with her mom when she introduced me to her boyfriend.

Hey, hey, nice to meet you.

Yeah, you too.

Cool.

Cool.

Now I can laugh at that situation a little. But that night ended up with me leaving, and I won't say it was the happiest time of my life.

But I didn't give up.

Winning Her Over

WHEN I MET Angie, she wasn't interested in wrestling. Worse, she thought wrestling was beneath her. She was too high end for it.

But wrestling helped me win her over. When she came to her first match—my first match in the ring—she saw that it was a whole different world. She saw how much fun it was, how into it everyone was. She couldn't help herself. She enjoyed it.

Angie was embarrassed walking in. She considered wrestling a lower form of entertainment, beneath her. But as soon as she saw the show, she became a convert.

"I never thought it was like this," she said.

With wrestling on my side, how could I lose? But even though I like to say it was love at first sight, it still had to grow. It took her time to realize we were meant for each other.

I never had any doubts myself.

Finally, there came a time when she had to make a decision.

"What are you going to do?" I asked.

"I'm going to tell him. I love you. I want to be with you. I'm going to tell him."

So she broke the news to the doctor. Fortunately, he seemed to be expecting it, and he took the news pretty well.

Her mom was a different story. She had a very strong reaction. And it wasn't positive. She thought I was still a kid, too young and immature for her daughter. And I guess that most parents would welcome a doctor into the family.

I wasn't making much money: I don't know, maybe ten, fifteen dollars a show, and that was once a week. Compare that to a doctor's pay. At the time, no one knew I was going to be famous, not even me.

It took time to win Angie's mother over.

Mrs. Alcantar was a strong woman, strict when she had to be, and very careful of her children. Her husband had died when Angie was only six. A trainer, he was warming up a racehorse around the track one night when the animal's leg broke. The poor man flew into a post at the track. His helmet cracked and the horse tumbled onto him, killing him.

Angie was the oldest child, with a younger brother and sister. Unfortunately, her brother—Adalderto, or Teto, as we called him— passed away in a car accident years later, when he was eighteen; I loved him as my own brother and I have a tattoo in his honor as a way of remembering him.

Mrs. Alcantar wasn't just strong; she was very intimidating, at least to me. I felt like I had to bow down just to talk to her. And once she heard that we were dating, her attitude became a lot harder.

A lot harder.

But as a wrestler, that's something you have to expect.

AS COLIBRI
IN 1992.

Rey Misterio Jr.

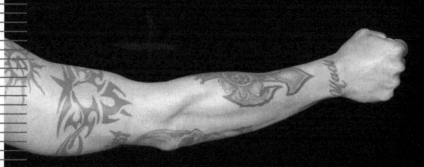

After my debut and early success as Colibri, I sort of forgot about becoming Rey Misterio Jr. I didn't *totally* forget, but I pushed the idea to the back of my mind. It became a distant hope, something I'd earn in a few years maybe.

I had a lot of other things to think about. My wrestling was improving rapidly. Within ten months of my debut, I graduated from the popcorn matches to the regular card. I wrestled in the opening match for six or eight months. Then, with less than two years under my belt, I was promoted to the second match.

In today's WWE, your position on the card isn't very important. You can be a Superstar and still appear in the night's first match. But in Mexico, the order you appeared in was very, very important, especially in those days. You worked your way up the card, earning every rise. Progress tended to be very slow. Where you appeared reflected where you were in the company: how much money the promoters thought you could earn for them, and how much prestige and pull you had with the owners. So moving up to the second match was quite an achievement.

A Special Night

ONE NIGHT I tagged with Thunderbird against Shamu & Gatonico. We walked out from the locker room, ready to go. Our music blared and we ran to the ring, jumping into our corner.

Then the music changed. The announcer took the microphone.

"We have a very special night here," he told the audience. "You are all going to be witnesses."

I was wondering what the hell was going on. The next thing I know, my uncle walked out, stepped into the ring, and grabbed the mike.

I still had no idea what he was doing.

"You know, Hummingbird has been wrestling for quite a while now," he said. "He is my nephew. From tonight on, Hummingbird will be Rey Misterio Jr."

It was a huge surprise. My uncle brought out a mask he had designed for me. He took off the Hummingbird mask and slipped on the new one—keeping my face hidden, of course.

It was a very emotional moment for me. Tears came down my eyes.

From that moment on, Rey Misterio Jr. kicked ass.

The Clique

I WAS PART of a group of young wrestlers who had all trained or worked with my uncle and were on their way up. We'd known each other for years, most of us. We wrestled together; we hung out together. We would train at the gym and finish around ten o'clock at night. There was a liquor store across the street and we would hang out there, eating Twinkies and drinking sodas.

And sometimes a sangria.

We'd just kick back and shoot the shit for a minute, then part ways. It was a tight little wrestling clique. Shamu—we called him Chon—was part of it, and so was Sergio, the mask maker. There were others—Felipe, Keko, my uncle sometimes, all friends whose happy faces I still dream of.

And there was Psicosis.

Psicosis

AT THE TIME, Psicosis was wrestling as El Salvaje, The Savage. Eighteen or nineteen years old, he had known me for several years. We'd met at the gym and instantly liked each other, training and hanging out together. He was taller than I was, so when we paired up he would base me.

When I use the word "base," I mean more than just catching me when I perform a jump, though obviously that's pretty important. My high-flying style puts a lot of stress not just on me but on the wrestlers I work with. They have to position themselves just right to receive my move. They have to first break my fall, then fall themselves. And they have to look good doing it. They can't just catch me or, worse, hit the canvas as I come down.

Even in the most basic wrestling moves, both wrestlers move

together and depend on each other. A vertical suplex, for example, relies on the victim subtly and artfully participating, adding just enough lift to amplify the attacker's strength without making the move seem artificial. The attacker must carefully guide the fall and prevent injury. In my moves, involving more energy and complex body movements than most standard moves, cooperation and coordination is even more important. And since many moves are unique, the wrestler basing me has to be fairly creative and adaptable.

Psicosis was extremely inventive, and he helped me come up with some cool moves. Every time we partnered it was high spot time.

I think the fact that we both had such a strong desire to become professional wrestlers and were at roughly the same level skill-wise when we first met helped both of us get better. We clicked right away and built a bond that I haven't felt with very many other wrestlers.

Psicosis—he still wears his mask in Mexico—stands about six feet tall. Today he weighs in at a little under two hundred pounds; he may have been a bit lighter back then, but he has always been extremely strong.

His strength added to what we could do. He would carry me like he was carrying a kid. It was almost like wrestling with your brother: I was his little brother, he was my big brother.

I think of that sometimes now when I wrestle with my children. I can pick them up and throw them around—that's how it was with me and Psicosis. My size against his size was a big entertainment factor. And he protected me every night I stepped into the ring.

A lot of wrestling fans don't understand that, no matter the outcome of the match, you have to completely trust the person you're working with. That's especially true when you use a high-flying style. A lot of people see my style and they praise me. What they don't realize is that the person I'm wrestling deserves just as much praise. He has to protect me one hundred percent. My opponent has to throw his body in front so I can throw my body against his. If he's not there, splat.

And worse.

If Psicosis hadn't been such a good wrestler, I would have had so many broken bones. And I could say the same for most of the men I've gone against. The injuries I've had over the years are minor compared to what could have happened.

Meeting Eddie

SOON AFTER I began wrestling as Colibri, I went on my first road trip. It was the first time I was away from home. I traveled with my uncle to do some shows in Ciudad Juárez, which is just across the border from El Paso, Texas.

The trip itself was very cool. It was the first time I saw what the road brings to you.

I say that because it does bring something to you. It's excitement, and something more—especially at that age, when everything is new, and everything is an adventure. The road opens your eyes and stretches you.

You don't know what to expect from the locker room, let alone from the different cities and the people you meet. Broadening your experience makes you a better person.

What this trip brought me was extraordinary. I met Eddie Guerrero.

Thinking back, I realize it may not have been the first time I saw him. He'd begun his career several years before, and it's hard to believe he wouldn't have wrestled in Tijuana by then. If he did, I almost certainly would have seen him, if not met him, at least to say hello.

But this is the trip that I remember shaking his hand for the first time. We were in the hotel. My uncle saw him and introduced us.

The Guerrero family is famous in Mexico as well as in America. Eddie's father, Gory—his full name is Salvador Guerrero Quesada— was an NWA and Mexican champ and wrestled with El Santo as part of La Pareja Atómica, The Atomic Pair, one of the most storied tag teams in all history. He was also a successful trainer and promoter. Besides Eddie, his sons Chavo Guerrero Sr., Mando, and Hector are also famous wrestlers.

Eddie would have been eighteen or so at the time. He wrestled the night I was there and really made an impression on me. From that point on, I made it a point to pay attention to his matches.

Sneaking into Bars

MY WRESTLING CAREER was really picking up. While Tijuana was my base, I would also go to Tecate, Mexicali, and to bars in Los Angeles, East L.A., and San Bernardino.

Wrestling in the bars was another new experience for me. I was only fifteen or so when I started—which is not only young but underage. I couldn't order a drink inside. In fact, the only way I could get in was to sneak in wearing my mask and a heavy coat. Otherwise the bouncers wouldn't have let me past the door.

I'd sneak in with the other wrestlers, as bulked up as possible with my heavy clothes. No matter what happened inside, I would not take my mask off. That was the laugh of the locker room: Hey, this kid's not even old enough to order a beer, and he's wrestling here.

I didn't mind the kidding. They were right, and I was having the time of my life. I remember wrestling Mando Guerrero, who at the time may have been close to twice my age. It was a great match. I just thought I was in the shit.

Konnan

I MET SO many other wrestlers during those years that I can't possibly talk about them all, even briefly. But one deserves his own page in this book.

Or a book of his own, now that I think of it.

His name is Charles Carlos Santiago Ashenoff.

You know him as Konnan.

Konnan is often called the Hulk Hogan of *lucha libre*. It's a good description. He is a huge star in Mexico, not just inside the ring but outside as well, appearing in many TV shows and even winning fans with his rap music. No accounting for taste—but they're Konnan fans, after all. Seriously, he was a major star with WCW during the 1990s, when the promotion was at the top of the ratings. He also starred with ECW and later with TNA, or Total Nonstop Action Wrestling.

What a lot of American fans don't realize is that Konnan has had a long career behind the scenes as well. He's been an important promoter and an influential booker or creative talent, one of the most important in recent Mexican history.

Konnan and I have a long history together. We met at the gym when he was first starting to train with my uncle, soon after he got out of the navy.

He was a bodybuilder, a big, jacked-up freak. He was a very big dude.

He lived in San Diego, and he came across specially to train with my uncle. My uncle started training him personally. He could see that Konnan had the look to go to the top of the profession.

I think I may have been eleven when I first met him. By the time I started wrestling in Tijuana, he had been a pro for a couple of years. By then, Konnan had an eye for spotting talent and bringing out the best in other wrestlers. He had a head for the business. Psicosis and I were just two examples of the people he helped.

What did he see in us?

"I loved Rey, because he was really, really short, and really, really skinny," Konnan explained much later. "He had that long hair and he looked good. He didn't weigh much. When I saw his size, I knew he would get sympathy whenever he wrestled against someone bigger. With his ability, and that sympathy, he would be a big favorite with the crowd."

Konnan arranged for us to work in the bars where he was appearing.

Soon after, he went down to Mexico City, to wrestle for CMLL and Arena Mexico. He went right to the top. He blew up big.

But he never forgot where he'd trained, and he didn't forget me. Which turned out to be very fortunate.

The Phone Call

CMLL, CONSEJO MUNDIAL de Lucha Libre, was not only the biggest wrestling promotion in Mexico at the time but, by some accounts, it was the world's oldest. Originally called Empresa Mexicana de la Lucha Libre (EMLL), it was started in 1933 by Salvador Lutteroth Gonzales, often called the father of *lucha libre*. A soldier, revolutionary, and businessman, Salvador Lutteroth was also a successful wrestler and the discoverer of El Santo.

In the early 1990s, CMLL had a weekly wrestling show on Televisa, one of Mexico's major networks and one of the biggest media companies in the world. Based in Mexico City, it had a large stable of superstar wrestlers and a virtual monopoly on big-time Mexican wrestling.

But trouble was brewing. A lot of wrestlers were unhappy with the company over how they were being treated and paid. When Antonio Peña, the owner's right-hand man, decided to break away and start a new company, many of these younger wrestlers agreed to go with him.

The most important was Konnan, who became a kind of alter ego to Peña. It was an important development for Mexican wrestling—and for me.

One day, when I was in my last year of high school, Konnan called and told me that there was a new promotion opening up and that they needed new wrestlers.

"This is your chance," he told me. "You have to come down and start wrestling with the new promotion."

"No, no," I told him. "I can't. I have to work, I have to finish high school. My parents won't just let me take off."

"There's no money in school," he said. "You're going to school and you're not making any money."

"But I have to finish."

"What are you going to do when you get out of school?"

"Wrestle."

"Why wait? Your chance is now."

"But I have to finish," I told him. But he wouldn't let up.

"Okay, Oscar," he said. "You've been training all your life to be a wrestler. What are you going to do? You're going to finish high school and then what? Get a part-time job and then stay in Tijuana? This is your chance. Don't blow it. You don't even like school."

I have to confess that was true. At that point, I no longer liked school very much. And he was right about my goal being wrestling. It was my whole world.

"Here's your chance," Konnan told me. "Do you want to take it? Or do you want to let the ball drop?"

I was torn. But his confidence in me was overwhelming. He was a big star and he thought I had what it took to succeed.

The decision wasn't entirely mine to make, since I was underage and still lived at home. And with the value my parents placed on education, I knew that getting their approval wouldn't be easy.

Konnan came up to Tijuana and talked to my parents with me. My mom was harder to convince than my dad. I think my father saw the logic, and he knew that my heart was set on taking this chance. But my mother believed I was too young to leave home. The new wrestling promotion was in Mexico City, far away from Tijuana. I'd be on my own there.

On the other hand, she had grown up with the sport herself and knew how important it was to me. So I think she wanted to give in, even as the mothering side of her came out.

"They knew you wanted to be a wrestler," Konnan told me recently, remembering back. "I assured them that I would take care of you. I think that did it."

And he did take care of me. He was like a big brother—then and ever since.

I have to confess that I don't think I would let my son leave at seventeen and go to another city and start living there, with nothing secure, no job, no money. It was an awfully big risk. But Konnan convinced them. My parents finally agreed to let me try it for a year.

That year would stretch into four—and beyond. But we didn't know it then.

AAA

THE NEW PROMOTION was called Asistencia Asesoría y Administración—Assistance, Consulting and Administration—or AAA, usually pronounced "Triple-A." It was a fresh company, devoted to new ideas in wrestling. Besides Konnan, many of the top stars left CMLL for AAA: Perro Aguayo, Octagon, Fuerza Guerrera were among them. Their defection hurt CMLL for many years.

CMLL had a reputation for being very conservative in its approach to wrestling. Antonio Peña, who'd been the booker or head writer at CMLL, had a very different vision. He wanted livelier wrestling, and he was more apt to break the old rules about what could be done in and outside the ring.

Looking back, I think he may have gotten a lot of it from watching World Wrestling Federation, World Championship Wrestling, and other American wrestling shows at the time. And, in my opinion, he was especially influenced by what Vince McMahon had done over the years. Remember, this was the period when wrestling was booming. With the help of Hulk Hogan, Vince had taken wrestling to an entirely new level.

Konnan worked very closely with Peña as they sketched out the direction of the new company. They both believed that pushing younger and smaller wrestlers would give the company and wrestling in general a new energy. Until that time, heavyweights tended to be favored no matter what, with little attention going to the others on the card. Konnan and Peña believed that audiences would love the excitement that others could bring to the sport.

I was very excited, and a little nervous about my chance. I had no promises from Peña, just Konnan's word that he would get me a shot.

My biggest risk wasn't with school or my career in Tijuana; it was with my girl. By that time, Angie and I had a very strong relationship. We'd been dating for almost two years.

That part was good. But I remembered how I won her.

"You'd better not pull the same stuff you did with your first boyfriend," I told her.

I said it in a joking way, but I was scared of losing her. I was big-time in love with her. Our relationship was so strong that I would even leave wrestling school at times to hang out with her, so that shows how much I really loved her.

She promised she'd be faithful. And Angie also urged me to go. She knew how much it meant to me, and she had a lot of faith that I was going to do well.

Our Little Gang

I HAD A few hundred dollars saved up, and my parents helped out a little, staking me with money for a few weeks. I took off with a group of friends, all guys I'd known and wrestled with for a while: Psicosis, Damián 666, Halloween, Thunderbird, and Vengador. I was the youngest cat in the group.

Damián 666 (Leonardo Carrera) and Vengador were the two veterans in the group. Both of them had been wrestling for longer than the rest of us. But even for them, it was a gamble.

We flew to Mexico City and found an inexpensive hotel to stay at, sharing rooms. From what Konnan had said, we thought the new promotion would be starting up any day, but we quickly learned there were problems. AAA was supposed to have its own television show on Televisa, which was also airing CMLL. Apparently this caused some trouble behind the scenes: The network wanted to continue airing both, and the negotiations to do so were delicate.

The television station was thinking: How do we not burn any bridges with CMLL by having their right-hand man leave, take all their superstars, and open up a competing promotion? How does that happen and not piss CMLL off? We see Peña's vision and we like it. It's going to be better than CMLL, but we want to keep CMLL happy.

Working that out caused quite a bit of delay.

So we hung around, waiting for things to happen. Konnan said, "Be patient," but it was hard. Fortunately, we were able to work out for free at a gym with a wrestling ring. It was owned by a wrestler named El Magnate, who was also joining the new promotion. He was a pretty good man who helped us out in a lot of ways.

As the weeks started to go by, we wondered if things would really happen. My uncle came down, but as the delays mounted he decided to go back to Tijuana. He had a lot of commitments there, and his own career and shows to worry about.

Money started to get tight. We would eat at little restaurants, conserving our money. We might spend as little as two or three dollars a meal for several people. But finally our cash was gone. El Magnate offered to let us stay in the gym. It was just a couple of mats on the floor, but it helped us make it through the night. He let a couple of other wrestlers in too, and his place became a hub for wrestlers waiting to join AAA.

I think the hardest times were on Sundays, when the gym was closed. The streets were empty and it seemed as if everybody was with their family. I would walk out to a pay phone and call home, then call Angie. There were days when I would just break down. I didn't have money to eat. I didn't have a real place to stay. I was far from home. I got a sense of reality, of what it feels like to be away from your loved ones. As important as wrestling was to me, I thought about quitting more than once.

Definitely.

I was ready to give up. Not on wrestling, just on the hope that this was going to start. But Angie was a big inspiration.

"You already went down there," she'd tell me. "You have to stay. Wait. Wait until they say no, that it's not going to happen. Don't turn back around now."

Besides the pep talks, she sent me some money, which helped keep me and my friends going.

My oldest brother, Lalo, was like that too, though he took a harder line.

"You know what?" he'd tell me. "Suck it up. You'll make it."

Our Little War

IT GOT TO be like a war, our own little war. During the week, we would forget our money troubles. We'd be so busy training, working out, lifting weights, running around learning about the city, that we didn't have time to wonder if the promotion was going to happen.

We stuck together every day, me and my boys. There was nothing we didn't do that we didn't do as a group. If we had three dollars and there were six of us, we figured out how to make that three dollars feed us all. If there was not enough food for all of us, none of us ate.

We got acquainted with tuna. It was the cheapest thing we could find. I can't tell you how many tunafish sandwiches I ate. In the gym, we'd open up a bunch of tuna cans, mix it with loads of mayonnaise, put it on bread—that was our big meal of the day.

Another month went by. Then another. Konnan told us we were getting close.

Finally, AAA was ready.

There were no contracts, no negotiation. Things were a lot different for wrestlers than they are now, especially in Mexico. Wrestling contracts were oral and pretty casual. If you were a superstar, you might be able to say what you wanted per match, and the promotion would say either yes or no. In our case, we weren't in a position to make any demands or even requests. We trusted that Konnan got us the best he could. We were happy just to get a chance.

Almost a Mini

THE QUESTION WAS, what sort of chance was I going to get?

When Peña saw me, he told Konnan I was too small.

I think he may have used the word "tiny." And it wasn't a compliment.

"He's not going to look good with the other wrestlers," he told Konnan.

"Give him a chance," said Konnan. "You haven't seen him perform."

"I don't know," said Peña. "I think we should put him in with the midgets. Or the minis."

"Give him an opportunity. If it doesn't work, then you can shit on me and do what you want."

In Mexico, midget and mini wrestling are much more important than they are here. But once a wrestler is in one of those divisions, it can be extremely difficult if not impossible to "graduate" to the larger weight classes.

I went over and talked to the midget wrestlers, even though I wasn't crazy about the idea. The truth is, they weren't too happy about the idea either, suggesting that I had to take tests and putting up some other barriers. Konnan explained later that he thought they might try to hurt me, just to keep me from taking the spotlight away from them.

Luckily for me, Konnan convinced Peña to give me a shot in the regular divisions. While Peña agreed, he made it clear I'd stay only if I did well in my first match. So everything was hanging on that performance.

It seems to have always gone that way for me, everywhere I've been. The first impression—*before* I wrestle—has always been that I'm too small. I've had to prove myself over and over. And usually I've only had one chance: Either I do well in my first match, or else I'm out.

I was determined. That first match, I was sure I was going to frickin' rock the house.

It Begins

MY FIRST MATCH was in Veracruz.

It was an eight-hour bus ride. The owner of the gym where we'd been staying, El Magnate, and his wife had befriended me by then. He generously offered to let me fly out to the show with him.

"Hey, hey, he wants to adopt you," the boys joked.

I wasn't going to take up the offer, but my friends insisted. The flight would mean I'd be rested for my match.

As soon as I said yes, they dished on me some more. That's the boys.

Traveling with El Magnate was a lot of fun, and a real taste of the kind of treatment stars get. We cruised around the city once we got there, and we even went to a fancy restaurant. It was like being with a rich uncle. It made me a little uncomfortable, but he was trying to pay back some of the kindnesses other people had shown him when he was a young wrestler.

By the time we got to the arena there was a massive crowd outside. I want to say there were eight or nine thousand people there, by far the largest audience I'd ever wrestled in front of.

I was in the second match of the night. My partners were Winners and Super Calo.

"Do a Good Job"

WINNERS (Andrés Alejandro Palomeque González) was a very popular *técnico*, very over with the ladies because of his good looks and style. Later on he became an even more popular *rudo*, working with some of the top talent in Mexico. Super Calo—Rafael García, unmasked finally in 2007 by Super Fly—was another popular *técnico* who later wrestled in WCW. We went against Psicosis, El Picudo, and Magnate. Both El Picudo and Magnate come from famous Mexican wrestling families: El Picudo's father was Espectro I, and Magnate (Erick Francisco Casas Ruiz) was one of the Casas clan, which includes Negro Casas.

I remember it was a Two-Out-of-Three-Falls, which is the normal thing in Mexico. The first match performers came back to the locker room and the place was pumped. My adrenaline was going sideways. We were up next.

Konnan came over and whispered to me, "Do a good job. You got to do a good job in front of the boss."

Not putting any pressure on me at all, right? Keep me nice and relaxed.

The crowd had no idea who the hell I was. I'd only been a local boy in Tijuana. Rey Misterio Jr.? Never heard of him.

But they were about to find out. I went out like they'd been watching me forever, like they knew exactly who I was. I shook hands, I gave high fives; I acted like a top dog.

My confidence level soared once I hit the ring. When the match started, I began to fly. Every high spot I did, the fans came unglued. They loved it.

I spent a lot of time in the ring with Psicosis. We had our chemistry that night. We'd been wrestling together for years, but these fans had never seen us before. And they had never seen half the moves we pulled.

I still remember the move I made at the end of the match, though to be honest I can't remember who I made it against. I know I drop-kicked my opponent. Then I ran almost parallel to the ropes, with the turnbuckle to my left. I jumped to the second rope and did a flip over the top rope to my right-hand side. It's very similar to a move Chris Jericho does these days, where he comes over and gives the guy on the apron a shoulder tap. But as I came over, I did a front flip and landed on the ground. I got the pin and the crowd went crazy.

There was no more talk about putting Rey Misterio Jr. in with the midgets or minis.

Punching

I DON'T WANT to give anyone the impression that I was perfect right from the start, or that I didn't have room to improve. Like every wrestler, especially young ones starting out, I had my strengths and my weaknesses.

One of my weaknesses was punching. My punches didn't look convincing, at least not to Antonio Peña. After a while, he told Konnan about it, and Konnan came to me with an ultimatum: Either I improved my punches, or I was out of the company.

"Peña likes you, bro," I remember him saying. "And the people like you. But you punch like shit."

So I went to work punching walls.

Konnan—who'd been a boxer—showed me how to do it without hurting my knuckles. It took a while, but I got it.

To this day, Konnan's not sure whether Peña really would have sent me back to Tijuana if I didn't learn how to punch. But I certainly believed it at the time, and that extra incentive—do or die—helped step up my game.

Getting Over

WE DROVE HOME on the bus and watched the show when it was televised that Saturday. It turned out that the commentators had put me over *huge*. They called my dive for the pin the "move of the year" and replayed it four or five times. They were going crazy.

"Look at this kid from Tijuana. And this is only his first match on TV!"

They built me up big. They made me look like a million bucks.

It was big praise, but it was also a challenge. I had to live up to the description. I had to make their words mean something. Once again, I promised myself I would work even harder to succeed.

Peña now was on my side. I started getting a good push from the company. I busted out moves that I'd been practicing or thinking about for years and years, waiting for the right time to try. This was the time.

Each week, I got a bigger push.

"Look at this," the commentators would say. "We've never seen this before. Where does this kid come up with this?"

I had always wanted to innovate, and now I saw that I could do it on a huge stage, in a televised match, and people would respond.

At the end of October 1992, I faced Fantasma de la Quebrada in a match that decided the National Welterweight title. Fantasma had just come into the promotion from CMLL and was the heavy favorite to win.

He didn't.

I ended up holding the title for several months. To get a championship at such a young age, wrestling with and against veterans I'd admired for years, was an unbelievable experience. It pushed me to do better, to come up with new ideas and moves every week.

Running Out of Ideas

PEOPLE ASK IF I ever worry about not being able to come up with new moves. Usually I brush off the question: "Oh no, man, something always comes up."

That's true enough, but I should confess that sometimes I do worry about it. *A little*. A few times in the past I got a little lazy and stopped pushing myself as hard as I could. But I've caught myself and gotten back in the right direction.

I have moves that I still haven't had the chance to try. I have a whole list I want to do, but I've held back. Either I'm not working with the right person, or I want to unveil them at a big show. There are many moves fans haven't seen yet. And I'm pretty sure I can keep coming up with things to surprise them.

By Bus

AAA STARTED WITH one TV show every week. Very quickly, the promotion began adding nontelevised or house shows to its weekly schedule. Promoters started calling, asking to arrange shows in their area.

It worked like this: A local promoter would call and ask AAA to bring a show to his city. He'd ask for a few of the top stars. The bookers would set that up, then give them two undercards, say, matches with wrestlers who weren't quite as well known. Me and my boys would then be added, usually as a Tag Team match, along with other up-and-coming wrestlers, to fill out the program.

Soon things were really rolling. People began to know who we were and to ask for us special. Within a few months of starting, we were working anywhere from five to six days a week.

The shows were all over Mexico. The stars usually flew and some guys drove cars, but for me, everything was by bus. Some of the rides were fifteen hours or more. There were times I'd wrestle, then have to run over to the bus station to catch the bus back to Mexico City to make another show.

Most of the time, AAA would arrange for the buses to take the wrestlers and crew to the various shows, so we'd all travel together. The road trips were a lot of fun, rolling parties. We'd meet at the AAA offices, usually early in the morning, though if the ride was going to be more than eight or nine hours—many were—we'd start out the night before the match. We'd go for a few hours, stop somewhere to get our grub, then continue on. We'd watch movies and wrestling tapes. Going home, we'd take beers and party a bit. The atmosphere was loose and fun.

One time we were traveling—I forget where we were going—but I remember that "Love Machine" Art Barr was on the bus, along with the rest of the crew and the *edecanes*—the ring girls. The girls were an important part of the show in AAA, escorting wrestlers to the ring as well as working the crowd.

This was back when chewing tobacco was considered pretty cool. Anyway, we made a pit stop in Puebla to get something to eat. Love Machine had a big lump of chew in his mouth and he had to spit it out somewhere. So he spit into a soda can.

Somehow the can ended up in a ring girl's seat. We went out to eat and forgot all about it. She got back on the bus, thought it was her cola . . .

Half a gulp later, she ran down the aisle, straight out the door, and threw up. I've never seen anyone throw up that badly. It was nasty. We were lucky she made it off the bus in time, or the ride would have been hell.

Love Machine had come over from CMLL and teamed with Eddie Guerrero as members of Konnan's stable of *rudos*. Along with Madonna's Boyfriend, they were known as The Crazy Americans, Los Gringos Locos. Love Machine was one of those guys you could see the tobacco bursting out of his cheek. (Love Machine passed away in 1994. God rest his soul. Madonna's Boyfriend was Louis Mucciolo, who later wrestled as Louie Spicolli and Rad Radford; he passed away in 1998.)

Nonstop Wrestling

WITHIN MONTHS, I was wrestling seven to nine times a week. There were Sundays when I would do three shows. I might wrestle at eleven in the morning at Reynosa, for example, then travel a few hours for an afternoon show, then go even farther for a night show.

I mention Reynosa because that arena really stands out. The locker room consisted of a tiny hallway, centered around a toilet—open, so if you had to go, you went in front of everyone. To flush, you filled up a pail and threw it into the toilet.

You'd have all these smells, cigarette smoke, everything around you, while you went over your spots. Then you'd go out and wrestle in an auditorium that was probably no bigger than the gym where I'd first trained. Part of the space didn't have a roof. The house would get hot, and it would heat up to like a hundred and five. The sunlight would hit directly in a corner of the ring, and every time you got slammed into that corner it was like hitting a frying pan.

Oh yes, a lot of the boys would slam you into that corner. On purpose. Count on it.

That's the boys.

The turnbuckles were all torn up, so you had to be careful about the spots you ran. After going so many times you'd be smartened up. You picked your corners and turnbuckles, not wanting to get too cut up.

But that little arena sold out every Sunday we were there. I think instead of going to church, people would go to the wrestling show. Maybe once or twice I saw the local priest in the audience.

As the years went on, some of the attendance started to drop, and there'd be a few shows that didn't sell out. But that run lasted quite a while, and it was a hell of a ride while it lasted.

One of the things that helped me was the variety of the matches and spots. I didn't do the same spots or wrestle the same people in each show. Being young, I was able to get up for each match.

Mask versus Mask

AS I MENTIONED before, the mask has a very special place in *lucha libre*. It becomes part of a wrestler's identity and, by extension, one of the most valuable things he has.

Because of that, losing your mask in a match is a big deal. Wrestlers who are involved in a big feud together will sometimes wager their masks. The loser gets unmasked. It's a symbol of ultimate submission and defeat.

It's also a sign of honor and respect for the profession and tradition: A wrestler who loses his mask in this way is telling the world that he realizes the sport is bigger than he is. A man who lost a Mask versus Mask match and then didn't take off his mask—that would be lower than low.

A Mask versus Mask match can be the highlight of a wrestling year—or a wrestler's career.

I still remember my first Mask versus Mask match. It was against Mr. Condor (Vicente Cruz Hernández) in 1992, and we were at the convention center in Acapulco.

They would hold a festival there every year, and the city would be flooded with people. A lot of American wrestling fans came into the auditorium that night.

I remember Art Barr was my second. He had a mask on, pretending to be my uncle, and they announced him as Rey Misterio. Mr. Condor's second was Blue Panther (Genaro Vásquez Nevares). Blue Panther and Art Barr had a long rivalry in CMLL, but it ended when Blue Panther went over to AAA. What the crowd didn't know was that Art Barr was now in our promotion—and that his rivalry with Blue Panther would flare up again at the end of my match, when Art revealed himself.

But first Condor and I had to get it on. During the match before ours, the second rope broke off the ring, so we had to wrestle with just the two. The unexpected complication spiced things up, but we were still able to hit all of our spots.

Things started a little slow between us, but as the pace picked up, the crowd got more and more into it. I fed off the crowd's energy, and I kept fending off Condor's moves. He was bigger than me, and he used his size to his advantage, but I didn't back down. Gradually the tide turned in my direction. I managed to get him down a couple of times but then got some very slow counts from the referee, which allowed Condor to kick out of two or three sure pins.

I climbed a turnbuckle for a splash but missed him as he rolled away while I was in the air. The match swung back in his direction, and it looked like he was going to take me. I managed to turn the tables, got his shoulders on the mat—then once again lost the pin on a long count.

Another exchange sent him flying out of the ring. I flew out after him, and we ended up rolling in the middle of the event photographers.

And then, back in the ring, just when he thought he had me, I bounced off the ropes into a hurricanrana: I leapt up to his shoulders, wrapped my legs around his neck in a headscissors takedown. As I went down backward, he came after me—and found himself pinned to the canvas, with me holding both of his legs. The slowest count in the world would have taken him out this time.

The crowd roared.

It was an emotional moment—not just for Condor, but for me. I'd seen my uncle take masks in Tijuana, but I'd never won one myself.

I still have that mask in my collection.

Hair versus Mask

I WON ABOUT half a dozen masks in Mexico over the years, but probably my favorite victory came at a Hair versus Mask match the next year—or, rather, three of them.

First, to explain about Hair versus Mask matches:

Losing your mask does not mean that your career is over. Most wrestlers continue wrestling after that happens, and some are even more popular than before. But if you've already given up your mask, what do you have that's valuable enough to wager against a wrestler who still has his?

Your hair.

That's what a Hair versus Mask match is. If the maskless wrestler loses, his head is shaved. There are also Hair versus Hair matches, where both wrestlers put their scalps on the line.

Los Destructores

TONY ARCE, VULCANO, and Rocco Valente were very popular *rudos*. Los Destructores—The Destructors or Destroyers—were billed as brothers, but only Tony Arce and Rocco Valente were actually brothers. They all wore similar costumes and looked alike. And they all had a similar, bruising style. These guys were the stature of, say, Fit Finlay. I was nineteen and skinny. I looked like a kid compared to them and, at least on the street, not much of an opponent.

In 1993, I started a feud with Rocco Valente. He was the youngest member of the group, and our individual matches were part of a larger series of contests that had me partnering with Volador & Misterioso against all three brothers. We were called La Tercia Del Aire, or The Team of the Sky. Later on, I teamed with Heavy Metal & Latin Lover. The series went on for months and is still remembered by Mexican fans.

Los Destructores were rough opponents. They'd come out of CMLL and jumped ship to AAA. They'd been around for some time and were the type of wrestlers who liked to test you in the ring. They would beat the shit out of me every match.

Talk about stiff. I went to bed every night covered with bruises.

At first I came out on the losing end of every encounter. I was doing the job for them, putting them over, and getting the shit kicked out of me in the process. I wondered if I'd pissed someone off or what.

The crowd, though, was getting more and more behind me. They didn't like seeing the little guy getting beat up.

Not that I did.

Rocco and I soon raised the stakes enough for a Mask versus Hair showdown.

I unveiled a new finishing move that Antonio Peña gave me. Peña had wrestled as Espectro and had used a pretty cool finishing move: You grab the guy by the left wrist, rotate his hand, then put him into a stretcher position. When he bends over to grab for his hand, you lock it under your right leg. You pin your leg under his leg, grab the loose arm, and pull it against his body. As he comes down, your left leg goes over his neck. It's a submission move; there's so much pressure around his neck that the other wrestler has to give up.

When I beat Rocco, I took the first clips of hair off his head before the barber went to work. Then the other Destructores came after me and tore my outfit practically off my body in revenge. This was the first time something like that had ever been done. It stoked the crowd and set the stage for our continuing feuds.

They got my tights, but I had his hair. I also had the crowd. The strong reaction from the feud convinced Konnan and Peña to keep things going, and sure enough, I soon found myself wrestling against Tony Arce.

Tony Arce had debuted in the mid-1970s. He stood several inches taller and weighed maybe forty or fifty pounds more than I did. Few people in the crowd thought I was going to win that match.

But I did, once more creating a convincing story in the ring.

We got to number three, same scenario. I got the shit kicked out of me in the buildup to the final showdown.

In the matches that led to the finale, I would take about thirty percent of the contest, doing my high spots, and get slammed around for the rest. That was exactly what Peña and Konnan wanted. I was the underdog, fighting impossible odds to come out on top.

I was also getting bruises on top of bruises, but the crowd loved it. I was their crash-test dummy, getting whipped on and selling, selling, selling.

Finally, Vulcano and I faced each other in a Hair versus Mask match. The fans thought it was impossible that I could win—no one could take three brothers' hair. But once more I won, and after such a brutal beating I had a new standing with the fans.

Jealousy

THE BEATING LOS Destructores gave me wasn't personal. It was just the way they were—stiff. But the way the feud unfolded, there were plenty of chances for jealousy. Misterioso and Volador were both experienced wrestlers, and I wouldn't have been surprised if they felt they ought to have won their matches.

The truth is, though, I never heard a word from any of them. There had to be some jealousy somewhere—I would have been very jealous. It's only human. Especially since Misterioso and Volador were at points in their careers where I think they could have rightly expected the trophies and the push that comes with them.

The way the business was at the time, jealousy was rampant and blatant. But I have to say none of these guys expressed anything, never any animosity or beef; if they had, I surely would have heard it. I think it says a lot about their characters: not just the kind of wrestlers they were, but the kind of men they are.

Just getting those matches meant my star was rising. Winning them—taking all three—meant I was getting the push of a lifetime. AAA was making me a star.

Why did Peña choose me? I don't know. Maybe I was the one getting over the most. Maybe he liked my acrobatic moves. Maybe he saw my potential as a sympathetic underdog. I didn't really think about it at the time. I just did my work.

Hazing

I HAD HEARD of new wrestlers being hazed in CMLL as part of an initiation into the sport. My uncle prepared me for that. Just in case I got into the ring with someone who wanted to shoot on me, he wanted me to be able to defend myself.

I was no fool growing up; if someone picked on me, they got more than they bargained for. I was very quiet, but the quiet guys are the ones you have to watch out for. We're the most dangerous ones. And by the time I went to Mexico, I was fully prepared to defend myself.

But despite the stories about CMLL, I wasn't hazed when I came into AAA. There were no initiations that I saw or heard about, not for anyone. We were all new there, all going through the same struggle and then triumph.

The guys I was wrestling with knew me and were my brothers. Psicosis had my back, and I had his. So nobody really could have screwed with us.

I don't mean to say that there was no jealousy at all in the company, or that we were all perfect teammates. Wrestling is one of those professions where envy and even some hatred are almost expected. Wrestlers start to think, *Why is this guy getting a push and not me?* It's natural. But in our little clique, there was none of that. It was really a special time. We were guys who had shared our last bits of food with each other and went through a war together—we couldn't help but support each other.

Who's Old?

I DID GET taken to school by some of the veterans early in my career at AAA.

I made the mistake of joking about Blue Panther and Fuerza Guerrera, calling them old-timers behind their backs. I meant it as a joke, but you know it got back to them pretty quick. I was going to wrestle them and Juventud one night, and they came over to me, smiling the kind of smiles that tell you to watch out.

One of them laughed.

"So, you think we're old, do you?"

"No, no, no, I didn't mean *old*," I said, realizing immediately that I was in trouble. "Not *old* old."

They weren't about to let me off that easy.

"You think we're old?" said the other.

"No, no, not like this. Not old."

They walked away smiling. I should probably mention that Panther would have been in his thirties and Fuerza the same—not really very old, unless you're still a teenager, as I was.

We went into the ring for a Three-Man Tag Team match. Not being fools, the other babyfaces threw me in first. Blue Panther tagged in. I won't say he beat the shit out of me, but he made me lose my wind within the first minute. He put me into so many holds I didn't know how I was twisted. I ran, he got me, I ran, he got me—*aiyeeguey*.

Then he tagged Fuerza. He had me for a few minutes. When he was done, Panther came back.

It seemed like an entire year passed before I somehow managed to get loose and roll out of the ring.

Escape!

No, not quite. My lesson wasn't over. Blue Panther came out, grabbed me, and threw me back in for more schooling. Twist, run, slam—I learned the ABCs of bruising.

Finally, one of my teammates tagged in to the rescue.

Panther and Fuerza were laughing back in the locker room when I came in following the match.

"You okay?" they asked. They didn't even try hiding their smirks.

"Oh, yeah, yeah, I get the point."

"You think we're old now?"

"No, no, no. I don't think you're old."

They laughed some more and hugged me. That was the last time I called anyone old.

Let me take a minute to give my ultimate respect to both men. To me, Blue Panther was a great base, an excellent wrestler. He knew everything from A to Z, and he was a hell of a technician in the ring. And the same goes for Fuerza, a true superstar in every way. His Fuerza Punt was a classic. Both men taught me a great deal—though usually under easier circumstances.

In with the Superstars

THE FEUD WITH Los Destructores rocketed me up the program, and I started finding myself in the ring with some of AAA's top stars. I think my first main event had me teaming with Octagon and El Hijo del Santo, both legends in *lucha libre*. On the other side were Psicosis, Fuerza Guerrera, and Blue Panther.

It seemed like every time I escalated, Psicosis would be in there, too, making me look good. We were both on the same ladder—everywhere I went he went, and vice versa. We moved up together.

I remember walking down toward the ring and thinking to myself, *Wow, I'm here with El Hijo del Santo, Octagon, Guerrera. I used to watch these guys on TV every week. Things can't get better than this.*

Every time I wrestled with Santo and Octagon, they let me take the spotlight. Here we had two top stars showing their generosity by letting the new kid get his cred with the crowd.

El Hijo del Santo had been watching me since back in Tijuana, when I was in the popcorn matches as the Hummingbird. Now it was four years later, and some of the promise that he spotted back then was blossoming.

"I saw the way you love this business," he told me after the match. "I always hoped you'd get the big break."

He did more than hope: He made it possible for me to go further by allowing me to take the spotlight. A lot of superstars, especially in Mexico, aren't that generous. You do your shit and watch your back. Somebody is always ready to tear you down and take your place.

Nowadays, I'm in the position where I can repay the respect and favor that stars such as El Hijo del Santo did for me. I try to give some of the younger guys a bit of a rub. It's a very good feeling. It's a chance to show my respect for the business and for our traditions.

Guerreras vs. Misterios

SOME OF MY most famous matches in AAA came with Fuerza's son, Juventud Guerrera. Juvy came into the promotion four or five months after we started. Like me, he had started wrestling at a very young age and had done very well both because of his training and his own efforts.

He quickly joined our little group: myself, Heavy Metal, Psicosis, El Picudoo, Winners, and Super Calo.

Whenever we were booked on the same card, the rest of the boys knew that we were going to go out and steal the night. We would go out with a different scenario every week. There'd always be a lot of high spots, with bodies flying around the ring—mine especially.

Besides our tag team matches, Juvy and his father were involved in one of my favorite Mexican feuds. It started out after I had been wrestling Juventud for a few weeks. His dad came in and interfered a few times, costing me a victory. With these interferences adding up, of course I had to find a way to retaliate.

What better way than to get my uncle involved?

My uncle joined us for a few months, and we had a great series of matches, us versus the Guerreras.

The matches brought back my earliest memories in the ring. Once again I was working with my uncle, who had been basing me since I was barely old enough to walk. I remember one move where Juventud would be on the floor. I would hit the ropes, and my uncle would fling me over the top rope. I'd do a crazy dive to the floor, smashing Juvy.

Champs

WE WRESTLED TOGETHER for two or three months, getting booked all over the place. We were Tag Team Champions and popular all over Mexico. There were stories about us in all the magazines.

But eventually my uncle decided to return to Tijuana. He was always the type of wrestler who would go on certain tours, then go home. He had a lot of offers, not just from AAA, but he never really wanted to move away from home. He had the talent. But I think being home and with his family was very important to him. And then again, he was very successful at home. He could make a good amount of money just wrestling in the Tijuana area and traveling every so often. He told me that the money he was going to make in Mexico City he could make in Tijuana and L.A. And he didn't like being tied down to one company, having to live with those kinds of restrictions.

"There's no way I'm going to sacrifice and go wrestle in Mexico," he'd tell me.

It was his decision and I respected it.

Fame

FAME WAS SNEAKING up on me. The TV shows, then the magazine stories, radio interviews—I didn't realize what was happening at first.

And when I did, I have to say that I let it go to my head a little. I got cockier. *Shit, I'm Rey Mysterio*, I thought. I'd drive my jeep in Mexico City and all, thinking, *I'm the shit*.

I didn't disrespect other people, but I wasn't really thinking right. I felt I was entitled to do whatever I wanted and get whatever I wanted. I was conceited, and I acted arrogantly.

It's a little hard to describe because I'm not that kind of person at heart. I was caught up in the excitement.

It didn't last long. Some of the veterans brought it to my attention that my feet were leaving the ground, as they put it. After that, I came back to my senses and acted more humbly, more myself.

But I still had a lot of fun. Back then I didn't have any tattoos, and without my mask I blended in pretty well in Mexico City. I didn't have a wrestling physique that stood out. My identity was kayfabe and I protected my face very well. Most people on the street not only didn't recognize me, they never suspected who I was. I could go wherever I wanted without being mobbed.

Don't get me wrong, I love my fans. But sometimes it's nice to be able to have a quiet meal or just a nice walk around town.

While I'm thinking about those days, I want to thank Octagon and his wife, Ofelia. They owned a condo in Mexico that they rented to Psicosis and me. When money was tight, they let us slide on the rent. We owe them a lot—maybe even a month or two.

Inspiration

I LIKE TO think that my rise helped inspire some of the young guys who joined AAA after me. I think wrestlers coming up saw me in the locker room and thought, *If he can do it, I can too.*

"Wow, he's so small—there's hope for me."

I heard a few digs here and there as time went on. You always hear stuff. But I worked my butt off, and people saw and respected that. I didn't kiss ass. I dedicated my life to the sport.

And hey, the guys who were jealous? Tough shit. That's the way life is.

I think the fact that I had already met a lot of the wrestlers at a very young age really worked in my favor. They had known me when I was eight or ten. They were almost like uncles, rooting for a nephew to do well. And my respect for them came from the heart, and they knew that.

Working with Eddie

AFTER I'D BEEN in AAA for roughly three years, I began wrestling Eddie Guerrero. Now people knew who I was; I had a strong following as a *técnico*. And Eddie was a pretty popular *rudo*.

Some wrestlers thought it was hard to do high spots with Eddie. But with me he was always very cool and easy. He would always make me look good.

We used to say that Mexican wrestlers would "heat each other out." Everybody was a hog spot, trying to make themselves look good without caring about their opponent or the match. But Eddie was an exception. I remember working with him the first time and he made me look like a million bucks. Every time after that, same thing: first time, every time.

We started to create a chemistry from our very first match. He told me he had seen a match where I came down outside the ring and my opponent took a certain bump. He suggested adding the frankensteiner, which took the move to a whole new level.

"Are you sure?" I asked. He was going to really take the brunt of the hit.

"Yeah, yeah. Do it."

So we did. He ended up on the floor, and I did a dive over the top rope, turning it into a front flip. I landed sitting down on Eddie. He caught me, pulled me in, then rotated me so that I could do the frankensteiner. I was light—a buck twenty, buck thirty—but still I was going pretty fast, and he had to muscle me, catch me, and then pull me to the side. It was pretty impressive.

We didn't practice it, we just did it. *Boom, boom, boom*: He caught me, pulled me to the side, I gave him the frankensteiner.

He'd told me that if I saw him coming after me to take off. I thought yeah, sure, he's going to take the bump and he's going to have to recover—*if* he can recover. Well, it turned out he jumped right up, looking really pissed off. I started to run. He chased me into the ring, out of the ring, back into the ring . . . we got a hell of a pop.

Eddie could base me with a couple of things I could never do with anyone else. I remember later on down the road in WCW I did two moves with Eddie that still stand out for me. One of them came at *Halloween Havoc*.

He was in the 619 position, hanging on the ropes. (The 619, where I run and swing around the ropes, catching my opponent in the face with a kick, wasn't actually named that until I reached WWE. But I'd been doing variations of the move for years.) I came up and flung my feet around. He grabbed me by my ankles and pulled me, rotating me into the ring, then brought me over the top rope and took some headshots from that position. I don't know how he pulled that off. We'd never practiced it, we just did it in the ring.

A Backflip DDT

THAT WAS EDDIE. He'd mention an idea backstage and you'd say, "Eddie, are you sure we can do it?"

"Sure, I'll base you for it."

"But—"

"Don't worry. Just do it."

Sure enough, we'd pull it off.

That same night, we did a backflip DDT. We didn't even call it; it just happened out in the ring.

He had me by my hands and I pushed him up with my feet, my back on the mat. As soon as I popped him up, he pulled me up too. I jumped up to the top rope and did a backflip, but he never let go of my left hand. As I was coming down, I overrotated by accident—I think I was supposed to just end with a backflip, but my arms came around his neck and he went with it. It turned into a backflip DDT.

"Sell, sell, sell," he told me.

So we both sold.

The Personality of a
Técnico

I GUESS THAT being a *técnico* really described my personality outside the ring too. I'm easy to get along with. I'm friendly. I don't like to cause any trouble. I have my times where I let loose, and I've had a few moments where I might get away with certain little things here and there, but I love good. I'm against evil. I don't wish any evil or harm to anyone. And I think that's my personality in the ring as well.

I love being the center of attention, which is also a *técnico*'s role. I'm the guy fighting for the force of good. There's even a little spiritual element involved: We are on God's side, protecting people from the devil.

The fans in Mexico really believe in their *técnicos*—and their *rudos*. They are pretty hardcore, I have to say. You go to a wrestling match, and it's like going to a KISS concert: Everyone's decked out like their favorite wrestler, dressed up like them.

In Mexico there's a special corner or spot in the arena for a group that attends every week to root for the *rudos*. They wear black T-shirts with the word *rudos* on them. While they're cheering their favorites, they're also booing the *técnicos*—they boo the fuck out of them. There are no exceptions.

Rey Mysterio? They boo me. Then, now, any time. No matter how

PSICOSIS AND ME IN 1994, WRESTLING FOR AAA.

big I might be around the world, they boo me. They are loyal to their wrestlers. It is very serious business.

I remember there was this fan back in the day. He was the biggest fan in AAA, kind of like the Sign Guy. They called him Guante Negro, the man with the black glove. He would wear a glove similar to what Kane wears, a big motorcycle glove with chopped-off fingers. And he would always sit in the front row.

I spoke to him a few times after the show. Outside of the cameras, he would give me my respect. But during the show, he would boo the hell out of me. I was a *técnico*; he cheered for *rudos*. That was the way it was.

When Worlds Collide

AS AAA BECAME more popular, the company began running shows in L.A. at the Los Angeles Memorial Sports Arena. The first time we did a show there, we sold out. The capacity is almost 17,000, so there were a lot of fans. They'd been watching us for years on local television, so they were really into *lucha libre* and knew who we were. When we came live, they wanted to check us out. It was great. We brought all the top stars to those shows: Eddie, Love Machine, La Parka, Psicosis.

The events were so close to home for me that I could drive up there with my girlfriend. I'd get to spend some time with her before and after the show.

Then in the fall of 1994, AAA came up with a plan to do something even bigger in L.A. They teamed up with WCW to do a Pay-Per-View called *When Worlds Collide*.

The buzz in the locker room was that Eric Bischoff was going to be there. Besides being an onscreen personality, Eric was the executive in charge of WCW for what eventually became Time Warner.

This was just before the start of the Monday Night Wars, where

WCW's *Nitro* and *Raw* competed head-to-head in prime time for television ratings. WCW was making a lot of noise in pro wrestling circles, beginning to challenge WWE for domination. Already the promotion was eyeing the Mexican companies for talent.

A lot of the boys hoped that being seen by Bischoff would lead to their big break. There was tremendous buzz backstage and in the media leading up to the show.

I was in a three-man tag team with Heavy Metal & Latin Lover against Psicosis, Fuerza Guerrera & Madonna's Boyfriend.

I'd been working with some of the heavier guys for a while. La Parka weighed in at well over two hundred pounds, but he was a guy I had really good chemistry with. He'd carry me around the ring and do some crazy shit. It was a little like wrestling against Kane or Big Show.

I remember burning the house down that night. I was a firecracker.

Standing Up to Bullies

BIG MAN-LITTLE man spots played an important role in my early career, just as they do now. They helped get me over with kids, especially. The kids were starting to pay attention to Rey Mysterio. They liked to see the little guy who flew around the ring. It may have been easier for them to imagine being me because I was so much closer to their size. But I also think they saw me as a model for how they could stand up to bullies. I was proof that being small doesn't mean that you're weak.

Not to slight my women fans, who always cheer for me as well. And I love the fact that I have a good fan base with people who have been watching wrestling for a while and appreciate the different moves that I do.

I never set out to win a specific segment of the fans. Even today when I wrestle, I'm not trying to think of how I can attract young fans or old fans, young women or kids. I'm just trying to do the best I can. I'm trying to entertain everyone. I don't stop and think about who the fans might be.

It's quite an honor when someone comes up to me and tells me about their son or daughter who has my posters in their room. And it's also an honor when someone says they've been watching wrestling for twenty or thirty years and have never seen anyone wrestling the way I do. Every compliment is an equal honor, and I enjoy them all. It's overwhelming. To hear people express themselves that way, it's overwhelming.

Rudos Prevail

THE BIG MAN-LITTLE man matchups were a good place to showcase my flying ability. But they also let me introduce a little slapstick and humor into the match.

There was a spot in *When Worlds Collide* when I was in the ring with Madonna's Boyfriend. He was really taking it to me—spinning me around, just going to town. Finally he sat me on the turnbuckle, pressed me, and dropped me behind. I hit the rope and did a baseball slide to tap in Latin Lover.

Latin Lover jumped in and Madonna's Boyfriend started back-pedaling real fast, worried all of a sudden that he had to face a big guy. The crowd loved it. He had just been revealed as a cowardly bully. They started hooting and stomping, and they got going off of that.

The *rudos* won that match, but the reviews were all very positive. Still, the WCW connection didn't play out for us, at least not right away. There were no fat contracts waiting out in the parking lot, no magic calls to make us rich.

But in my case, another American promotion did come calling: ECW. I didn't get rich, but I did move on to a new stage in my career.

Going to Extremes

Today ECW is owned by WWE and is part of the wrestling mainstream. But in the mid-1990s, ECW was a radical newcomer, shaking up the wrestling world with extreme action and some of the most irreverent and controversial storylines ever. It was considered outrageous and provocative—and the company liked it that way.

ECW started as Eastern Championship Wrestling in 1991. By 1994, it had left the

National Wrestling Alliance and changed its name to Extreme Championship Wrestling. It was headed, and eventually owned, by Paul Heyman, known onscreen as Paul E. Dangerously and in the locker room as Paul E.

ECW's wild, anything-goes style energized wrestling. Though the franchise remained small compared to World Wrestling Federation and WCW, it had a fanatic fan base. Conducting shows in a converted warehouse in South Philadelphia, it gained a national reputation as an innovator and rule breaker.

In 1995 Eddie Guerrero and a number of other cruiserweight wrestlers were invited to join ECW by Paul E. They brought a fast-paced, *lucha libre* style to the promotion. Their pure wrestling contrasted with the blood and guts that typically poured into the ring in ECW shows, but the crowd loved it.

Later on that same year, Eddie left for WCW. Paul E. also lost Chris Benoit, Dean Malenko, and Chris Jericho, all wrestlers whose speed and skill had brought the small promotion respect among fans. He decided he had to find some replacements.

I was one of them.

Philadelphia

ONCE AGAIN, KONNAN played a big part in my career. He was doing some shows with Paul E. when the promoter came over and started talking to him about bringing some *luchadores* into ECW. They were very tight at the time. Both of them had great minds for this business. They knew what would work, what crowds wanted to see.

They each have slightly different memories of how the discussion started—both take credit separately for the idea—but they agree on how it ended: Psicosis and I got two plane tickets for Philadelphia.

A lady by the name of Kathy Fritz picked us up at the airport and brought us to a Travelodge where ECW had arranged for us to stay. It was a tower hotel. I remember walking into the hotel lobby and seeing ten or twelve cops coming down the stairs, hauling ECW wrestling star New Jack out of there. He was handcuffed. I don't know what that was about—I don't think I want to know—but that was my introduction to ECW.

"Have Fun"

WE CHECKED IN and went over to the arena. It was an old warehouse that had been converted into an auditorium. The outside looked like an oversized bunker. The inside was a little nicer—but not much.

We walked into the locker room and found a *whole* different atmosphere from the one we'd grown up in. It was one of the best atmospheres in a locker room I've ever seen in the wrestling world. Everyone was friendly and welcoming. There was music, beers, and smoking—all sorts of smoking.

I don't want to go into too much detail, but basically everything and anything went in that locker room. You walked in and you were like, *Wow, this is wild*. It was exactly like I thought it would be from watching the ECW tapes. What you saw was what you got backstage.

Just before the show we went up to Paul E. and asked him to give us some guidelines. ECW matches made generous use of unconventional weapons and other items of destruction, ranging from chairs and tables to pots. Blood was regularly spilled.

I wasn't sure exactly how far we could go though. In AAA, we were usually given pretty strict rules—you can do this, you can't do that, that sort of thing. We learned to listen to the rules and to respect other matches. We wouldn't go past what we were told.

At ECW, there were literally no limits.

I didn't totally believe it at first. I may have asked Paul E. a couple of times whether he was serious that we could do whatever we wanted.

"We can do anything?" I asked.

"Yes, yes."

"Anything?"

"Yes."

"What can we use?" I asked. "What can't we use? Can we use a table? Can we grab a chair?"

"Rey, fucking go out there and have fun," he said. "Do whatever you guys want."

I was like, *Shit, okay. That's what we'll do*.

"*Rudos! Rudos!*"

I WALKED OUT for the show very nervous. Konnan and some other wrestlers had told me that the audience would either like us or hate us. A lot. Either way. There was no in between. I didn't know how they would react. Psicosis and myself went out and they were cheering for us.

Actually, mostly for Psicosis. Like Mexican fans, they were chanting, *"Rudos! Rudos!"* At least that's what I heard.

But once we got going with some of our high-flying moves, they cheered for both of us. It was one of the most exciting crowds I've ever experienced during my wrestling career. The auditorium may have been small—I'm told it sat sixteen hundred—but it felt like twenty thousand people.

Every little pop we got made us pop in our own way. By the end of the match we were flying. We ran into the back congratulating each other.

"We did it, bro, we did it," we both said.

Paul E. met us near the entrance to the locker room. He was smiling.

"You guys are going to keep coming back," he said.

We quickly agreed.

Crazy Stuff

PSICOSIS AND I were in three different ECW Pay-Per-Views matched up against each other over the next several months. We also appeared regularly at the weekend shows. Our Pay-Per-Views were called Mexican Death matches, something either Paul E. or Konnan cooked up. The name just referred to the fact that we were both Mexican—and that we were going all out. But I wouldn't be surprised if some fans thought we were really going to fight to the death.

This was ECW, remember. Anything went.

I remember in one of them—I think it was the second Pay-Per-View—we started brawling outside the ring near a camera tower that went up twelve or fifteen feet high. I gave Psicosis a DDT at the bottom of the tower, climbed up, then dropped off and gave him a frankensteiner out in the audience.

That's how I beat him. The crowd went wild.

We did a lot of crazy stuff night after night, throwing our bodies deep into the audience, against barriers, against each other. One time we went out into the crowd and I dropped Psicosis down onto the floor. I made my way to an upper balcony, and off I went.

With anybody else, I might have been a little scared. It was an immense jump, and catching me right was critical—for my opponent as well as for me. But this was Psicosis, who'd been basing me for years. He caught me with no problem. The fans loved it.

Getting Hurt

PEOPLE ASK ME all the time if I was worried about getting hurt when I was younger. I have to say I wasn't. At that point I just wanted to stand out. I wanted to give it my all. I never thought about getting hurt or injured. And always, when I was wrestling Psicosis, I never

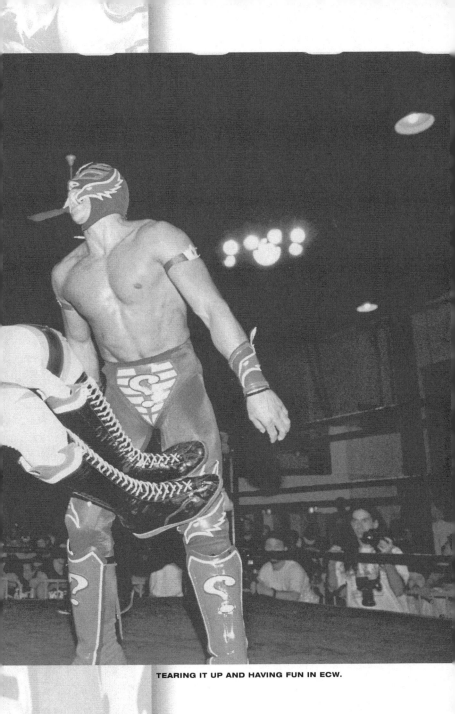
TEARING IT UP AND HAVING FUN IN ECW.

worried about getting hurt with him. Every night he put his own life on the line for me. I knew he had my back. There was no concern. I could jump off a building and he would throw his body in front so I wouldn't get hurt.

One time I was doing a Tag Team match with Konnan versus Psicosis & LaParka in ECW. Psicosis did a dive to the floor from between the second and third rope. Just before he came out, a fan gave me a chair. I swung the chair like a baseball bat, aiming for his head, but somehow I hit his lip instead.

His lip split in half. It was as if I had grabbed a scissors and cut it down the middle. Blood gushed out like water from a fire hose.

He insisted we keep going.

Finally, match over, we took him backstage and told him he was getting stitches.

There was no medical team or doctor there to help us. We started driving around Philadelphia trying to find this plastic surgeon Paul E. had hooked us up with. It was snowing, the wind was howling—it was like something out of a movie.

They took us to this surgeon in an underground house that looked like a place where a mafia guy might go after he'd been shot in some sort of crime. It was crazy.

But the doctor—or whatever he was—stitched him up in the basement. It was a good job, and Psicosis was good to go.

Conflicts? Who Has Conflicts?

WE SAW SO many of the other wrestlers doing things like that that we just wanted to be part of the atmosphere. We wanted to fit right in. And before we knew it, we did.

ECW had this thing where the fans would bring different items into the arena that could be used as weapons. One night early on, someone gave me a frying pan. I'm surprised no one brought a howitzer in, maybe after I left . . .

After each ECW show, Psicosis and I would return to Mexico and appear with AAA. We were wrestling practically every night of the week, in two different countries, for two very different promotions. That may seem unusual: Today most promotions frown on a wrestler appearing somewhere else, and many completely forbid it.

But things were different then. ECW didn't try to limit us at all. And AAA had never had contracts, so wrestlers weren't limited there either.

At the start, Peña believed that a wrestler who appeared in the States would be helping Mexican wrestling by increasing the *lucha libre* profile. Konnan had set everything up, and he was very close with Peña. They believed the arrangements with ECW and other promotions would open up new territory for AAA and add to its prestige in Mexico.

I have to give Peña a lot of credit. Once he saw what I had as a wrestler, he really pushed me. He had a lot of vision for the business, and I fit in well with his vision. We became pretty close as the years went on. I've never really been one to pal around with the boss—the boss is the boss—but we genuinely liked each other as we got to know each other.

With that being said, after our trips to ECW became a regular thing, Peña started to ask more questions. Wrestling full-time in ECW wasn't possible: They only ran shows on the weekends, compared to AAA, where we'd wrestle all week. But still, I think Peña was worried that he was going to lose us. He knew that Eddie—who'd left AAA to go to Japan before joining ECW—had gone to WCW. Maybe he expected we would try the same.

If so, he knew something we didn't at the time.

My First Promo

PAUL E. WAS cool. He believed that wrestlers knew their characters and their craft, and he encouraged us to put that knowledge to use.

I had never cut a promo in my life, but he let me make them in ECW. If I remember correctly, he paired me with 911 for a while against The Eliminators. That was my chance to cut my first promo.

Which sucked, by the way.

Not to say that my promos are good now, but that one was really bad. With my squeaky-ass child's voice, it sounded ridiculous. Maybe that was what Paul E. wanted to get across: that I was a kid in a big man's world.

Did I mention that 911 was about seven feet tall?

I think there's been a bit of an improvement in my promos over the years. But truthfully, I don't think I've found the reality of my character yet. I get caught up a bit too much in the character, rather than being myself. I need to get a little more of my humor in. But I'm working on it. It's a work in progress.

On the Fly

FOR ME, ONE of the big differences between ECW and AAA was the fact that the specific moves in the matches were usually not worked out in detail before we got into the ring. We'd just go out and wing it. Calling the match in the ring was new for me, and it took some adjusting.

Sometimes we'd call something out backstage and in the ring we'd switch it around. We took our cues from the fans, which really added something. There's an energy when that happens—and there was no energy like the energy in that small ECW auditorium.

I have to say that once I got used to it, it was very, very enjoyable.

Nowadays I can adjust to either method. Sometimes I prefer to not call the match, because it tends to be more fun for me as a wrestler. I get a chance to react to the fans, and the match feels more spontaneous—instead of Plan A and Plan B, I go by how I feel. It's like grabbing your car and going on a road trip without a set destination: I'm going wherever I end up. It's a journey, and the journey itself becomes the thing.

Of course, you're not going to do that all the time. A lot of times when you're driving from Point A to Point B, you absolutely have to make sure you want to get there in a reasonable amount of time, and in one piece.

Wrestling is a very creative art. When you put everything together, it comes back to the meaning of *lucha libre*—freestyle. You free your mind and feel it out.

A lot of wrestlers get nervous with not having a match prepared. I used to be that way, so I know what it feels like. Having a good match, either way, is your goal.

Japan

IN DECEMBER OF 1995, I took my first trip to Japan. Ultimate Dragon recommended me to WAR (Wrestling and Romance), the Japanese company sponsoring the Super J Cup tournament. A match between Psicosis and myself was booked as a special bonus in the tournament finale.

At the time Ultimate Dragon—Asai Yoshihiro—was known as Último Dragón (Last Dragon), a name I believe came from or was influenced by his time and training in Mexico, where he learned the *lucha libre* style. We would meet later on in WCW and spend quite a bit of time together there.

The Super J Cup tournament was first held in 1994. Hosted by New Japan Pro Wrestling, it was an invitation-only tournament that

I LOVED WRESTLING IN JAPAN.

featured some of the best young cruiserweights in the world. Among those wrestling there were Negro Casas, Dean Malenko, Chris Jericho, Justin Liger, and Chris Benoit, who appeared as Wild Pegasus and eventually won the cup. For all of those wrestlers, the contest brought new recognition, catapulting them to international fame.

The success of the tournament practically guaranteed a second one the following year; that's the one I attended. Like I said, Psicosis and I weren't in the actual tournament. Instead, we were booked as a special match on the final night. We did our best, though, to steal the spotlight.

Right before I was going out, Ultimate Dragon pulled me over and told me that both the owner of WAR and the person in charge of the J Cup competition told him that they didn't want me to wrestle.

"Look how small this guy is," they said. Once again, my size was an issue.

"Wait until you see him wrestle," he argued. Then he came over to me and said I had better not make him look bad for sticking up for me.

So now I was nervous as fuck. I'm confident, because I'm wrestling Psicosis. But I'm still nervous as fuck.

The crowd was loud, very excited, as we were introduced. My fear started evaporating.

Then the bell rang. The auditorium went silent. You couldn't hear anything. Nothing.

Nothing.

You could hear a pin drop in that arena. Fortunately, I had been warned that the Japanese fans tended to be very quiet once the match got under way. Otherwise I don't know what I would have done.

As I started to go out to meet Psicosis, I heard a sound from way up in the stands.

"*Wah-ka-ki!*" yelled some fan.

What did it mean? Nothing as far as I know. None of my Japanese friends have ever been able to figure it out. But it sounded cool.

"*Wah-ka-ki!*"

There was this entirely quiet auditorium, and then that sound, coming out of the rafters somewhere.

"Wah-ka-ki!"

After a while he was drowned out by the fans yelling, *"My-sterio-san!"* They'd adopted me.

Psicosis and I locked up; we did our thing. The very first high spot was this thing where we did a sunset flip: Psicosis would grab me by the hands and launch me up. My knees would go up to his shoulders. I'd stay there for a second, then slide down and give him the sunset flip. As soon as I did that, the fans were *"Ooohhhhh."*

My-sterio!

Very good, Rey-san.

Even that guy in the rafters was yelling: *"Mysterio!"*

I had Psicosis down. The ref dropped, did the count. Psicosis kicked out.

The fans went crazy. Then on some sort of magic signal, they just stopped cheering. The place was silent again.

It kept going like that through the match. At every high spot, they erupted. The more we did, the louder they got. We took them all the way to the top, and we got just a volcano of applause at the end.

And one last, final *Mysterio!*

"You Should Have Told Us . . ."

THE PROMOTERS WERE singing a different song in the back when we hit the locker room.

"Hey, why haven't you told us earlier about this Rey Mysterio?" one of them asked Dragon. "You should have brought him over a lot sooner."

Chris Jericho was in the locker room as well. I'd met him in Mexico, and he had watched the match backstage with Chris Benoit.

They looked at each other at one point and said together, "How the fuck does he do all this shit?"

I went back and took a look at the tape the other day. I almost wondered the same thing.

Frankensteiners

IF YOU LOOK at that match now, you'll be amazed at how many frankensteiners I did. Watching my video brought back memories of Scott Steiner, who was probably the first person I saw use the move. If I'm not mistaken, Hurcán Ramirez, a *luchador*, invented the move and gave his name to it.

Some younger fans may not be familiar with the frankensteiner or its close cousin, the hurricanrana. In the basic frankensteiner, both wrestlers move toward each other. The wrestler doing the move— me—jumps up on his opponent's shoulders, putting his legs around his neck in a headscissors. Your opponent is usually moving with some speed, charging you, so momentum is in your favor for what comes next—a backflip. Your opponent then tumbles over you and finds himself pinned to the mat after you land. One-two-three and down.

Technically, the hurricanrana is the same move, except that it ends with a rana—a double leg cradle. A lot of times the terms are used interchangeably in American wrestling. And of course there are many different variations in how they work—a number of which I've either invented or made my own by adding personal twists.

But it was Scott Steiner who inspired me to work on that move. I was always a big fan of Scott's. Early on in his career he used the frankensteiner as a finishing move. He would shoot his opponent to the ropes, leapfrog him, then on the way back hook him in a frankensteiner.

The first time I saw that move I thought, *Wow*. Scott is a pretty big guy, and for him to do that took incredible strength and agility. He also took a pounding: He'd land on his head just about every time.

I altered the move just a bit to make it my own. I'd leap off the top rope onto the guy's shoulders and then use the frankensteiner. Or I'd start in the middle of the ring, do a springboard to the top rope, and then do a frankensteiner. Or I'd do a cartwheel in the ring, get to the guy's shoulders that way, and do a frankensteiner.

I think now that the move may have put a lot of stress on my knee, which led indirectly to my first surgery. As my opponent took the fall, I would land on my knee. For some reason, my body always twisted to the left, putting a lot of stress and strain on that knee. And sure enough, all my surgeries have been on that knee.

But at that point my injuries were in the future.

Incredible Fans

OUR GOOD SHOWING won us some more invitations. Ultimate Dragon booked me and Psicosis on a couple of other tours. They were always great fun. He and Genichiro Tenryu, the promotion's owner, always took good care of us.

They were good for me financially as well. Before I went over for my first show, my war buddy Damián 666 gave me the heads-up on what to do in Japan. He'd been wrestling there for years, and he knew that the fans were very personal when it came to showing their appreciation. They wanted to buy souvenirs, and they would often present you with gifts and other tokens. He also said that they would know a lot about me and about *lucha libre* in general.

"When you go over, take yourself about fifty masks," he said. "The Japanese are going to want to buy them. They're going to call you to go eat, they're going to invite you and pay for everything."

Sure enough, when I got to the airport, there were fans waiting to greet me. I came out with my mask on, said hello, then went on to my hotel. I was in the room maybe three minutes when I got a phone call from a fan. I found out later that his name was Masahiro Hayashi.

"Rey Mysterio?" said Hayashi.

"Yes?"

"I made an outfit for you."

An outfit? This was something I'd never encountered before. I told him to come up.

I met Hayashi with mask on, of course. I opened the door and he was standing there with the outfit.

"Presento, presento," Hayashi said. That was all the Spanish he knew. He held out the costume.

It was a black wrestling outfit with a yellow falcon on it. Not only did it look pretty cool, it was the right size. None of that Green Lizard–style squeezing.

"You wear please for the ring," he told me.

My new fan had also made two masks. He wanted me to wear one in the match. Afterward I would give it to him and he would give me the other. It sounded like a good deal to me.

I was blown away by the whole deal, but I realized later on that this was a business for him and that I was helping him out by wearing the costume. We became very good friends, and he's still one of the guys who makes my outfits to this day.

Masks on Display

AFTER HAYASHI LEFT, I got another call. I picked up the phone.

"Can I buy mask? Can I buy mask?"

I said, *Oh shit*—to myself—*here we go*. Damián had told me all about it but I guess I didn't really believe it, not until it happened.

"Sure, give me five minutes," I told the caller. "Then come up."

I set up my little swap meet stand on top of my bed. I put about forty masks in a row, arranged real nice. He walked in.

"Oh my God," he said. "Oh, very nice. Ahhh."

He was really excited. It was a pretty impressive display, I have to say.

"How much for this one?" he asked.

So I gave him a price.

"How much for this one?" he asked.

"Oh, that one's a little more expensive."

"And this one?"

"This one is a little cheaper. But look at this one. I've used it many times."

"Ah, yes."

I was in Japan only three days. By the time I got back on the plane, I had sold all of my masks. Forty or fifty masks, all gone. I sold them for three or four hundred dollars each, mostly, with the most expensive

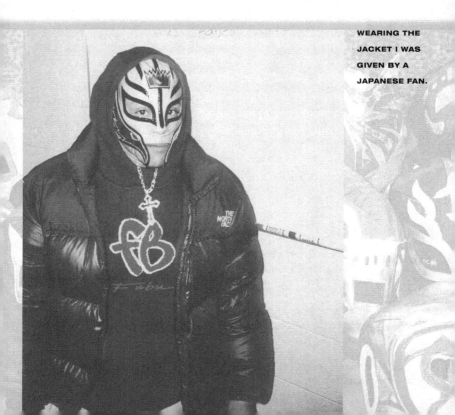

WEARING THE JACKET I WAS GIVEN BY A JAPANESE FAN.

close to eight hundred. I made more on masks than I got paid for the show—and I got paid really well for that show.

Japanese fans are unbelievably generous. People would come up and give me presents. One guy gave me a North Face jacket: It was really cold in Tokyo that winter, and I definitely appreciated it. There were all sorts of souvenirs in my luggage when I headed home.

Food

NOT LONG AFTERWARD I returned to Japan on a five-day tour. We went by bus up and down the country. We got to see more of Japan, visiting Tokyo, Osaka, Nagasaki, and some of the smaller cities. We would get into each town maybe four hours before the show, so we got a chance to see some of the city and meet fans.

I got to like Japanese cooking. On my very first trip, I went to the famous Rivera Steakhouse. It's a great restaurant, loved by wrestlers. All the boys go there, and everybody who's been there has a picture on the wall. I drank two tall beers and had a forty-two-ounce steak (I only ate about a quarter of it).

But after that, I began to experiment. One thing that really fascinated me was *yakiniku*-style cooking, which is popular in a lot of restaurants. You order your food, and when they bring it out, you cook it yourself on a little grill at the table. I understand it's a style that actually started in Korea and was brought over to Japan.

I don't care where it came from; for me it's the ultimate. You have your meat and your vegetables, and then there are different sauces that you dip in or add. You get a bowl of white rice. It's really a guy thing: It's do-it-yourself, and you're cooking on the grill.

I can sit there for hours, talking, drinking a little beer, and grilling. I get my grub on. My favorites are Kobe beef—and tongue.

Speaking of Food

THIS IS OFF topic, but since I'm talking about food . . .

When I'm on the road, I like to ride with a bunch of the boys. My usual riding team includes Randy Orton, Santino Marella, Michael Chioda, and Charlie Haas. When we're all together, we have a hell of a time. We even got Santino out on a bucking bronco machine one night. (I'll make the pictures available for a price.)

Anyway, when we're all together, we'll set one night aside to have a really fine dinner at a nice place. We fill up the table with appetizers to start, and it's like a little party.

The reason I'm bringing this up right now has to do with food. I've turned the boys on to a number of dishes, including escargot.

Snails, in case you don't know.

I didn't tell them what they were until after they tried them—and liked them. So if you're ever in a restaurant and see a wrestler ordering escargot, you can blame it on me.

One of these nights, we'll find a Chinese place that serves fried tarantulas. Mmmmm, spiders.

Seriously, fried tarantulas are a specialty in parts of China. They're so common that vendors sell them on the street.

I can't wait.

Autographs

RESPECT IS A very important concept in Japan. The fans treat wrestlers and the entire profession with a lot of respect and honor. Especially when it comes to an autograph.

People all over the world ask for autographs, but sometimes you wonder. In Mexico they'll give you anything to sign. A lot of times they would hand me a bus ticket right after the show.

I'd look at them and say, "Are you really going to keep this? I mean, how are you going to get home?" I don't know how many bus drivers have ended up with my signature in their pocket.

The worst is when fans give you a napkin. They're not only hard to sign, but you know they're not going to last.

I was with MVP one time when someone gave him a napkin. He took a hard line.

"Dude, what do you do with a napkin?" he asked the fan.

"I don't know."

"You wipe your hands on it and throw it out. You really want me to sign a napkin? Go get yourself a piece of paper."

The fan did. That's an autograph that lasted, I'd bet.

In Japan fans give you an eight-by-ten piece of cardboard that is white with silver around it. Very, very fancy.

Putting Dragon Over

I BELIEVE IT was on that tour that Ultimate Dragon and I did a tag match together at Korakuen Hall right next to the Tokyo Dome. It's a very important venue in Japan. It's almost like a miniature Madison Square Garden.

One sign of my new status internationally came at that match when he asked me to put him over. In other words, he wanted to wrestle me—and win—in a way that improved his standing with the fans.

He understood that I was getting popular. Dragon also had a lot of status in Japan; he was very well known. So booking this match helped me as well.

I never mind doing the job for anybody. To me, win or lose, it's the same as long as you give the fans what they deserve and you make sure you put on a good name for yourself and the company you're working for at the time. And I was always very appreciative to the

Dragon, because without him I would never have gotten to Japan. I had followed his career for years, from the first time I saw him wrestle in Mexico. He'd been one of my heroes, and it was an honor to step into the ring with him.

Even though Dragon had a *lucha libre* approach, we have slightly different styles. I did most of the high flying in the ring; he did a lot of the power moves. I don't see that much of a size difference between us—not compared to a lot of the other people I wrestle—but I think fans do. And I think that increased some of the interest.

He had one move—the torture rack—that I think brought the house down. He'd get me up on top of his shoulders and spin me, spin me, spin me, then drop to his knees—it hurts talking about it. It was almost a backbreaker with me on top of his shoulders.

Working with Dragon was always fun. No matter what was happening, he gave me room to do my moves too. It was fifty-fifty, no spot hogging involved.

TOMMY DREAMER.

The Biggest
Year Yet

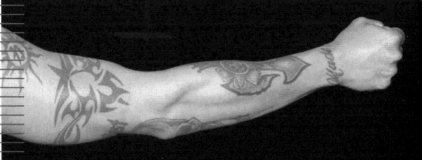

The year 1996 was an incredible one for me.

By now I was a star in Mexico, headlining the

card. And I was going up to the States most

weekends to do shows with ECW.

Everything just rushed by. I knew I was

entering a new level. I just didn't know how

big that level was going to be.

Tommy Dreamer

I THINK TODAY when fans think back to ECW, if there's only one wrestler they remember well, it's Tommy Dreamer. People have called him the heart and soul of the organization, and there's no better description of him. Even today, with WWE, he really lights up the arena when he goes out there.

But when I think about Tommy, I remember how generous and respectful he was when we first met at ECW. He was a big star in the promotion. He was the king, the shit—however you might want to describe it.

You might expect some guys in that position to be a little full of themselves or to act like they're above everyone else, especially a new guy coming in. They might even look at you with some suspicion, like, *Who the hell do you think you are?*

Not Tommy. He was very cool. Still is. He was friendly, and he went out of his way to make you feel welcome. And I think he was that way with everybody. Didn't matter what was going on with him, he was just way too good a friend.

Not everybody was like that, even at ECW. Take Raven. He was in his own world back then. When he was in a good mood, he'd make you feel good. At other times, he just acted out like he was the big dog.

I didn't have any problems with him, personally. He definitely has incredible knowledge about the business. Some of the angles he did, especially what he did with Sandman—I still remember the angle they did with Sandman's kid.

But locker room wise, he had his ups and downs. A lot of people didn't get along with him. He was just a weird dude offstage.

But I almost had a date with Dreamer. Or so the story goes.

The version I heard runs like this: Early on I was riding in an elevator with Paul E. I hadn't been introduced to most of the guys yet.

Tommy Dreamer saw us get out, gave Paul E. a puzzled look, then turned away as we walked on.

Later on, he went over to Paul E. and asked, "Hey, who was that chick you were with? She looked hot. A little flat-chested, but hey."

He lost interest real fast when he found out it was me. It's a good thing he told Paul E. The boys would have set us up for a date, then hidden around the corner to see what happened.

That's the boys.

Sandman

SPEAKING OF SANDMAN, he was another cat who was cool from day one. I partied with him and had some great times. But he was another guy who was in his own world. He always—I mean *always*— had a beer and a cigarette in his hand. He lived his gimmick.

Younger wrestling fans may not have had a chance to see his work. He was an edgy character, one of the guys who helped give ECW that reputation. He'd smoke a cigarette, drink a beer—this is in the arena, in the ring, during a show. And there was a famous ECW storyline where he used a kendo stick.

They called it a Singapore Cane, because of a story in the news at the time about a kid who was punished for a crime in Singapore by being caned rather than going to jail. He had a feud with Cactus Jack that eventually saw him use barbed wire in a match.

This was all new stuff at the time, very cutting-edge for pro wrestling. I still go back and watch some of the old tapes. They're incredible.

I don't think he had any limits. His attitude was always: *Fuck it. I'll do it.* Incredible. That's the kind of guy he was.

And for real: If you were in a bar fight, and he was there, he'd back you up no matter what. Even if we both got our asses kicked.

It's funny, but according to legend, there were all sorts of bar fights in those days. But, swear to God, I never saw one, let alone got involved in one.

There haven't been many bar fights in my time—from Mexico to ECW to WCW to WWE. I won't say there have been *no* fights; there have been a few. But for some reason, I've missed every single one of them. I've always either left before they started, or didn't get there in time, or whatever.

Just my rotten luck, I guess.

Cactus Jack and Sabu

CACTUS JACK, OTHERWISE known as Mick Foley, was wrestling in ECW at the time. He was doing some wild stuff, pushing the limits not just on wrestling but on the entire definition of "extreme."

At the time, he pretty much kept to himself. He and I got to know each other better down the road. But I was impressed when I found out that he already knew who I was.

Foley is a real student of wrestling. Certainly at the time I don't think there was anything going on or anything that had gone on that he didn't know about. For all his crazy stunts, he was very serious, a real scholar when it came to the ring. One thing you can say about a lot of wrestlers, certainly the good ones: There's a lot more to them than you see at first glance.

Of course, I got to know Mick a lot better later on at WWE. There were so many guys I met at ECW who I crossed paths with later on. One of the most famous, of course, was Steve Austin. We'd say hello out of respect and everything, but at the time we didn't have much of a chance to get to know each other or work together.

On the other hand, Sabu and I had a chance to work together several times, not just in ECW but at some independent shows in northern California. He and I hit it off really well. He'd studied up on me somehow and knew who I was when I came in. And he was all over the ECW tapes I'd been watching, so I knew exactly who he was.

Sabu was one tough dude. Most fans who know ECW history have probably heard the story about him duct-taping his jaw in place during a match with Sandman. He broke his back twice that I know of. He is just an incredible machine. His high-flying style worked well with mine, and when we were in the ring together we gave the fans an aerial show I don't think any of them can forget.

I had heard about Sabu from Damián, who'd worked in Japan with him and Sabu's uncle, The Sheik. We became fans of each other's work, and to this day I like to watch him on tape.

In 2007 I had a chance to work with him again at the *One Night Stand* Pay-Per-View. I was World Champion then, and the title was on the line. He nailed me through a table outside the ring with a DDT, but he used so much force that not only did he send me through the table, he put himself through it as well. The medical people came out and the match had to be stopped. If it wasn't for that, he probably would have won that match; he was really on fire that night.

The match was up in New York and we had a great crowd. A lot of them were ECW people, cheering for him even though I was the champ. But to tell the truth, I wish the contest had been down in Philadelphia in the old arena. The atmosphere and the crowd would just have sent it even higher.

And if it had been back in the day—that would have been *phenomenal*.

Of course, ECW fans have gotten older and the crazy shit they used to pull has toned down quite a bit these days. Don't get me wrong, I really appreciate today's wrestling fans. They're so knowledgeable, and they really get behind their favorites. But back in the day, when extreme wrestling was new, it was as if we were all exploring new territory together.

Joey Styles

ONE OF THE people who really helped put me over in ECW was Joey Styles.

Joey started as a commentator on ECW right around the time it changed its name from Eastern Championship Wrestling to Extreme Championship Wrestling. By the time I got there he was an institution. He called all of my matches. He had a name for every move we made. I swear he invented a couple, but even if he made them up, they sounded perfect.

His commentary spiced up the matches. He wouldn't stop. He'd take you on that roller-coaster ride. He made us look and sound good, and I think he added to the fun for the people at home. The emotion was real.

I remember going back and watching the Pay-Per-View *November to Remember* and getting excited all over again just because of his descriptions. *Oh. My. God!* That was one of his catchphrases. It was perfectly matched to the action.

It's not an easy thing to do. I've taken a few turns behind the mike at the commentators' table, and I can tell you firsthand. I'm sure if you put Joey in the ring and asked him to do a few of my moves, he'd say no way. I have to say the same thing about trying to do his job.

To this day, when I see him, we talk about old ECW moves. He's a big fan, and a lot of times he reminds me of moves that I haven't tried in a while and he urges me to bring them back.

No Problems

AFTER PSICOSIS AND I proved that the crowds would get into Mexican-style wrestling, a few other guys from AAA came up. I remember Juventud Guerrera's first time in the locker room. He used to have really long hair. While he was dressing for that match, Tommy Dreamer spotted him from the back.

He whistled or something and went over to him, saying, "Hey, who's this cool chick?"

He went to present himself—put on a move.

Man, he got the shock of his life when Juventud turned around. We just about died laughing.

Hell, I'm *still* laughing.

I got the same kind of reaction myself when I started wrestling, back when my hair was very long.

At ECW, it was understandable. There were a lot of women hanging around in the ECW locker room in those days. Oh, yeah. The girls who were in the show didn't dress with us, but everyone was together in one big room before things got going. I think there were a couple of little kayfabe spots around the corner, if you know what I mean, but I never saw anyone get down and dirty in the big room.

That was one cool locker room.

Paul E. would have a speech right before the show started. There was a stairwell that would take you up to an office. Paul E. would come out, hop up a couple of steps, then give us a quick pep talk. Then he'd end it with something along the lines of "All right. Let's kick this motherfucker off," and we'd blast out of there.

ECW

PRO WRESTLING HAD exploded in the U.S. at this time. WWE, then known as World Wrestling Federation, was going head-to-head with WCW. The two promotions had prime-time television shows and a lot of money to spend; that eventually hurt ECW in a lot of ways. For one thing, it tempted talent away. That was great for wrestlers—it definitely helped me—but ultimately it made it hard for the original ECW to survive.

There are a bunch of places where you can get a history of ECW if you're interested. One of them is a two-DVD set called *The Rise and Fall of ECW,* which I believe is put out by WWE. There's a book with the same name written by Thom Loverro. Loverro talked to a lot of the original ECW people, including Paul E., Tazz, and Tommy Dreamer, when he wrote it.

Eventually, ECW crashed and burned financially. The organization was forced to declare bankruptcy in 2001.

I was gone by then, but I heard a lot of stories about wrestlers not being paid at ECW. I'm not discounting them, but I do know that I never had any problems. We were always paid fairly, and right after the matches. For us, it was always cash. I never had a problem with Paul E. Always had our plane tickets, always had our hotels, and always paid our money after our shows.

WWE has since taken over ECW and revived it, recapturing some of the old spirit. Maybe the best testimony about the original's success is the fact that the brand still counts fans from the old days when the cramped auditorium next to the highway was its home.

Mexico

I LOVED WRESTLING in America, getting a chance to be around the American wrestlers and to use my native language. Going back and forth meant I was almost always working, but for some reason I didn't feel that tired. When you're young and the whole world is opening up to you—and especially when you're living your dream, as I was—you don't have time to get tired.

Mexico was still my base, though. I had a big following there, and of course I knew all the other wrestlers. I'd grown up with them. And for the most part, they didn't show any jealousy or anything like that. They were all, like, *Rey, way to go, yeah.*

Mexican vs. American Wrestling

PEOPLE ASK ME about the differences between Mexican-style wrestling and American. It can be hard to explain.

Konnan likes to point out that in American-style wrestling, there's generally a lot of storytelling and psychology, while in Mexican wrestling the focus is usually on the spots and the match itself.

"American wrestling has a semblance of logic," he says. "Mexican wrestling—no logic. There's more comedy and cheesy stuff."

He usually laughs when he says that, though he's being very serious. As Konnan describes it, Mexican wrestling is like riding down the Autobahn at 180; American style is a scenic train ride.

With the help of people like Dean Malenko, Chris Benoit, and others, I've tried to take the best of Mexican wrestling—the dives, the high flying—and incorporate it into a logical match. I hope it makes Americans appreciate *lucha libre* better.

Superhero Outfits

IT WAS AROUND this time that I started wearing more and more elaborate costumes. If you look back at some of those early ECW tapes and the Mexican matches from around the same period, you'll notice I wear a cape. I was really getting into the superhero gimmicks back then. I did a riff on a Batman and a Superman cape, and a number of others. My idea was to make a nice presentation, look a little different—me being me.

Everybody knows who Batman and Superman are, and I think the costumes gave the younger fans a little something to hook on to my character with. The funny thing is, even today a lot of fans mention some of these costumes.

MY TRIBUTE TO
THE FLASH.

Hey, I saw you wearing this Batman-style cape. Hey, hey, that was cool.

So I guess it worked.

As the years went on, I brought my costumes to another level. But I still love the superheroes, and a lot of times I'll pay them tribute with my costumes. All but one of my *WrestleMania* outfits have been inspired by superheroes. I either modeled my look on their costumes, or I had them designed as a tribute in some way.

For my first *WrestleMania* in WWE, I had a Daredevil outfit made up. It was right after the movie starring Ben Affleck came out. I've paid homage to Silver Surfer, Incredible Hulk, and Iron Man. I love the movies, especially the characters and comics they're based on.

I have to confess that lately I've been getting some of my best ideas from my kids, who inspire me with their thoughts. I'll ask them who they'd like to see, and go from there. That's where my Iron Man tribute came from.

It's very important to stand out and do something different, and costumes help me do that. They're also a good way to keep in touch with my younger fans.

A Tribute to Our Ancestors

BUT THERE'S A serious side to the costumes as well, just as there's a serious side to me. When I won the World Heavyweight Championship at *WrestleMania 22* in 2006, I was wearing a special Aztec warrior costume. For me, it was a connection to my heritage.

It was an idea that I'd had in the back of my mind for a long, long time. Back in the day, Canek—also known as The Mayan Prince— would wear colorful costumes that celebrated the original inhabitants of North and South America, most especially the Mayans. I wanted to bring that back in my own way.

My Aztec costume is extremely elaborate and was actually made for me by someone in Mexico. My wife and I had been talking about having a Native American costume made. She and my friend Emiliano—who owns a wrestling magazine in Mexico—found a vendor in Mexico City who could do it for me while we were touring there. It is an elaborate, custom-made costume complete with feathers. It cost several thousand dollars, but there's nothing else that compares to it.

Just for comparison's sake, my regular wrestling gear can cost anywhere from a few hundred to eight hundred dollars. Those too are custom-made by hand.

Because it's so elaborate, I've only worn my Aztec costume once. It has to be put together, feather by feather, and adjusted just right each time it's worn. It's the sort of thing that you want to take out only for special occasions.

The costume represents who I am down deep inside. It's a form of homage to my past and my ancestors, not just a piece of wrestling gear. It has a meaning to it that's hard to describe. It's almost magical in a way—as if the spirit of an Aztec warrior descends on me whenever I put it on.

Outfits and Rosaries

MY REGULAR COSTUMES are made by two friends of mine: Hayashi in Japan, and Gustavo Bucio in Mexico. They're both excellent craftsmen, with slightly different styles and tastes. Hayashi likes to use rhinestones and other little jewels, making things a little more intricate. Bucio is very good at finding exotic colors and materials.

The designs come from many different places. One of my most recent masks, for example, is based on a mask my uncle once wore. I added a cross and an Aztec calendar to his falcon, making the design my own.

My masks and costumes are changing all the time, but some parts of the designs keep coming back and back. Besides the cross, you'll often see a rosary. Rosary beads are a special set of prayer beads that Catholics use to help them keep track when they're reciting a set of prayers known as the Rosary.

I've always been very religious. Every night before I go to bed, I kneel down and pray. You remember Hogan praying in the ring? For me it's real. I kneel and say my prayers before I get into the ring too. So for me, the rosary beads feel like a symbol of protection. Some fans noticed at some point, and for a while giving Rey Mysterio rosary beads became kind of the "in thing" to do. On my way back from the ring, they would put a rosary around my neck. I have quite a collection right now, in different colors, different sizes. Some are made out of wood, some are made out of metal, some crystals. One of my favorites is a set blessed by the Holy Father, the Pope, that came from the Vatican. It was kind of a nice tribute.

One day I left for the road without my rosary beads and I felt a little—I guess "unprotected" would be the word. I didn't feel complete. So I decided I would never go anywhere without them again: I had a set tattooed around my chest. It goes with me wherever I go.

A couple of other Catholic medals and tokens mean a lot to me. I keep them in a little sunglass case and carry them with me wherever I go. There's a little wooden cross that a fan in Italy gave me when I visited Rome a while back. And a statue of San Judas Tadeo, or Saint Jude the Apostle. He's the patron saint of miracles and lost causes—and my wife's favorite saint.

Not to say that I'm a lost cause, I hope.

She gave the statue to me as a reminder of the saint's protection. With his help, and God's, I leave the house every week and come back safe to her and the family.

No Belief in Evil

I OUGHT TO mention that the skull and the skeletons I wear on my outfits and masks don't represent evil. In fact they have no connection with it. They are reminders of our mortality and a chance to honor ancestors who have passed on.

The ideas of mortality and eternal rewards are very important to Catholics, especially those of us with Mexican backgrounds. We celebrate All Souls' Day—also known as the Day of the Dead, or *el Dia de los Muertos* in Mexico—every November 2. The day before is All Saints' Day, a holy day of obligation when Catholics go to mass and honor the saints. All Saints' Day is also known as All Hallows, and nearly everyone is familiar with Halloween, or the day before All Saints' Day. There are huge celebrations throughout Mexico for All Saints' Day and the Day of the Dead, with festivals that are bigger than any Halloween party in the U.S. Often children who have died— the little angels—are celebrated on All Saints' Day, with adults on the Day of the Dead. Some people connect the festivals and observances with early native practices in Mexico, as well as Catholicism.

A lot of other cultures do similar things. The Japanese, for instance, honor their ancestors with a very similar holiday.

Star in Mexico

BY THIS POINT in my career, early 1996, I was starting to go from being a national star in Mexico to an international star, both in Japan and the U.S. The foreign appearances gave me more credibility in Mexico. The local wrestling magazines carried a lot of stories about me and Psicosis going to the U.S. That increased my following and prestige in Mexico. I started main eventing with the biggest names in the company, real legends in *lucha libre*.

I'd arrived in Mexico City with a lot of potential, but I was far from a superstar. Even with Konnan's backing, I'd had to convince the owner just to let me wrestle. I worked hard, climbing that ladder and earning every step of the way. So when I finally reached the main event, I felt honored.

There was pressure to perform. But it was a good pressure. I'd learned to deal with it as I progressed through the ranks. I think there's a lot to be said for that. Starting out at the bottom and working hard when you start a profession or a career—any job, not just wrestling—really helps prepare you for the challenges you face later on. It definitely did for me. I could see what was expected of the more experienced wrestlers, how they dealt with the fans and fame, the pressures of life on the road, everything, without being exposed to them so much at first that they broke me.

I would have been excited to start out as a main eventer when I came in—but I would also have been nervous as hell, probably too nervous to do a good job.

But by 1995, 1996, I was ready for the pressure and the attention. I knew I had busted my ass to become a main eventer. I knew what to do. I was the same person—still hungry, still trying hard—but with just a little bit more experience.

One thing was a constant, from the popcorn matches to the main events:

I enjoyed myself. I loved wrestling. I still do. Every night.

"Didn't I Tell You?"

KONNAN WAS IN my corner, pushing me just as he had at my earliest AAA matches. He was always there. If I was tempted to coast, he'd give me a kick and get me straightened right out.

"Rey, you're in this spot because you earned it," he'd tell me. "This shit wasn't handed to you—you can't act like it was. Do what you're capable of doing."

He would add a little pressure, but it was in a good way.

"Bro, you gotta look good tonight," he'd say. "Our boss is counting on you, I'm counting on you. Don't fuck up."

And I didn't.

Konnan and I were such good friends that it got to the point where I could give the speech myself. I'd hear him in my head: *Come on, Rey, turn it up, turn it up. Do it for your people, do it for your fans, do it for your family, do it for yourself.*

Always the pep talk.

But he'd also be the first one back in the locker room to congratulate me. "I told you, fucker. I told you you could do it. I told you."

Special matches called for turning it up. I'd go out and find some way of stealing the show. I really liked the challenge. It set me off.

Misterio vs. Misterio, No Bull

THERE WERE SO many matches during this time that they tend to blur together. We had contests all over the country, in big auditoriums, small auditoriums, bullrings. I remember a contest between me and Misterioso in a bullring in Tijuana. It was a Mask versus Mask contest.

Roberto "Beto" Castillo had once been Rey Misterio #2 before changing his name to Mysterioso. My uncle had trained him, and he bought the right to use the name. Beto wanted to be part of the Rey Misterio dynasty, and they worked out an agreement.

I even trained with him for a while. He wrestled in CMLL, and then came over to AAA.

Misterioso and Volador—his name means "the flier"—had given me the rub during my early days with AAA. They were both veterans when I joined them; already their two-man tag team was considered one of the best ever in Mexican history. During the course of that storyline, Misterioso turned on Volador, which broke up our team and set them against each other for some memorable encounters.

Now he and I were back together, but as opponents.

People who haven't seen a bullfight are probably wondering how you can have a match in a bullring. Maybe some people who have seen one are wondering that as well. It's not too hard, actually. A bullring is really just a large stadium with an open area at the center. They would put a wrestling ring in the middle, add some seats around the ring, and it was ready.

It can also be dusty and hot, since you are out in the sun. Depending on the size of the ring and the match, the fans might be pretty far away.

Our showdown came at the bullring in Tijuana at a *TripleMania*. *TripleMania* is AAA's equivalent of *WrestleMania*, sometimes held twice or even three times over the course of a year.

Misterioso got things going outside the ring, jumping me before I got to the ropes. The fans were just crazy, pumping us both up. We'd been building the feud for a while, and the fact that we were both local added to the tension. Chairs flew in the air. Then, after the first fall, Misterioso started working on my leg. We both got a little help from our seconds—my uncle was in my corner and got a few whacks in with the kendo stick—and finally faced off for the third pin, tied at one.

In the last fall of the match, we must have both had half a dozen near pins, the other wiggling away from defeat at the last moment. Finally, I managed to jump on Misterioso and rolled him up for the pin.

It was an emotional moment for everybody, Misterioso especially. At that point, I think he went back to America for a while, then returned later on and continued his career in Mexico.

A Mask of a
Different Kind

BEING A STAR in AAA brought some perks. We had started televising our matches most Friday nights from Mexico City, but of course there was still a lot of travel for house shows and other events. As a main eventer, I didn't have to take long bus rides anymore. I got to travel in planes—most times, anyway.

Of course, that could be an adventure on its own.

I've always been able to fall asleep while traveling, even on airplanes. I may have all sorts of trouble sleeping at home, depending on what's going on, but once on a flight, I just lean my pillow against the window and I'm gone.

This one time I was traveling to Monterrey. I check in, jump on the plane. It's a short flight, hour and fifteen maybe. I tilted my seat back and passed out before the plane took off.

The next thing I know, I feel this pat on my shoulder. I blew it off for a second, but then the tapping became pretty urgent, like I was back in the ring. I woke up and turned to the passenger next to me.

He was wearing a mask.

Not to wrestle with: The plane's oxygen masks had dropped down. Everywhere I looked, everyone was wearing them.

As I grabbed for mine, the plane jerked hard to the side. I saw a mountain looking in the window.

How many prayers do you think can be said in the space of three seconds?

A lot, believe me.

We spun back upright, missed the mountain somehow, and eventually landed. Apparently one of the doors hadn't shut properly, and we'd lost pressurization; fortunately, the pilots were able to deal with the situation and we were back in the air a short time later.

But it was months before I could sleep on an airplane again.

Riot

THERE WERE TIMES in the arena when things got out of hand. It didn't happen all that often, but when it did, it could be hazardous to your health, especially if you were on the wrong side of the fans.

Mexican fans feel free to voice their opinions about matches, and sometimes they go a little overboard. There are plenty of videos around showing fans tossing chairs into the ring in disgust, and those are pictures of some of the tamer incidents.

I remember one time I was with Konnan, La Parka, and Psicosis, wrestling for AAA. We were the main event; it was Konnan and myself against the others. It was in Durango.

Now, that city has a reputation for being a rough place. You see policemen driving around in trucks with machine guns in the back. That's the kind of reputation it has.

Well, after the match, Konnan and I left the arena first. I was high-fiving the fans, and Konnan was behind me somewhere as I came down the aisle.

I gave this kid a high five, and the next thing I knew, somebody smashed me on the back of the head. I turned around and the kid had a guilty grin. I grabbed his hand and told him, "Don't ever do that. That's very disrespectful."

The next thing you know, the kid's uncle or older friend jumped over the rail and kicked me in the back. He took me by surprise and hit me so hard I flew into the locker room door a few feet away.

Konnan knocked him on his ass.

I looked back and saw Parka in the ring, going at it with someone. Psicosis, meanwhile, was under attack in the aisle.

Then all hell broke loose.

Parka got out and we all made it to the locker room. We managed to lock up the door and sat inside, trying to figure out what to do.

"You see that?" I asked Parka. "You see Konnan?"

"Shit, man, I was in the ring with two or three guys," said Parka. "You guys missed everything."

Parka was a good fighter—it would have taken half a dozen to put him away. He can really throw down. But there were more than enough takers outside the door.

There was only one way into the locker room—and one way out. We were trapped.

The owner came in. He was freaking out.

"The fans are out there, and they want your fucking heads," he told us. "Parka, man, they want you worst of all. And you, Konnan—they say you started hitting fans."

I explained what had happened. The promoter calmed down, but explanations weren't going to cut it with the crowd outside. They wanted blood.

"We'll wait until tempers cool," said the promoter.

"Fuck that," said Konnan finally. I think he wanted to go out the front and take them all on.

Under Arrest

WE AGREED THAT if one of us went, we'd all go. But other than that, we weren't sure exactly what to do. Could we take them on? Should we try to sneak out? Without masks, we might not be known.

While we were discussing it, the police stormed in, heavily armed and in riot gear.

"Who's La Parka?" they yelled. "Who's Konnan?"

Funny thing, but my name never got mentioned in that fight. Maybe that's the benefit of being a babyface: They don't think you're in the middle of the shit.

To make a long story short, the police handcuffed La Parka and Konnan and took them out, pretty much dragging them because they didn't want to go. Before they went, Konnan and Parka told Psicosis and me to get away. In streetclothes and without our masks, we weren't recognizable, so we were able to sneak out. I hid with the promoter and managed to get away in a car.

They threw Konnan in the back of an open troop truck; I'm not sure if La Parka was with him or not at that point. About halfway through the ride—once past the crowds—Konnan started arguing that they had no right to take him and they had to let him go.

Their answer was this: They stopped the truck and started beating the crap out of him.

He was handcuffed, but he managed to get out of the truck. He took down a couple of the cops before they maced him. Konnan was a little worse for wear by the time he reached the station.

Meanwhile, I snuck over to the police station. There were a bunch of people there, screaming about wanting to press charges.

Or be paid off in exchange for *not* pressing charges. I swear, there was an army of supposed fans with their arms in slings and their legs in casts as they hobbled in on crutches. Everybody thought the riot was going to be a big payday.

It took three or four hours, but the police finally let Konnan and Parka go. By then, the crowd was gone.

Did money change hands somewhere?

I don't know. But I can say I witnessed a medical miracle: The cripples I'd seen on the way to the station walked away without crutches. It was a miracle any saint could have been proud of.

Enjoying the Ride

INCIDENTS LIKE THAT aside, I was enjoying the ride at AAA.

Barely twenty-two years old, I was a big star in Mexico. But more than that, I saw opportunities everywhere. If there was a tour coming up to Japan, I'd think, *Jeez, I want to be part of that*. Not because I had a plan to climb to the top of the world or anything, but because I just thought it would be cool. I wasn't following a master plan to advance, let alone to get rich as a wrestler. It was all just fun, and I wanted to be right there, where the action was.

That was the overwhelming emotion and aim: I wanted to just keep having fun. But maybe underneath it there was a little bit of—I can't call it fear, but maybe the knowledge that status can be very fleeting. When you get up toward the top, you don't want to go back down. I kept pushing myself to come up with things to stay there. My desire to keep innovating helped me, because the new moves excited the crowd and gave me an edge.

I think I also felt that I didn't want to let anyone down, especially Konnan and my boss, Antonio Peña. They had both shown enormous confidence in me, and I felt like I had to prove that they were right. I think I did prove they were right. There was no denying that when the bell rang, Rey Mysterio turned it up.

The people responded well.

Pumpkin Head

ECW INFLUENCED HOW we wrestled in Mexico. Konnan especially pushed us to incorporate the extreme styles in our shows.

I remember one match that we had, a Cage match between Psicosis and Halloween on one team, and Konnan and myself on the other. We had cans, lids, kendo sticks, and a pumpkin in the ring. The plan at one point was to stick the pumpkin on Halloween's head, then whack it with the kendo stick. We'd hollowed out the pumpkin to make it easier to get on, but there was enough on the sides to form kind of a helmet buffer to soften the blow.

The match went on and we went at it, back and forth, to the point where the time came for Konnan to put the pumpkin on Halloween's head.

The only problem was, it wouldn't quite fit. The hole we'd cut at the bottom was too small for his head.

The crowd was up—we were close to the finish—and we didn't want to lose the pace of the show. So I picked up the kendo stick, ready to swing.

"Bro, the pumpkin doesn't fit," warned Konnan.

"Well, hold it," I told him.

I started swinging the stick like a baseball bat. He held the pumpkin on Halloween's head. But as I swung, Konnan let go and the pumpkin slid off. My aim swerved, but instead of hitting the pumpkin, I whacked poor Halloween right on the side of the head.

Still to this day he has that lump on his head.

Payback

HALLOWEEN GOT ME back a short time later, when we were doing a Six-Man Tag Team match at Palenque del Hipodromo in Tijuana. I was down on the canvas and my legs were spread open. I heard him tell me not to move. He was going to hit me in the balls with the kendo stick.

I didn't move. He stood over me, milking the crowd, then he swung.

I don't know if he swung hard or not, but when he hit me it felt as if I had been punched by a rocket ship. I rolled out of the ring. I couldn't catch my breath. I had to leave the match, go back to the locker room, and give my boys some air.

Bad aim? Or revenge?

You decide.

Juventud Title Match

ONE OF MY favorite matches was a title bout against Juventud. It was a main event in my hometown. The fans had been watching me for years, and I was definitely amped. It was at the Palenque del Hipodromo, in Tijuana, where the arena is shaped like a dome and the audience surrounds the ring.

We came up with some special moves just for that night. Juventud and I had been studying Japanese tapes, watching Tiger Mask and some others. We were big fans of their work, and we decided to model the match after some of Tiger Mask's encounters.

The cramped space around the ring made things a little tricky. We really didn't have enough room to dive out to the floor—but we did it anyway. For some reason, maybe because it was so cramped and no one thought we'd wrestle out there, the floor wasn't covered at all—no mats broke our falls. We just kissed the concrete and kept going.

The speed was incredible. We'd go from move to move, building, building, building. The crowd had come in knowing that we had history, and knowing that the belt was on the line, but I think our energy took them to another level.

My parents, my oldest brother, and my girlfriend were in the audience, which added another dimension for me.

Early on in the contest, I did a version of what later became the 619. Juventud grabbed my legs and we spun out into the center of the ring, where we traded some moves. I got Juventud into the corner and literally ran up his body, kicking him in the chin before flipping over and landing on my feet.

But Juventud got me back, launching himself off the top rope and kicking me in the shoulders with an incredible flying leap. Then, with the match tied at one fall apiece—like most Mexican matches at the time, the winner had to take two out of three falls—I threw Juventud out of the ring. I followed him, diving past the barrier and into the first row of the audience. We struggled back between the ropes, then went at it some more until I managed to clamp his shoulders against the canvas.

I could see my girlfriend and my parents as I got the count, then the ref grabbed my hand to declare me champ. It was a special moment.

We had so much planned out that sometimes there were just too many moves. I'd hit about nine out of ten, though—sometimes ten out of ten. That night was ten out of ten—a perfect night. The crowd chanted my name the whole night.

ECW Angles

WE BURNED THE Tijuana territory down. Konnan was promoting the city matches, and he was using ECW angles all the time. We went on for about a year, amping things up, until we finally got to the point where we just couldn't top ourselves any more. People had seen us jump off ladders and break tables so much, it just didn't look that scary.

Cage matches, fire—we kept amping up, and the wrestling commission started to clamp down even harder. New members came in, determined to get us back under control. They had a point: They were worried about us endangering the fans with some of the things we did.

The fans, on the other hand, were loving it. We had a huge crowd most nights. We may have turned off a few families with our antics, but we had developed a steady following among teenagers and men in their early twenties.

Eventually, the commission clamped down totally. We could no longer use any type of weapons in the ring. The promotion lost popularity. Konnan soon started a new venture—but I'm getting ahead of myself.

Marriage

WRESTLING WASN'T THE only high point of my life in that period. Romance was huge as well.

Most teenage romances don't last very long, and wrestlers are notorious for having love problems. With that combination, most people would have figured that my relationship with my first real girlfriend would never last.

But they'd be wrong. Angie was and is the love of my life.

Angie and I were married May 11, 1996, in Tijuana. It was a traditional Catholic ceremony, which led to a fantastic celebration with our family and close friends. Her mom gave us her best blessings. She and I had had a rocky start, but over the years I'd managed to win her over. I think she knew true love when she saw it. We've grown close over the years.

Psicosis was my best man—and no, neither one of us wore masks at the ceremony.

Unfortunately, my wedding happened to coincide with a *TripleMania* held in Chicago, which limited the number of my wrestling friends who could join us, including Antonio Peña and Konnan.

I took some ribbing from the wrestlers, asking which I'd rather do, wrestle or get married, but there was never a contest in my heart. As much as I love wrestling—it's my life—I'd waited four years to tie the knot with Angie, and nothing was going to stop me that day.

After we got married, we started thinking about buying a house where we could raise a family. We had a lot of options, both in Mexico and the States. For me, though, there was only one place I really wanted to put down roots: San Diego.

I wanted to be around family, both mine and my wife's. We liked Tijuana, but San Diego had always been my first love. And I wanted my kids to be able to go to school like I did in the U.S.

Kids.

Our original plan was to wait a few years before getting started on that road. But God had other ideas. Not too long after we came back from our honeymoon, we discovered that Angie was pregnant.

It was a surprise, but a really, really good surprise.

Rolling Big

AT THIS POINT, I was rolling pretty big in Mexico. I was main eventing, going north of the border every week for ECW, doing big shows in Japan. And on the personal side, I was now a married man. I was feeling mature and ready to do the things a man does, taking responsibility for his life and his future. I thought things were going really well.

What I didn't know was that they were about to take another huge leap upward.

I remember we were all on a bus going to an AAA event. Konnan had just gotten back from the States, where he'd wrestled for WCW in an audition match. He brought back a tape and we watched it on the bus.

"That's really great," I told him after it ended. "Good luck."

"Yeah, bro, thanks. I'm going to try and get you there."

"Yeah?"

"Yeah."

"That'd be real nice," I told him, and I went back to whatever I'd been doing before he put in the tape.

Sleep, I think.

Little did I know . . .

Prime Time

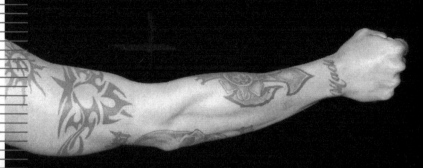

It wasn't exactly a grand plan, but with Konnan only a few words were enough. He started appearing as a regular with WCW in early 1996. As soon as he got there, he started talking me up. By June, they had decided to give me a try.

At this point I could see the big picture. I wasn't the local hometown boy anymore. I understood that the world of wrestling had become massive, and that the best opportunities were in the States, with either World Championship Wrestling or World Wrestling Federation.

And I also knew, from my trips with ECW, that America was ready for a *lucha libre* style. Fans wanted high-flying action, and I could deliver it. I may have only been twenty-one, but I'd been wrestling professionally for seven years. That was a lot of time in the ring, and it filled me with a lot of confidence.

Which isn't to say that I was cocky about it, or that I had a bloated head. You always have a little doubt, in the back of your mind. Always before a show—then and even now—there are knots in your stomach.

Can you do it again? Can you entertain these people?

The knots and doubts disappear once the show starts. Maybe the fact that they're there to begin with helps me keep my edge. Maybe, in some ways, they help push me to succeed, and exceed.

If you want to be the best, you have to keep your edge. That means believing in yourself—but also believing that you still have something to prove.

And that's how I felt in 1996 when Konnan called up and said WCW wanted me to audition for them.

Wrestling for Peace

KONNAN HAD BEEN pushing me for a while. Besides our friendship, he felt that having another strong Mexican-style wrestler in the promotion would help the company. He saw the potential of Mexican-style wrestling in the States, and he thought WCW should capitalize on it.

At the beginning of June, Último Dragón and I faced off against Heavy Metal and Psicosis at the *World Wrestling Peace Festival*, held June 1 at the Sports Arena in Los Angeles.

The peace festival was promoted by Antonio Inoki, who was

hoping to promote international understanding by holding wrestling events around the world. The L.A. show was held in conjunction with WCW, and a lot of their stars were there. According to rumor, so were Eric Bischoff and other key WCW execs.

People later said my performance at that show convinced WCW that they would be fools if they didn't give me a shot. All I know is, Konnan called me and told me to come to Baltimore for a match on June 17.

What he didn't tell me was that the match was going to be held at a Pay-Per-View and that it was considered one of the biggest WCW events of the year. It happened to coincide with Father's Day, which meant a big crowd at home as well as at the arena.

Dean Malenko

MY MATCH WAS going to be against Dean Malenko. I'd heard of Dean, but I don't believe I'd seen him work in person before. Konnan gave me a few tapes so I could study his style.

When I saw them, I thought to myself, *He's a shooter. I better be ready.*

He looked pretty damn intimidating. Dean was an excellent mat wrestler—his nickname was The Man of a Thousand Holds. To be honest, while I can mat wrestle, I've never really considered that the best part of my game.

Some younger fans may not know who Dean Malenko is. If so, that's a real shame. Find some tapes and go to school on him, because it'll be an enjoyable education.

Dean Malenko is one of the all-time greats, a wrestler who defined professionalism and blazed a trail for cruiserweights. We're all still trying to live up to the standards he set in the 1990s.

Dean's father, Boris, was a professional wrestler, so he came from good genes. He'd made a name for himself in ECW, where among other things he was called The Shooter, before going over to WCW with Eddie Guerrero and Chris Benoit in what became known as the cruiserweight revolution. Together, they brought a new level of excitement to prime-time wrestling at WCW.

Dean mostly played a villain in his early days at WCW. Onscreen, he looked cold and really mean—so mean they called him The Iceman. Besides a powerful, athletic style, he was a virtual encyclopedia of wrestling moves and holds.

At the time of my audition, he was WCW's Cruiserweight champ: the number-one attraction in that division.

Just Entertain

WAIT—I WAS wrestling the Cruiserweight Champion in my very first match in the promotion? For my audition?

At a Pay-Per-View?

"Bro, why didn't you tell me?" I asked Konnan when I got up there and realized what was going on.

"Hey, you're here. All you have to do is entertain and do your thing."

I walked into the locker room and said hello to everybody I could, though I didn't really know many of the guys. Scott Steiner and his brother Rick were there; I knew them slightly from ECW and went over and said hi. Otherwise, the faces all belonged to strangers.

I knew who they were, though. They were all famous. Hulk Hogan was there. Ric Flair. It was like an all-star team of professional wrestling.

Mostly they ignored me. A few may have made fun of me behind my back, or snickered, thinking I wasn't going to put on much of a show. I remember hearing a couple of guys say, "Hey, who's that kid? What's that kid doing in the locker room?"

There were other comments:

"Are we starting a new midget division?"

"Are we filming Willie Wonka Part II?"

Maybe I can't blame them. I was real skinny, short, and had a total of one tattoo. To guys who weighed two and even three times what I did, and who stood a whole foot taller, I didn't look like much of a wrestler.

The comments didn't bother me. Hell, I was tripping. Here I was, a twenty-one-year-old, in with guys I'd watched on television for a long time. I was hanging out where the big boys played now. I had made it. It couldn't get any better than this.

I found a spot to dress in the corner. When I was done, I went over and met Dean.

He was the nicest guy in the world. And in the ring, contrary to what I had thought, he turned out to be smooth to work with.

Dean was very familiar with Mexican-style wrestling. He gave me advice on what to take away and what to emphasize. We went over the match beforehand, and then we went out and tore the house down.

The Match

WE HAD CHEMISTRY right from the get-go. I was wearing my tights and mask, looking very different to the American crowd. Not knowing who I was, they were pretty quiet when I came down.

A few made fun of me because I was wearing a mask. I tried not to let them get to me. The Baltimore crowd was pretty knowledgeable about wrestling, and maybe one or two had seen me on ECW. But for the most part, I was unknown.

The announcers were giving me a good push on air. Mike Tenay was already calling me "the human highlight film."

I couldn't hear that, though.

We traded some handholds and acrobatic flips at the top of the match. We started moving a little faster. I spun around Dean's neck and he flew out of the ring, and all of a sudden the crowd was into what we were doing.

Dean went to work on my left elbow, unleashing a few of his thousand holds. That gave him an advantage into the first third of the match, until I used his hold to help me climb the ropes and dropkick him to the mat.

Malenko got me into a press and nearly pinned me. A kickout saved me—but it only set me up for some more abuse as he got me in an armbreaker leveraged by his ankle-locked legs.

I'd break out, springboard, and take him down, but Dean was relentless, punishing my elbow and working for the pin. He put me into an upside-down surfboard—or, as it's known in Mexico, a Rita Romero. I slipped out of the pin, then resisted a series of submission moves. The story of the match was simple: He was going to try and punish me and take away my air game with his strength and full range of moves.

The crowd started warming to me because of my endurance.

Then I managed to get Dean out of the ring. As he flew out, he bopped a cameraman and was momentarily dazed. I did a springboard somersault off the top rope, planting him on the concrete. A dropkick to his face back in the ring, and it looked like I was going to win. He kicked out at two and we exchanged some bridges, both just missing the pin.

My frankensteiner failed to get a pin. Then we worked into the corner, where I put him down with another frankensteiner off the turnbuckle.

The crowd was psyched for an upset, but it wasn't to be. Dean managed to turn me around and powerbomb me to the mat, holding me there—just barely—for the three count.

A Great Job

WHEN WE WALKED into the back, everyone applauded. They'd stopped what they were doing and had gathered around the monitor to watch. We got a standing ovation.

That just doesn't happen in wrestling, especially in those days, in that company. It was a tremendous feeling.

You can tell when you have a good match out in the ring. You just know, from your reaction to it and from the fans'. But the real test is when you go back into the locker room. When everybody stands up and starts applauding, then you really know.

No more little guy jokes. Now it was more like:

"Great match, guys!"

"Hell of a match!"

"That's the way to do it."

I was on Cloud 9. Hogan, Flair, Nash—they were all applauding us.

Applauding me.

Dean's Professionalism

DEAN AND I went on to have a series of memorable matches over the next few weeks and months. We wrestled together throughout my career at WCW. He was always one of my best opponents.

I was very impressed by Dean's professionalism. He was a very enjoyable man to work with, from that very first match to the last time we worked together. He knew my style right away. I didn't have to adapt at all or change anything. He knew exactly where to position himself as I did my moves. He really displayed me well for the crowd.

Dean and I would always try to come up with a few different moves and holds—holds for him especially. I think that at every match

we had he brought out something new. The fans looked forward to that, and so did I.

Dean was as creative with his holds as I was with my moves. Every time I stepped into the ring with him, I knew we were going full blast. He had a way of bringing that out in you. As we went on, I got comfortable with his style and was able to take my own game to a new level.

Dean told me later that he had worked with a lot of Mexican wrestlers in Japan, and that helped him when he was facing me. He seemed able to adapt to my style pretty well.

He came across as a different person on television: You were sure he was going to tear you up. But he was the nicest guy going in person backstage.

I still can't believe it. How many guys get an opportunity to work for a company, and they throw you off the bat into a Pay-Per-View with Dean Malenko?

It was a real break, and Malenko made me look like a million dollars.

Day Laborer

WE DEFINITELY ROCKED the house. But I didn't get a contract with WCW.

Not that night, anyway.

I didn't complain. The pay for one night was a lot more than what I got in Mexico. I remember thinking, *If they pay me this much, I could make some pretty good cheese.*

People always think that wrestlers are rich. I'm not complaining at all. It's a job I love, and it certainly doesn't pay poorly compared to most work.

But the truth is, most wrestlers don't really make as much money as people think. Many wrestlers in Mexico work other jobs to keep food on the table. And when WCW did offer me a contract—it happened a couple of weeks later—I was making far less than six figures.

Not that I didn't *feel* like a millionaire.

It wasn't just the money. The contract represented security. It included health insurance, which I didn't have in Mexico. And it was a future with one of the two biggest wrestling franchises in the U.S., and therefore the world.

I was married, my wife had become pregnant during our honeymoon, we were looking into buying a house—things were really turning out good for me. I was at the top of the world.

Problems in Mexico

WCW AND WORLD Wrestling Federation were locked in a head-to-head fight to dominate the American wrestling scene. Besides their head-to-head shows on Monday nights—*Nitro* and *Raw*, respectively—they did a variety of other shows, from Pay-Per-Views to house shows. By the beginning of 1998, WCW would launch another show on Thursday nights called *WCW Thunder*. All of this competition meant a lot of opportunity for wrestlers, including some of my friends in Mexico. With the success of people like Eddie Guerrero, Konnan, and myself, WCW naturally looked to Mexico for more talent.

Konnan helped bring new wrestlers in. Eventually, Antonio Peña began to take offense.

Konnan had been his right-hand man, so it couldn't have been an easy time for either one of them. Mixed into the conflict was a dispute over how the wrestlers from Mexico should be paid: whether the money should go to AAA, who would then pay them, or to them directly.

I don't know exactly what happened with that, whether AAA was looking for a cut or not. Since I was an American citizen living in San Diego, I was paid directly and the issue never came up.

Some people may have had their conflicts with Peña, but I was never one of them. He would occasionally give me advice on how to sell or work the crowd. We were very close toward the end. He was always very cool with me, very nice. He passed away of a heart attack in October 2006. God rest his soul.

Promo Azteca

TOWARD THE END of 1996, the conflict over money convinced some of the Mexican wrestlers to leave AAA completely, rather than splitting their time between the promotion and WCW. Psicosis, La Parka, Juventud Guerrera, Super Calo, and a few others were wrestling a lot in WCW, but they were actually wrestling on limited contracts. That meant they were being paid only for the nights they worked. That was nothing new, but it meant that they had a lot of downtime when they weren't working for WCW. Once they decided they didn't want to work with AAA anymore, it left a hole in their schedules— and an opportunity.

Konnan and Peña had a falling-out over money as well. Konnan decided to leave AAA and start a new company in which the Mexican wrestlers connected with WCW could work. He got a contract with TV Azteca, one of the largest networks in Mexico, and began packing the house.

My schedule was busier than most of the others', but I still worked with him when I had the chance.

Konnan's Promotion

KONNAN HAD PROMOTED shows in Tijuana for a while, filling the void for AAA when it lost its Tijuana promoter in the early 1990s. He would work with the wrestlers before the shows, doing the booking, helping them with music—all the creative, behind-the-scenes things that help make modern wrestling so interesting. So Promo Azteca, even though it was a big step up, was just a natural progression for him.

Konnan's plan was to take the underused Mexican stars, mix them with some guys who were getting big in the States, and bring ECW-style wrestling to Tijuana. He succeeded, changing local fans' views about wrestling. But at the same time he caused an incredible amount of controversy.

He brought in tables, ladders, trash cans, sticks—all the shit you would see in ECW. The people loved it. But there was one huge obstacle: the Wrestling and Boxing Commission of Tijuana.

They were not flexible at all. Even before Konnan's promotion, wrestlers would be fined for using chairs. If you were on the ground and shot someone into the rail, you would be fined or suspended or both, even if no one got hurt. They were very conservative.

Some people call them conservative. I call them dicks. Total dicks.

"When I worked in wrestling," one of the commissioners told Konnan, "we ate on tables. Now you're putting people through them."

"That's evolution, bro," he told him.

These tables were only tables in the most theoretical sense: They had legs and a top. I wouldn't have eaten off them, not without expecting to get my dinner in my lap. We'd put someone on top and expect it to snap before they were hit.

Our ladders were the same way. They were dangerous to even climb. But they looked good collapsing, which was the one thing you wanted.

We had tables on fire, ladders falling, wrestlers flying all over the place. The commission would come in after just about every match and penalize us in some way. Konnan tried working with them, negotiating back and forth.

Sometimes they were just making it look as if they were giving us a hard time. Other times it was for real. The different commission members had different attitudes.

WCW Steps In

AT LEAST AT first, WCW had no problem with the arrangement. They were rotating guys through the house shows, so it was easy to set up a schedule that didn't conflict with theirs. And Konnan would book TV on days when WCW was dark. So you might wrestle on the weekend for WCW, then head down to Tijuana in the middle of the week for a televised show there.

After a while, WCW decided that there was too much risk for the wrestlers and they put a stop to it. If you had a contract with WCW, as I did, you were told that's where your energy belonged.

Losing the big stars hurt Promo Azteca. The promotion kept going for a couple of years but eventually fell apart. Before it did, though, it treated fans to some fantastic shows, with plenty of high flying. Super Crazy, Super Muñeco, and Halloween were just a few of the other stars who were featured in the promotion, winning fame there before going on to other companies.

The fans were pretty emotional and hardcore. There's a video on the Web somewhere of me interfering in a match with Konnan. The fans didn't like the ending that much. It's overhyped on the Web as a riot, but still, Tijuana fans were pretty passionate about their wrestling, and they still are. A number of matches ended up with bottle-throwing and *very* passionate fans. *Rudos* who won with their underhanded tactics were sometimes lucky to get out of the arena alive.

REY MYSTERIO JR.
FLYINGFURY

WCW
MONDAY
NITRO
TNT

THE RULES HAVE CHANGED

WCW Style:
Quickening the Pace

ONE OF THE differences between Mexican wrestling and most American wrestling is the mat wrestling that starts off a lot of the Mexican matches. In ECW, we would start off with mat wrestling too, since Paul E. wanted the *lucha libre* style. But in WCW, I changed my style, tightening the pace. I stopped doing a lot of the mat wrestling.

For one thing, I was wrestling under a time limit. I might have six minutes for a match. I learned from Dean Malenko, Eddie Guerrero, and the others that sometimes you have to jumpstart the match with a high spot.

But the biggest change wasn't in the ring. From the start, WCW spelled my last name with a *y*: Mysterio. I'm not sure why; probably it wasn't done on purpose. I'd guess that whoever first wrote it down knew the Spanish word meant "mystery" and thought that's the way it was spelled.

Anyway, the change or mistake stuck. I didn't realize it until a few months in. I was signing my autographs with an *i* when one day I realized as I signed a promo picture that they had printed *y*. So I changed it. I was now Rey Mysterio Jr., instead of Rey Misterio Jr.

As you can tell, it wasn't a big deal to me.

Another of the differences between Mexico and WCW was just the sheer size of the guys. I've always been small, but in Mexico and ECW, the size difference wasn't as glaring as it was in WCW. I really stood out in the locker room.

Whenever I worked the bigger guys, I had to change my style. Usually I couldn't do the normal headscissors and frankensteiners, unless I was working with someone who really knew how to base me. There'd be more action down on the mat. Maybe I'd hit him with a crossbody or get a leg onto him off the rope while he was flat.

People who don't really know who I am sometimes assume that

I had a language problem when I came to the States. Of course that wasn't true. Not only am I American, but English is my first language. So I was plenty comfortable. Looking back, that probably helped the transition. Not knowing the language can be a big barrier to making friends. Once you start making friends in the locker room, you know you're part of the family.

A Friendly Lift

THE FIRST PERSON who offered his friendship to me after I joined WCW was Kevin Nash.

It was a few weeks after I started, right around the time I signed my contract. We were in Daytona for the July 7 *Bash at the Beach*, one of WCW's big Pay-Per-Views that year. Psicosis and I wrestled in the opening match.

That was a huge night for WCW: It's the show when Hulk Hogan did his heel turn, still remembered as one of the great moments in pro wrestling history.

I had to go over to Orlando the next day for a match at the Disney/MGM outdoor arena on *Nitro*. Konnan was coming with me. Kevin came over right after the Pay-Per-View and offered to give us a ride the next day.

A car ride may not sound like much, but at the time we didn't have rental cars and were stuck taking cabs everywhere. I believe I had my American license—I honestly can't remember—but I know I didn't have a credit card; things were still a little different back then. One time we took a two-hour cab ride. It's funny now, but at the time it wasn't a laugher. I think it cost something like three hundred and fifty bucks.

We had to take cabs from the airport to wherever we were: land in Atlanta and take a cab to Macon, Georgia. Another time we took a Greyhound bus that stopped maybe a million times before we got to wherever it was we were going.

So a friendly ride meant a lot.

"I'll pick you guys up at 7:30," Kevin said.

We said great. Then back at the hotel, Konnan and I started debating back and forth.

"You think he's really going to come?"

"I don't know."

It would be just like a wrestler to pull a little joke on the new guys: to leave them waiting while he laughed all the way to the show.

"Maybe he was ribbing us."

"No, no, I don't think so."

"He must have been."

"No, I think he meant it."

Sure enough, Kevin was waiting in his Caddy when 7:30 rolled around. We jumped in his car and headed to the show.

Cruiserweight Champ

IT WAS ON that *Nitro* show, July 8, that I won the cruiserweight title from Dean Malenko.

WWE collected that match on my *Rey Mysterio 619* video DVD, so you can watch it if you want. One of the interesting things for fans watching today is the fact that the match was held outside. You don't see too much of that in the States.

Unlike our first showdown, I got to use my speed a lot more in this match. Both of us were literally flying around the ring, Dean almost as much as me. We had tumbles and jumps out of the ring, jumps in the ring, a lot of near pins. At one point, I did a moonsault out of the ring and onto the floor, landing on the concrete. Dean was just getting up, and he couldn't catch me. I think the senior citizens in the front row were ready to call for an ambulance.

"It's hard to wrestle a man if you can't grab him," said one of the commentators, and that was the game plan. From my side at least.

At one point in the match, Dean had me down solidly. He could have had the pin, but in the story of the match, I had infuriated him early on with my speed and moves, and now he wanted revenge. He pulled me up as the ref counted so he could inflict more pain.

A fatal mistake.

Dean flipped me around back and forth for a bit as if I were a rag doll. But I was gathering my energy, getting a second wind. Finally I worked to a spot for a frankensteiner. He hit the mat, and as I came over, I grabbed his legs.

"We've got a new Cruiserweight Champion!" shouted Mike Tenay from the announcers' table.

The fans were on their feet—even the old lady in the wheelchair.

It was a crazy feeling. I'd been with WCW a little more than three weeks, and now I was champion.

My Deal

THE NIGHT BEFORE that match, Kevin Sullivan called me over to his car. I don't remember exactly where we were—I think we were in Daytona, but we were definitely in a parking lot. Sullivan was handling talent at the time: His job was roughly the same as the head of talent relations in today's WWE.

He offered me a full-time contract. I took it.

Antonio Peña took the news that I was leaving very well. I'm sure he didn't want to lose one of his best draws, but he didn't give a hint of whatever pain it may have caused him. He wished me well.

I've been blessed with some very understanding and supportive bosses. Every time I've been ready to move on with my life to something better, they have wished me well. And I've done the same from my side. I've always left with a thank-you and the promise that if I could come back in the future and help them in some way, I would.

A Human Lawn Dart

ONE OF MY most famous bits ever occured during my early months with WCW: the infamous lawn dart incident.

In the weeks after I became champion, the Outsiders tore WCW apart, literally as well as figuratively. Hall and Nash did most of the damage. One night on *Nitro*, they staged a fight in the trailer we used as a locker room. Their target was Arn Anderson—and anyone else who got in their way.

The cameras switched to the back just in time to see the fight roll outside, where they were pummeling Arn and Marcus "Buff" Bagwell with baseball bats. Deciding to help, I climbed up on the trailer and dove off into Kevin's arms. He spun me around and tossed me headfirst into the side of the trailer.

I bounced off, tumbled down, and landed on the concrete.

The bit had been my idea. I told him I'd jump from the trailer, then he could pick me up and throw me.

"Yo, bro, isn't that dangerous?" Kevin asked.

"Nah. Just throw me in."

And that's exactly what happened.

It looks impressive, but it actually didn't hurt. He threw me perfectly.

People talked about that for quite a while. The incident became known as the Human Lawn Dart, and I still hear comments about it from time to time.

Our WCW Crew

A LITTLE GROUP of us started working and traveling together at WCW. There'd be the Mexicans, with Konnan as kind of our leader and negotiator. He got Psicosis hooked up after me, and eventually some other *luchadores* joined us. Often we'd have Eddie, Chris Jericho, Chris Benoit, and some of the other cruiserweights on the same loop.

That made it a lot easier. All of us had come from more or less the same backgrounds and were trying to work our way up. Eddie and the others were always helping us with rides and giving us the little pointers that made living on the road easier.

After a while, we started renting minivans. I remember squishing seven people inside a van. We did that plenty of times.

I ended up handling the driving a lot. One time we were packed in: I think Halloween was there, Psicosis, Damián . . . I can't remember who else, but it was a packed van—two in the front and five in the back. We were in Florida somewhere and it was late.

Everybody in the back was passed out. Damián and I looked at each other, and we cranked up the heat. If one person was awake, we *all* had to be awake. About fifteen minutes later, they all woke up and started complaining.

"What are you doing? We're sweating."

"Nobody goes to sleep," we told them. "That's the rule."

We either all slept, or we all stayed awake. Besides, there was a lot to see at midnight.

Funny to say, but we didn't get lost too often. The only time I can really remember was once with Eddie.

We took a wrong turn and went an hour and a half in the wrong direction before we finally figured it out. This was in the days before GPS systems were common. Back then our GPS was finding someone on the street and asking where the hell we were.

Strict for Some People

GETTING TO A show late would get you in a lot of trouble at WCW—depending on who you were. Which basically meant that if you were one of the Mexican wrestlers, you were always nervous.

They wanted to be strict and have everything in order, but they were only strict with certain people. The younger talent, the Mexicans especially, had to be very careful.

It sometimes seemed that we were there to obey rules and do whatever we were told to do. Wrestle, yes, but otherwise everything was completely at their command. Things got worse as time went on. I don't know if it had to do with the fact that we were Mexican or Hispanic; I don't know if it was prejudice. It might just have been because we were the new guys and low on the totem pole, so we were the ones they could push around. But there was always a tone in the air, as if we were going to be punished—and maybe deported—if we screwed up. Thank God I was born in the U.S.; they couldn't hold anything over my head like that.

Of course, none of us were illegal. We were either American citizens, like me, or we had all the proper work papers and everything else you need to have a job. We were all legit. No one was ever in the States crooked. But there was definitely the feeling that you would get heat if you didn't go straight by the book. *Their* book.

Hogan

I'M NOT COMPLAINING about the fact that WCW's top stars were treated differently than the rest of the wrestlers. There were definitely cliques in the locker room. Hogan had his people, for example, and how they were treated depended a lot on where the main star in the group was ranked in the company.

But you know what? I respect that to some degree, especially in Hogan's case. The guy turned this business around. That's Hulk Hogan. I always respected him. You have to give the man credit. And some of the credit works out to him having more privileges than anyone else.

At the time, people complained about him, claiming he treated them like a dick, that sort of thing. But he was never bad to me. He was always straight, no bullshit.

As a matter of fact, he used to bring his son Nick around at times, and I'd kick it with him in the ring a bit. Nick was a good kid, and fooling with him reminded me of when I'd been his age and got a chance to work with my uncle and other Mexican stars. So on a personal level as well as a professional level, I can only say the best things about Hogan.

Cliques

HOGAN WASN'T THE only wrestler with a clique. There was a DDP clique—a group of guys who hung with Dallas Diamond Page. Bagwell had a little group. Scott Steiner had his people. There were a bunch of them. I got along with them all. I didn't have any trouble.

But each group had different pulls with management and Eric Bischoff, who was in charge of the company. Or at least it seemed that way. You saw who ran with who, who had stroke and who didn't.

You can't just go into a new place of that magnitude and expect to have stroke. You have to earn your stripes. But the behind-the-scenes maneuvering for status caused some problems. There'd be friction in the locker room, with people complaining about not getting a push or having to obey rules when others didn't.

I know it cuts both ways. I have a little stroke myself these days. If we're going to be late, I can tell the other wrestlers to chill. "Relax, put the heat on me." It's not a huge thing, but it is definitely something the newer guys can't get away with.

And it wasn't something I could do back in WCW.

"What Are You Saying?"

THE MEXICANS BECAME their own group, and we rolled in deep. We had our own little section going. Every so often, just for fun, we'd talk in Spanish so no one understood.

Of course, we'd make sure they were listening.

"He thinks we're talking about him," we'd joke, saying it in Spanish, of course. "Keep talking."

"What are you saying?" the other wrestlers would ask in English. "What the fuck? You talking about me?"

"No, no, no, bro, it's nothing. Just saying hello . . ."

We'd go on, playing with their heads. It was fun to do with people who had big opinions of themselves.

Bagwell bothered some of the guys—not me, actually—and they'd pull that on him all the time. Lex Luger was another victim, but he was out there to begin with. A cool dude, never a beef with me . . . but out there.

The Mexicans were definitely on the low end of the status chain at WCW. It was the attitude of the office and of Eric. I don't know if he thought we were slaves or didn't like us or what. He was just a dick at points. Not all the time—but enough.

Dominik's Birth

ONE OF THE times where the company seemed to have no respect for me personally came when my wife was just about to give birth to Dominik, my first child. This was in 1997, when I'd been with the company for a few months.

We were going into a Pay-Per-View. J. J. Dillon was my talent relations guy, the executive I had to attend to. He worked under Eric.

A word about Dillon. Old-time wrestling fans may remember that he was the original manager for the Four Horsemen, probably the most famous heel stable in wrestling history. He had an important part in the early storylines and deserves his place in the history books. By this time, he was working in the front office and occasionally appearing onscreen as the head of the WCW executive committee. As far as I was concerned, he was the real-life executive who would deal with me on company matters.

I remember it was in early April, the weekend of *Uncensored*, a WCW Pay-Per-View. I was booked to wrestle Prince Iaukea for the WCW World Television Championship. They wanted me to come in Saturday afternoon, a full day ahead of the show. Not for promos or anything; just to be there.

The baby had been due right around that time. If you haven't been through it at least once, you probably can't understand how nerve-racking it is to have a kid, especially the first time.

So when I say I was nervous even though I didn't have much of a direct role in the proceedings, believe me.

Any Minute

THAT FRIDAY, MY wife was due any minute. We were walking around, trying to push the baby down. "Come on, Dominik," we were saying. "Come on."

She felt a little something and we went to the hospital. But she wasn't ready and they sent her home.

I managed to get out of the Saturday afternoon flight. I had to lie to do it. I called and said, "My wife is in the hospital right now. I can't leave her."

"Okay. We really need you to get in here," answered whoever it was I spoke to. "Call as soon as you can."

If it was their wife, I guarantee they wouldn't have been thinking of leaving. Hell no.

They rebooked me on a Saturday night flight. I told my wife I wasn't leaving her.

"No, no, you have to go, you have to go," she said. She was worried about my job.

"No. I'm not leaving you. You're not giving birth without me."

The flight kept getting closer.

I called the office again and I spoke to J.J.

"You know what, J.J.?" I said. "We're still in the hospital."

"All right, get the last flight tonight."

I hung up the phone and told my wife, "I'm staying with you until you have the baby."

That night, she went back in the hospital. We went in and then Dominik was born at 6:59 P.M., Saturday, April 5, 1997.

I didn't want to leave. Seeing your son or daughter born is a really cool experience. I was right there, right next to Angie as our son came out into the world. But I could only enjoy so much—and then I had to rush right off.

They got me a flight for Sunday morning. My match wasn't the biggest one on the card, but they still insisted on getting me there. When I got to the building just before show time, J.J. Dillon was waiting for me like I was Hulk Hogan.

At least I felt important getting out of the cab.

Injured

NOT TOO LONG after that, I got seriously hurt for the first time.

I remember it very clearly. I was doing a show with Dean Malenko. I did what I now call the West Coast Pop, starting with a frankensteiner and then going for the pin. When I landed, my knee went sideways. I felt it right away. I started to get up and my knee just folded. It felt like a noodle.

But it wasn't the end of the match. I kept going.

When we finally got back to the locker room, the trainer took a look and said it might be my ACL, or anterior cruciate ligament.

It felt bad when it happened, but the next morning when I woke up in the hotel I couldn't lift my leg from the bed. I was in so much pain I had to use my hand to lift my leg onto the floor. I dragged it with me across the room to get dressed. It was swollen and puffy, and needless to say, it hurt like hell.

I was so hurt I couldn't walk. I flew to Atlanta and got an MRI. When they saw the results, they scheduled me for surgery.

At the time, reports claimed that Konnan had hurt my leg. That was just something that was done for story purposes; it wasn't real. In fact, I don't even remember the storyline at all.

Frankensteiners at Fault?

I HAD LANDED off a frankensteiner when I hurt my knee. Naturally, I thought that the injury came from that particular move, that one time, but as I mentioned earlier, now that I've been able to think about it and watch the old tapes, it's clear that I had been putting too much strain on my knee for years. I had been doing the same move for years on the hard rings of Mexico. When I entered WCW, I think my knee said enough's enough. "You've got insurance here. I'll blow out now so they can take care of your surgery."

I can make a little joke about it now, but it wasn't very funny back then. The anterior cruciate ligament, or ACL, is a small piece of tissue that helps hold your knee together. A tear can lead to even worse injuries to your knee. While the nearby muscles can be trained to do some of the ACL's work, it's pretty hard to imagine wrestling without one. Mine had to be fixed if I was ever going to get into the ring again.

Back Together

I WAS VERY, very nervous about getting surgery. Other guys had had operations for different problems and injuries; as far as I could tell, the results weren't always that good. Ultimate Dragon had a problem with his hand that I think got worse after the operation. You hear things like that and it makes you worried.

But you know what? The surgery itself went fine. The doctor used a cadaver tendon to put my knee back together. It was a full surgery, and he left a big scar in the middle of my kneecap. But, with a lot of rehab, I was able to wrestle again.

My style puts a lot of pressure on my knee. As I mentioned earlier, the way I used to land after the frankensteiner may very well have set me up for the injury. But when the doctor finished, I felt almost as good as new. The repair served me well . . . for a while, anyway.

Daddy Time

THE INJURY SENT me home for a few months. It was the longest time I'd gone without wrestling since becoming a professional. In fact, if you don't count the rehab, it was probably the longest time I was away from the ring since I had started training.

I was worried about losing my spot in the company. I'd been on a roll and I didn't want to lose the momentum I'd built. But at the same time, it was good being home. Dominik had just been born, and the time off gave me a chance to watch him grow.

Being able to feed him and even change his diaper turned out to be very special experiences. The daddy thing has really been an important part of my life. I had the opportunity to spend time with both of my kids during their early years. It's hard—and with the wrestling lifestyle, it can really be impossible. So getting hurt had some sweet compensation.

My Mask

MY WORST CONFRONTATION with WCW's management happened later that year, when rumors started going around that I was going to lose my mask.

The rumors turned into a confrontation, though it was weeks before anyone actually approached me about it.

I'm not sure where the idea came from. I think Scott Hall said something along the lines of, *Hey, he's a good-looking motherfucker, man, why is he wrestling with the mask? Take his mask off. You should have him in commercials.*

It's a story I've heard from various sources. If it's true, I'm sure he thought it was a compliment: Nobody calls you good-looking because they're trying to put you down. And I was getting along with Scott and Kevin Nash, hanging out with them, so I have no reason to think it was meant in a bad way.

Or do I?

Anyway, the rumor started to spread. I don't know if Eric had the idea himself at some point. He wasn't the one booking the shows, which is wrestling terminology for writing the storylines, though he could have been directly involved in the decision.

A match was scheduled between me and Eddie Guerrero for *Halloween Havoc* in 1997. Eddie had the title, and the match was billed as a contest between Eddie's title and my mask.

He loses, I get the title. I lose, I take off my mask.

Somehow, I heard that I was going to lose. It would mean my mask.

I didn't believe it at first. Then, sure enough, I got the word from a reliable source.

The source was Kevin Nash.

Kevin was my friend, and I didn't make any secret of how I felt about it.

You have to remember, losing a mask in Mexico is a very, very big deal. When it happens, there's a big buildup and the whole event is very emotional. A lot of thought goes into it. It's a career-shaping event. It doesn't necessarily mean the end of your career, but it's definitely not something taken lightly.

"You Better Show Up"

BUT THE WHOLE significance of my mask—the tradition behind it, its importance—seemed lost on the people in charge of WCW, including Eric. At the least, it should have been discussed with me. But it wasn't.

When Kevin told me about it, I told him I wasn't going to do it.

He was pretty sympathetic. He agreed I shouldn't go.

"Tell them you're hurt," he said. "Tell them you can't wrestle. Get a note from your doctor, and don't show up. Then you have a legitimate excuse."

I decided I'd take his advice.

Well, the word got back to Eric somehow. Who told him? I don't know. Somebody stooged me off. I hope it wasn't Kevin, though the timing of what happened next made it seem like one pretty big coincidence if he didn't.

Eric called me at home that Friday, the day before I was supposed to leave for Vegas to get ready for the Pay-Per-View, which was on Sunday. I think it was the first time Eric ever called me, certainly there.

I never pick up my phone at home, but that day I happened to.

Eric said hello.

"Hey, Eric, how you doing?"

"I heard you're not going to be going to *Halloween Havoc.*"

"Well, that is my plan."

"I just want to let you know that if you do not show up, you're in breech of contract, and I will fire you."

"Wait, hold on. You want to take off my mask, and I'm not cool with that."

"You are going to do what you are told, and you have nothing to say about that. So you better show up, and you better be there for the Pay-Per-View."

"Well, what if I don't show up?"

"You just better show up."

The conversation is still burned into my memory. He was pissed off—which, looking back, is kind of funny, because I was the one who should have been pissed off.

Intimidated

I WAS INTIMIDATED by him and he knew it. I had nowhere else to go.

I remember asking Kevin at a bar in San Francisco whether he thought I could get a spot with World Wrestling Federation. Straight up, he told me it'd be hard to go over to the other promotion, so I knew I was pretty much boxed in.

I took my flight to Las Vegas on Saturday. That night, I ran into Eric in the hotel lounge. We said hello to each other, but he did it in almost a mocking way.

"You ready for tomorrow?" he asked.

"Yeah, well, I'm here."

"Good."

That was about the extent of the conversation. No explanation, no real courtesy, just "Good."

The next day, Eddie and I set up the match.

Eddie knew what was going on. He told me not to worry about it.

WHILE EDDIE AND I SET UP THE MATCH, THE OUTCOME KEPT CHANGING.

"Show these motherfuckers what we're all about," he said. "Show them what you're about. Let them take your mask."

"This wasn't the way I wanted to go down. This has a lot of meaning to me."

"I know, bro. Who do you think you're telling?"

I think if I had asked Eddie, he would have thrown the match somehow. He was that good a friend. But I didn't. I didn't want to get him in trouble.

"Come on," he told me. "Don't worry about it. Get your head in the game."

So we set up the match. About half an hour before the show, Arn Anderson came over. I think he was our agent for the match, but whatever, he came over and told me, "Keep your head up."

A little while later, someone came up and gave us the outcome of the match, basically a script that said how it would end.

I was going over, not Eddie. I was keeping the mask.

Power Play . . .
Or a Work?

I SAID TO myself, *Motherfuckers*. Were they fucking with me all this time? What was the purpose of this? To test me? To get me down psychologically? To show me who was boss? To play with my mind?

I'm not sure to this day.

If it was a rib, they never came back and told me. I think they were serious from the start. But who knows? It may just have been a shoot between Eric and myself—to what purpose, I have no idea.

In all honesty, no one in the WCW hierarchy understood what the mask meant to me, or what the tradition meant to Mexican wrestling fans. There was very little interest in any of us as individuals. It wasn't just me. Take a look at Chris Jericho's book or Eddie's, and you'll see they came away with the same conclusion. We were there to fill out a card and to basically do what they wanted, when they thought of something.

Compare that to WWE. If Vince McMahon sees talent, he explores it, pushes it, and gets the most out of it. He's a businessman, no doubt about it.

It's ironic, because Eric had a tremendous stable of wrestlers at the time. There was a lot more he could have done with us. A lot more.

If I had known back then about business what I know now, I would have spoken up—about not just the mask, but coming up with much better ways to use my talent and to make the most of it. There was a lot more promotion, a lot of items that could have been sold: WCW never marketed my masks, to give just one example.

These sorts of problems eventually led to Eddie and Chris leaving WCW, along with other guys like Big Show and Dean, who felt they weren't getting the chance they deserved.

But I'm getting ahead of myself.

Those early days in WCW whipped by in a blur.

Not only was I riding high, but the company

was too.

WCW's dominant storyline involved a take-

over of the company in what came to be

called the New World Order, or nWo. The heat

generated by that story helped usher in an era

of excitement that took mainstream wrestling

to a new level. While much of what WCW was

doing had been done to some degree before,

prime-time exposure led to an explosion in popularity for our profession. Audiences grew to a size unimaginable a few years before.

The Company Line

DEFECTING FROM WORLD Wrestling Federation, Scott Hall and Kevin Nash joined WCW as the Outsiders. They were rebels with a cause, and that cause was to overturn the established order at WCW. They acted a lot like a street gang. While they were portrayed as villains or heels in wrestling slang, they were very cool heels. So cool, in fact, that everyone wanted to join them, including Hogan and Eric.

As the storyline continued, nWo split the company in half, and it then would itself split. My character, like most of the Mexicans and cruiserweights, remained with the company. For the most part, I had no role in the conflict, except to play a good guy on the company's side.

People who have followed my career know that I've had most of my success as a babyface or good guy. I believe that's partly due to the fact that that's who I am—that I believe in good rather than evil. But I didn't have any say in selecting the character when I was in WCW. They pretty much handled everything. The management made its decision and handed me the lines. At that point in my career, I didn't feel I had any other choice but to follow along and do it.

It's possible that I had more stroke than I realized, at least with the audience. Right from the start, I was on every TV show WCW had, I did just about every Pay-Per-View, you name it. Besides Monday night *Nitro*, we started airing a taped show called *Thunder* beginning in January 1998. We also did weekly house shows and occasionally some TV specials. I was at almost every one of them.

That wasn't an accidental thing. The fans were reacting to my style, getting into my high flying. So I was making money for them— or, as Eric used to say, I was "putting asses in the seats."

And that was without a strong storyline, at a time when storylines were supposed to be the biggest part of the entertainment. People were interested in seeing me work.

My T-shirt

ONE OF MY early milestones with WCW came when the company developed a T-shirt for me. It was very cool. It was all black, with the outline of my mask with its birds and everything in red. On the bottom it had my signature.

Me, with a T-shirt all my own. It was pretty cool.

Merchandizing was starting to become a big deal at the time. Just the idea that I had my own T-shirt told me that I was on a real roll. So despite the hassles about my mask, I felt as if things at WCW were going pretty well.

Down with Regis

I EVEN WENT on *Live with Regis and Kathie Lee* at one point. (The show is now *Live with Regis and Kelly*, with Kelly Ripa.)

For those of you who don't know, Regis Philbin has been a wrestling fan since his early days in my hometown, San Diego. He's become a star since then and now broadcasts every morning from New York City, but he still has a soft spot for wrestlers. All of the greats have been on with him, and it was a real honor to step onto his set.

It was the first talk show I'd ever done. Ever.

It was nerve-racking a bit: They were so famous, and I knew the audience was huge. I was on for about two minutes; it rushed by so quickly I don't remember a word I said. But I liked the chance to talk with their audience and maybe expand our own following a bit. Plus it added to the mystery of the mask—because you don't see many people with masks on when you flip on the TV.

It's very rare to see a guy with a mask on *anywhere*, even in New York, at least not in public. Robbing a bank, maybe—but that's a whole other story.

I've worn my mask on the street a few times, either for a promotion or for fun. One time I was in L.A. We were on Hollywood Boulevard doing a photo shoot or some other type of promotion for an upcoming show. After we got out of the car someone suggested I wear my mask as we walked. So I did.

People started flocking around me. There was a group of Japanese tourists who came over and thought I was some sort of freak who hung out on Hollywood Boulevard.

We were over in London not too long ago, and I tried the same thing. A lot of people know who I am in Europe, and I was mobbed. But it was a fun little thing. We got some photos of me coming out of a tube stop and near some double-decker buses for a European magazine, and then I did a bunch for the fans.

Me and Jennifer

BUT FAME CAN be a strange thing. People tell stories and rumors about you that aren't true, and the next thing you know, everyone believes them.

I remember in 1997 there were some stories going around that I was dating Jennifer Aniston, the actress who at the time was in the popular TV show *Friends*. The *National Enquirer* even printed a story about how we were an item.

I have no idea what that was about or where it came from. Maybe somebody wanted to get my name out there and started the rumor. Anyway, I thought it was funny. I even showed the story to my wife— best coming from me, no?

The locker room got on me for it.

"Hey, Rey, what's up with you and Jennifer?" someone would ask.

"What do you mean?" I answered. "What's up?"

They wouldn't let it die. Over the next few weeks and months they were ribbing me in all sorts of ways. I'm lucky Photoshopped pictures of me and Jennifer didn't appear on television somewhere.

That's the boys.

One thing I never let on about: I was the first guy to grab the magazine. And I still have a copy.

A Who's Who

MY OPPONENTS DURING my first two years at WCW read now like a who's who of famous cruiserweight and Mexican wrestlers. The series with Dean went off and on for months; he got the title back at *Halloween Havoc* that October. By then I had defended against Último Dragón, Billy Kidman, and Super Calo.

Super Calo had come into WCW in 1995 after leaving AAA. He and Winners—who unfortunately passed away under tragic circumstances recently—were tag team partners during my early days there.

After I lost the championship, I worked with Psicosis, Bobby Eaton, Jerry Lynn, and Juventud Guerrera, Syxx, Steven Regal, and even got into the ring with Kevin Nash. I'm probably leaving a dozen people out. I got the championship belt back at *Halloween Havoc*— the match where my mask was on the line against Eddie, remember— only to lose it back to Eddie a few weeks later on *Nitro* in Memphis.

Jerry Lynn—also known as Mr. J.L.—was at WCW for only a short time, but I enjoyed working with him very much. He would base me for all my moves, positioning himself very well. He knew how to take my bumps.

Before I came in, Jerry had been doing a lot of high flying himself. I think that because of that he knew exactly what my style was like, where he had to be when I wrestled, how to set up—all the little things that make a wrestler a professional.

THAT'S
SUPER
CALO
BASING
ME.

SOULED OUT IN '99 WITH CHRIS.

When you wrestle with a guy like that, you end up a lot more confident. You can't look good in the ring unless the other guy in the ring is working hard along with you. It takes two wrestlers to make a match.

As 1997 came to a close, my career rocketed along. I took the title back, this time from Juventud, on *Thunder* in January 1998, hoisting it over my head for the third time. I was looking forward to holding on to it for a while, even though I was working into a conflict with Chris Jericho, a tough and physically stronger opponent.

Then my knee went out again.

Jericho Tops Me

CHRIS AND I faced off at *Souled Out* with the cruiserweight belt on the line. My knee had been bothering me for a while, and I was wrestling in a heavy knee brace. I was still able to move around the ring; early on I remember I caught Jericho by surprise as I vaulted over the top rope and lassoed him with my legs. But the knee was hurting too badly, and Jericho took advantage. I managed to get on top of him and put him down with a forward roll, but I missed the pin.

From there, Jericho started inflicting punishment. I managed a one-legged inverted DDT and got him outside of the ropes. Then I climbed up, did a springboard off the top rope into a somersault flip, and landed on him out on the concrete. The announcers were writing me off by that point, but I wasn't ready to quit.

I threw Jericho back into the ring, then climbed on the ropes, ready to spring at him. But he threw himself forward, whacking the ropes and upsetting my timing. My ankle grabbed on the rope and I crashed to the mat.

Jericho got me on the turnbuckle and I was ripe for the picking. He leapt forward, leveraging me into the Liontamer, his trademark submission move. I had to tap out.

And if that wasn't enough, he hit me with a toolbox after the match ended.

Injured

THE MATCH LAID the fictional groundwork for the real injury I was suffering, setting the stage for my operation and recovery. But this time I hadn't actually hurt my knee in the ring.

When I had been operated on a few months earlier, the doctor replaced my tissue with some from a cadaver. It was a standard operation at the time, and usually it worked well. But there was always a possibility that the new tissue wouldn't get along with the rest of my body. And it turned out after a few months that my body rejected it, sending me back to square one.

I guess the cadaver didn't like wrestling.

With the pain ramping up, I got an appointment with one of the top orthopedic surgeons in the country, Dr. James Andrews in Atlanta. Dr. Andrews has operated on a lot of wrestlers and other athletes. I can tell you personally that he is an incredible surgeon. He's also a very caring doctor, with an incredible bedside manner.

He's an older man, with a confident and easygoing manner. He also knows a lot about "wrassling," which is his slightly Southern, slightly old-fashioned way of referring to wrestling.

Dr. Andrews put my wife at ease right away, which was something I was very grateful for. Angie had studied medicine, and he offered to let her watch part of the operation. Well, she had a little peek, but that was all she could stand.

She may have seen a lot of things at school, but it's a lot different when you know the person on the table, I guess.

Dr. Andrews removed the other tendon and used a patella tendon to reattach the ACL. The operation went well, and I started rehabbing the next day.

Back to Work

ONCE AGAIN I had time off to be with my family, which was some consolation for being out. Dominik was rounding the corner toward one year old, and I got to see a lot of his firsts. I watched him learn to crawl, then walk. I was there for his first word, which I'm proud to say was "papa."

Becoming a father was one of the great events of my life. Learning to deal with the responsibility that goes with that title isn't easy, but I want to say that it's as satisfying as anything that's ever happened to me.

I worked hard at rehab, exercising my knee and getting the rest of my body back into shape. I came back stronger and better than ever physically. Mentally, I was never tougher.

I returned for *Bash at the Beach* that July in San Diego. The location itself was special: I was performing in front of my hometown crowd.

Chris Jericho had spent a number of years in Mexico. He made a lot of our height difference during the match—he put his hand on his chest where he claimed I came up to—but our styles were very similar. That made him easy to work with. He was an excellent base.

I remember one move in that match. It goes back to my love of the frankensteiner and its many varieties.

We had a tower near the ring. I worked Chris outside of the ropes, and I took him back to the tower. I climbed up and gave him a frankensteiner from the top. It was the highlight for me, though Chris kept on fighting.

Dean Malenko distracted Chris at the end of the match, helping me get the pin. It was the fourth time I wore the championship belt, tying Dean for the most turns as Cruiserweight Champ in WCW.

In case you're keeping track, as of this writing I've held that title eight times, more than anyone else. The championship is officially retired, at least for now, so it's a good bet that record will last a few years at least.

Jealousy

THERE WAS DEFINITELY jealousy at WCW, and more than a little between Juventud Guerrera and myself. Juventud had the Cruiserweight Championship for just one week that January before losing it to me. While I was out for surgery, Dean Malenko and Jericho battled back and forth over the title; if I'm not mistaken they traded it at least once, and it was on Jericho when I came back.

Juventud had spent the time working to move up, hoping for a long stint as champ. He got a good push, but then when I came back—the first night I came back—I got the shot at the title, not him. I guess he talked to Konnan and let him know that he thought it wasn't fair.

"I've been busting my ass while he was gone," he said bitterly. "He comes back one day and they're going to give him the title."

Coming from Juvy I believe it. He was the friend you love to hate sometimes.

Eddie

EDDIE GUERRERO HAD been at WCW for about a year when I came in. He was at a higher level with the company than I was. He'd worked quite a lot in ECW and Japan, and between that and WCW he was pretty well known. He was working with the Flairs and the Benoits, the stars of the company.

But every so often I would get a chance to work with him. It brought back a lot of history from my very early days in Mexico City.

With Eddie you didn't talk out the match beforehand. He would tell me, "Just listen to me in the ring." That's all I would do. I would go into the ring and have my ears open. I'd follow his lead.

Eddie could always sense what the crowd was feeling. He knew what they were reacting to. I might suggest a move or two, and he'd tell me, "Fine, I'll work it into the match." But that would be it, one move or two out of the whole match. Everything else would evolve.

On live TV, that can be nerve-racking. You're working without a net. But Eddie made you feel confident about what you were doing. And he was just a true professional. You didn't have to sweat it. All you had to do was listen.

Stiff

A LOT OF the bigger guys, especially the first time I wrestled with them, didn't know how to take my bumps. We'd work something out, but I'd go into the ring a little skeptical of them. If they moved or positioned themselves wrong, even by a small amount, we could both get very seriously hurt. If you don't have confidence in your partner, you increase the chances that something will go wrong.

Some of the bigger guys didn't have control over how hard they were tossing me around. I was pretty light, even lighter than I am now, and very literally they didn't know their own strength.

Some of the bigger, American-style wrestlers were notorious for that.

I remember working with Gangrel one time. Now, he was a good guy, down to earth. I love him to death. And he was trained by Dean Malenko, so he had an excellent background. But he was just naturally stiff. He doesn't mean to do it, but when he hit you—oh, fuck, it hurt. You'd think to yourself, *Take it easy, I'm giving you my body*.

Of course, you don't say that. You suck it up. After the match, you just say, "Thank you." No way you complain, even if your head is hanging sideways down your back.

"Babyfacing You"

BUT I WAS talking about Eddie Guerrero.

WCW had never really done much in the way of a storyline with him, or with any of the Mexican wrestlers and cruiserweights for that matter. Eddie was very serious about his career, and he understood, way earlier than I did, how storylines were helping to shape wrestlers' images and their position in the promotion.

He knew he was ready to advance, but the company didn't seem that interested. Worse, the cliques and the politics were working against him. He would tell me in Spanish to be careful about who we were talking in front of. Some guys, he'd say, were just stooges for management. Everything we said would go right back to Eric.

"This guy is babyfacing you," Eddie would tell me. That meant he was saying one thing to my face and another to my back. Maybe he'd be squealing to management as well. Eddie was definitely aware of the politics there, and how they worked against certain people.

Maybe I'm naïve, but I usually take friendships pretty seriously. If someone shows affection, invites you to their house, hangs out, you tend to trust them.

Me, I take things like that very seriously. Family is important to me, and friendships are important. That's just the way I am.

That wasn't the way things went in WCW. Somebody could hang out with you one day, then go and sabotage you the next. It was just the way it was.

Things are different in WWE. I think there's more of an openness and friendship among wrestlers now. The wrestling world has changed dramatically. Maybe it has to do with the Internet—*everything* is out there now. So we all try to get along. We make friends a lot easier than we would back in the day.

There are a lot less cliques as well. Back then it was hi and bye if you weren't in the group. Now I feel as if everyone is more on the same level; there's no separation between stars, and not a lot of politics.

From Fill-in to Takeover

POLITICS PLAYED A huge part in people's careers, because politics often determined who got airtime and who got a push. And a lot of that had to do with the storylines. A good angle meant more airtime. But only certain people got good storylines. Or any storyline at all.

You'd think that the company would have paid attention to all parts of its show. *Nitro* was on the air for two and then three hours every week. That's a lot of air to fill. A lot of the matches featured cruiserweights and Mexican wrestlers. But there were rarely any storylines for them.

WCW had a good lead in the ratings, and maybe because of that they focused on the stars. The powers-that-be didn't give a shit about the rest. The rest of the card was a fill-in.

Part of the problem probably came from the top guys. They didn't want anybody else to escalate. Maybe the way they saw it, there was only so much room for stars. They didn't have enough vision to realize that the more stars there were, the better the company would do—and the better the company did, the better they would do.

That's the background that you have to remember when you consider the conflict Eddie and some of the others had with management. He wasn't just concerned about his own career, though that was definitely part of it. He saw what the potential was for *everyone*.

We could have had more big stars. No question—look what happened to the guys who left WCW: Eddie, Jericho, later on myself. WCW had all of that potential but couldn't find a way to use it.

LWO

POLITICS ASIDE, EDDIE finally decided he'd take matters into his own hands. He came up with his own storyline. And that was when LWO was born.

His idea was to band the Latino wrestlers together as a little clique, a band of rebels. The group would take the name Latino World Order, after the New World Order. It played on some of the themes about national heritages, friction with immigrants and races—real stuff in America. It also capitalized on rumors that

LWO
VERSUS ME.

were popular in the media about friction between Eric Bischoff and
Eddie.

The idea in WCW at the time was to mix reality with wrestling,
using storylines that came, or seemed to come, from the real lives of the
wrestlers. The idea was to make what we did seem real and immediate
to the audience. If we could suspend the audience's disbelief, they
would enjoy the show that much more.

The conflict between the company and members of LWO, rumored

in the trade press every time they reported on something Eddie did, was pretty well known. That made the storyline that much more powerful.

But that was just a small part of Eddie's idea. He wanted there to be conflict within the group—say, with a popular guy who everybody thought should be part of it, refusing.

That popular guy was me.

I'm Not a Joining Kind of Guy

EDDIE WENT AROUND getting different members for his group. Psicosis, La Parka, Héctor Garza, and Juventud were all involved. Some of the other wrestlers were Silver King, Damián, Ciclope, El Dandy, and Villaño V. He came up with T-shirts and colors that members were supposed to wear.

Eddie recruited on the air. When he tried to talk me up, I told him I didn't want to be part of it.

I pushed him, he pushed back.

Things escalated. He started a campaign to get me to join. They handed out T-shirts, gave me one, threw me another—but I kept refusing to join. Soon his whole gang was trying to beat me into submission.

Then getting me to join LWO wasn't good enough—they had to humiliate me. I remember the size of the T-shirt when I finally gave in and joined: It must have been a 4XL.

I thought it was kind of funny. In real life, that is.

A Big Deal

THE STORYLINE WAS a big deal for me. It was the first time I had been in an extended story at WCW. Plus the way the story was set up, there was a lot of attention on me. It helped boost my name up.

We had our own logo: *LWO* in green, white, and red—just like nWo had. Eddie rallied the troops by telling them they would win the respect they deserved. And by hosting parties with plenty of good-looking Latino ladies.

Fans made signs and brought them to the arena. There was plenty of high flying in the matches that revolved around the story.

One of the subplots that developed was dissension and backbiting among the different members. I remember teaming with Billy Kidman and facing against Psicosis and Juventud for a tag team aerial spectacular. Double the trouble, double the fun. Even though I had joined by then (Kidman was not a member), Psicosis and Juventud went out of their way to give me a beating.

Unfortunately, Eddie was in a car accident in early 1999. His absence hurt the storyline badly. Not only was he not there to wrestle, but he wasn't able to contribute the ideas. He'd been the driving force behind the angle, and without his energy, it started to fade.

Giant Killer

MEANWHILE, NWO HAD split into two factions in the company: nWo Hollywood, led by Hogan as Hollywood Hulk Hogan; and nWo Wolfpac. There was a shakeup in the factions, and Konnan ended up teaming with me for yet another round of feuds where the competing factions tried to bully me into submission. From having been a reluctant member of LWO, I became the last holdout, proudly wearing my T-shirt—or the threads that were left of it—as an act of defiance.

At the same time, I started being worked into matches with much bigger guys . . . and finding a way to win. People started calling me a giant killer. My star kept rising, but I had a bad feeling about it, and that feeling only grew as time went on.

Unmasked

I didn't really like my new role.

The name Giant Killer bothered me. I didn't like it. It didn't have the kind of ring to it you like to hear.

But the real problem was with my size. I was a fly compared to these guys. There were some almost comical moments when the Wolfpac surrounded me in the ring. They must have had a few tons on me.

In mid-January, I faced off in the ring against Lex Luger. Luger had vowed to take off my mask at the match.

Two of me would have added up to one Lex, but I wasn't backing down.

"Rey, you're a cute little wrestler," said Luger, taking the mike when I came out. "I'll give you one last chance. Take off the [LWO] shirt, hand me the mask, and I'll let you walk."

I shook my head. Taunting me wasn't enough. He had to kick me in the balls when I wasn't looking.

Half the crowd hated him. The other half wanted to kill him.

I'd been taking a lot of beatings over the past few months, and this match started out with a few more. Lex picked me up and threw me to the mat, then tossed me this way and that. Finally I ducked out of his way as he ran across; he impaled himself on the ring post.

Now the advantage was mine, and I swarmed over him like an angry bee. Legdrop from the front rope, dropkick to the chin, a moonsault into a lateral press.

Luger's weight and height advantage came into play again, as he withstood some of my blows and once more began slamming me around. He press-slammed me to the mat. But when he went to grab my mask, I got a burst of adrenaline and unleashed a flurry of punches and desperation moves. When it was clear I was going to beat Luger, Kevin Nash came in and interfered. It was two against one—figure their weight in, and it was more like five or six against one.

My mask looked like a goner—until Konnan ran in with a chair and chased them off.

Just like in real life, he had my back.

The Mask

THE COMPANY HAD launched a plan to take my mask. When they finally smartened me up about it, I told them I was all right with it.

I wasn't, not entirely, but at least they went about it much differently than they had before. It was a *little* more respectful.

Not as good as it could have been—nowhere near—but better.

I sat down with Scott Hall, Kevin Nash, and Eric. Things were okay between me and Eric by now. We all sat down and hashed it out. There was a lot more consideration, or at least there seemed to be, than the last time. They were giving me a push, so they kind of reeled me in.

"If that's what you want to do, all right," I told them finally. "I'm here to work. I don't want to do it. But if you guys feel it's going to take me to a different place in my career, all right."

We were talking about commercials that we'd be able to do, how showing my face would help me move higher in the company. It sounded like they were going to use me a lot better than they had.

And this time they promised a buildup and a storyline with a payoff. I saw it as an opportunity to do something more, not a punishment.

Still, I wasn't totally convinced. Good thing or bad thing, I wasn't really ready to take off the mask. I'd envisioned wearing it for most, if not all, of my career.

I remember calling my uncle to talk about it. I told him I wasn't really ready, but that they wanted to do it. He said I should do whatever I had to do to keep my job.

I was asking him for permission, I guess. Not directly, but I wanted to hear from him that it was okay.

He was very supportive.

"Do it," he said. "Show them you have balls and do it. Show them you're a man of your word."

That's what I decided to do. I figured one of two things would happen. Either it worked out and I shot up . . . or I'd go straight down the drain.

Kevin

THE ORIGINAL PLAN, I believe, would have had me wrestling Lex Luger again. But Lex got hurt, so I faced Kevin Nash at *Superbrawl IX* in Oakland on February 21, 1999. My mask was at stake.

The weird thing was, he didn't have anything personal at stake: I was wrestling for Miss Elizabeth's hair.

They still didn't quite get how important the mask was. And the way the storyline evolved, moving so quickly, it was clear to most people in the auditorium who was going to win. But I'd already given my commitment.

The event was set up as a contest between Scott Hall & Kevin Nash, versus Konnan & myself. Konnan had been by my side through nearly all the big moments of my career, and here he was again. Just to have him at my side, in my corner, on my back—it really meant a lot. It was good to have a brother with me when I went down for history.

The match itself was a good one, but it was a screw finish, and it's questionable whether anyone really thought a guy basically twice my size was going to lose to me. Especially in that company.

Tagging Toward Oblivion

HALL AND I started things off. The size mismatch was of course pretty obvious. I had him down a few times, but finally he slammed me to the mat and tagged Kevin in.

How tall is Kevin Nash? Seven feet?

It felt like he threw me down from the Empire State Building every time he sent me to the mat.

After getting pummeled for a few minutes, I wriggled out of a hold and tagged Konnan in. He cleaned up—until they double-teamed him and sent him down in the center of the ring. The ref was no help, letting them gang up on him.

I got the tag and used a pair of springboard dropkicks to send both men to the mat. A spinwheel kick set up a move where I used Kevin as a jumping board to kick Hall. Then Konnan came in and I vaulted from his legs to take Nash down.

My broncobuster on Kevin in the corner put him asleep for a bit, but there was one man we hadn't counted on: Luger. Though injured, he was prowling the apron, and he knocked Konnan out cold.

It was now two against one, but my opponents were still stunned from the earlier attacks. I did a springboard and then a moonsault from the center of the ring. I caught Kevin with my knee brace and put him out, flat on the mat, ready for the pin.

That exchange was a variation on a finish Scott Hall had with the 1-2-3 Kid back in the day. (The 1-2-3 Kid was Sean Waltman. Sean also wrestled as Syxx.)

But Miss Elizabeth distracted the ref, and with my back turned, I was vulnerable to Hall, who knocked me out and arranged the pin for the comatose Kevin Nash.

My mask was history.

A Tense Moment

THE MOMENT HAD come for me to unmask.

I was tense, more tense than I'd been throughout the match.

I'd been working all my life for a moment like this, losing the mask. But it had come way too early. I knew I hadn't gotten the kind of juice that could have come from a better buildup. And now, without the mask, I was afraid I was going to be just another wrestler. What would set me apart?

My size?

That wasn't a plus.

EVEN WITH KONNAN IN MY
CORNER, THE ODDS WERE
AGAINST ME.

I remember Konnan trying to undo the mask. He got a couple of laces off in the back—I used to tie it from behind. I grabbed it from the top and slid it straight down my face.

It was an intense moment, one of the most emotional moments I've ever had in the ring. Probably the second most, actually: The first would have been my uncle naming me Rey Misterio Jr.

I remember taking the mask off. The fans were stunned. Nash and Scott Hall were saying, "Hey, he's a kid. He's a kid—put it back on."

A Matter of Pride

IN MEXICO, WHEN a wrestler loses a mask, it's the high point of the night and maybe the year. There's a moment of pride: The winner takes the mask and treats it like a sacred trophy.

It's a matter of respect to the profession as well as to the wrestler.

But in America, things are different. Nash and Hall started playing with the mask in the ring. Kevin stuck it on the back of his head.

Not exactly a lot of respect for tradition there.

In all honesty, people knew Liz wasn't going to shave her head. Nash and Hall came up with the angle, and it played out the way they wanted—not the way I would have done it, not the way someone who understood *lucha libre* would have written it.

Maybe I should have said something and had it changed. I wish they would have done it in a better way.

It's funny, though, and ironic. Looking back, I think I would have rather lost it against Eddie, that first time back when I took the cruiserweight title. It would have been such a classy thing, and it would have meant a lot more to lose to Eddie. He understood and was part of the tradition.

But that wasn't the way it went.

My boys—Psicosis, Super Calo, everybody—were waiting for me in the back when the match ended. They were very encouraging, complimenting me and everything.

I gave them the good face, but I broke down in tears when I was alone.

Would I Have Been Bigger?

I THINK NOW that, if I hadn't lost my mask then, if I'd kept it and been able to protect my image, my name would be even bigger today. Not that I don't have millions of great and faithful fans, but unmasking took a little edge away, a little bit of the mystery.

Imagine if I had come into WWE with the mask? Imagine if, to this day, no one had seen a photo of Rey Mysterio without his mask?

I never signed autographs, never took pictures without the hood. If Eric had just listened . . .

Taking Down Kevin

THEY DID THAT to Juventud Guererra, too. He was unmasked. His father's name was very strong in Mexico—he still wears a hood.

The night after I lost my mask, we were in Sacramento. I had a match against Kevin Nash. I was still feeling a little ornery about the whole thing.

At one point he picked me up for the powerbomb and I began punching the shit out of his face.

Was I a little stiff that night? Did the punches connect a little harder than normal?

Who remembers?

He dropped me, and I got my first win off Kevin. Not really revenge—there's no making up for a mask—but a victory nonetheless.

A Harder Edge

ONCE I KNEW I had to lose the mask, I decided I'd make my new identity work for me. I gave the thing a lot of thought.

Losing the mask meant taking a new direction with my character. If I lost my mask, I thought, I wasn't going to go out there with my regular tights. That would be cheesy. My tights and my mask were part of my identity.

So I started wearing baggy pants. I had a new suit made with a new pattern: gray, black, and white camouflage pants. I started wearing beanies to the ring. I had my cross around my neck and my beanie.

The new look had a bit of an edge to it. A hard edge. So did my wrestling.

More Giants

OVER THE NEXT few months I racked up an impressive number of wins against the company's big men. At that point in my career, I was working out more and had a bit more weight. I was looking good, better than when I started. Bigger. But I was still pretty small, especially compared to my opponents.

I was taking on some of the biggest guys in the company. I took down Scott Norton. There was a bump in that match that still stands out. He grabbed me from the mat and chucked me over the top rope. I took a bump to the floor, nearly putting a permanent dent in it. Later

BAM BAM
BIGELOW.

on, he got me in a pie-face position, mocking me, mocking—then all of a sudden I kicked him in the nuts.

Make fun of the little guy?

He dropped down. I covered him. The people went crazy.

I also remember working against Bam Bam Bigelow. To me, that was a real honor. I had grown up watching him. It was exciting just to wrestle against him and to have him put me over for the crowd.

Bam Bam had started out during the days when there were still a lot of independent circuits. After working his way up, he became a star with World Wrestling Federation. From there, he did some work in Japan and ECW before going to WCW.

I still admire his professionalism. When we wrestled, he was all work, ready to go. He was all business when he came down to the ring.

I won most of the matches in this streak. But I never had a problem doing the job for the bigger guys. For anyone.

Recognized

NOT HAVING THE mask changed things for me with the fans. Now they knew who I was.

I was a little awkward with it, and I think they were too. They didn't know how to deal with it. I was working on a new identity, and they had to adjust to it just as I did.

When I was wrestling with the mask on, I could go into a mall or somewhere else and no one would recognize me. After the mask came off, little by little people started recognizing me. My private life was gone.

Don't misunderstand: It's cool to be a star, to be famous. In that part of my career, it was definitely cool to have fans come up and ask for an autograph, a picture and everything. But it does affect your private life. And in my case, it happened almost overnight. Those were big adjustments.

Most fans were very nice. Occasionally, one might say something like, "Hey, you're little!" or "You're young, man." That was the harshest thing that happened. And that didn't bother me. Hell, from day one I was told I couldn't be a wrestler, so someone pointing out that I was small or looked like a kid, that really didn't matter.

Master P

AROUND THIS TIME, Master P and the WCW management started talking about doing something together.

Master P—Percy Miller—was topping the charts in the late 1990s, with *Ghetto D* in 1997, *MP Da Last Don* in 1998, and *Only God Can Judge Me* in 1999. He isn't just a rap star. He's a businessman with a lot of interests in clothes, films, you name it. He's also made a name for himself by being involved in numerous charitable enterprises. He's done a lot especially for kids and education.

At the time, WCW was looking to expand its audience, and the execs thought rap would help. I don't know exactly how it all came about, but Eric arranged a meeting between Master P, some of his people, Konnan, and myself.

It happened that Konnan and I were listening to a lot of gangsta rap while we were traveling, so we were really hip on his music. We were listening to him, Tupac, Dr. Dre, the whole scene. We really liked the music.

I can go with a lot of different styles: Guns N' Roses, Kid Rock, Metallica, Pink Floyd, Led Zeppelin, Little Wayne, Eminem. I have pretty wide tastes.

And Konnan was already doing some rap on his own, performing with Mad One. They did "Psyko" and some others in 1998. It debuted on *Halloween Havoc* that year and got some good airtime.

One of Master P's cousins and bodyguards—Randy Thorton, who was known as Swoll—wanted to be a wrestler, so WCW decided to team him up with Konnan and myself. That's how we got rolling with the No Limit Soldiers. We were part rap group, part babyface stable.

There ended up being a bit of controversy over the angle. Master P never thought he got the reaction he deserved. But we got a lot of mileage out of that whole angle once Curt Hennig got involved. Hennig came up with this fantastic gimmick. Declaring "Rap is crap," he fronted a country music band made up of wrestlers known as the West Texas Rednecks and became our archenemies.

He may have come up with that angle on his own. The company wasn't doing all that much with his character at the time, and like a lot of wrestlers, he kind of got lost in the nWo thing. Which was a shame. Curt was a really creative guy and popular as well. Though he was playing a heel, he was really over with the crowd.

The Rednecks' first few "songs" were horrible—on purpose. But as the storyline went on, the music got better and better. Those cats could play. I liked their sound.

Curt

BEING ABLE TO work with Curt was fun.

Earlier in his career, he'd used the nickname Mr. Perfect. He was incredibly successful with a gimmick that had him perfect in every sport. And I mean *perfect*. He could bowl a perfect game, throw a football a hundred yards—you name the activity, he was perfect. He presented that perfection with a smiling, really fun personality. It was like: *Of course I'm better than you. I'm perfect.*

And as a technical wrestler, he *was* just about perfect. A lot of people think he was one of the best if not *the* best wrestler of his generation. He's in the WWE Hall of Fame, one indication of his skill.

Once again, I was working with someone I'd grown up watching, and it was both a thrill and a learning experience. Curt taught me a lot about the psychology of American wrestling, and he helped me

CURT.

move from someone who did high-spot fests to someone who could hold up his part of an angle. Between him and Konnan, I stretched into a new phase of my career, growing as a wrestler and performer.

Rednecks

CURT PLAYED GUITAR in his group. The other members were Bobby Duncum Jr., Barry Windham and Kendall Windham, and Curly Bill. Even though officially they were the West Texas Outlaws, most people called them the West Texas Rednecks. Their song "Rap is Crap" can still be found in a bunch of places. So can their theme song, "Good Ol' Boys."

Curt, Bobby, and the Windhams were all second-generation wrestlers, and it was a thrill to work with them. These were all big guys, so I adjusted my in-ring work.

We had a big tag match at *Bash at the Beach* in Fort Lauderdale that year. It was an Eight-Man Elimination match: myself, Konnan, Brad Armstrong, & Swoll against Curt, Barry, Kendall, & Bobby. There was music everywhere, country *and* rap. It was hot.

I remember I started out wrestling with Barry. His huge height advantage didn't help him fend off a couple of backflips, but he managed to tap Curt in. I tapped Brad and chilled.

When I got back in a few minutes later, I managed to send Kendall flying out of the ring and brought the crowd to its feet. Konnan and I teamed for a pair of catapult somersaults and a broncobuster on Hennig.

Konnan and Kendall starred in the next third of the match, with Kendall flying around the ring before Konnan took him out. Then Barry and Konnan continued things outside the ring and were officially counted out, leaving me and Swoll to face Curt.

I climbed on Swoll's shoulders and did a splash onto Curt's body for the final pin. The crowd, which was about evenly divided between the teams, loved it.

That was a fun angle. Konnan and I worked with Mad One on a rap for the show. Elow was our producer. We did the music and shot some video at a studio in San Diego. Again, we were trying to take things to a new level.

Hunting with Curt

FOR A WHILE I rode with Curt, going to house shows together. It was an experience. I got to hear a lot of his stories about breaking into the business and some of his early matches.

One day, he invited me and Juventud, along with some other friends, to go out hunting in Georgia. Rick Steiner, Big Boss Man, and another friend of Curt's were there, if I'm remembering correctly. We went all out, bought camo hunting clothes, put boots on and all. We had quad runners and everything. We were really excited. We camped out the night before, then got up at like four in the morning, very early, and we were out looking for deer.

Curt posted us in different places where the deer usually came through. He put Juventud on this little trail, hiding in some shrubs.

"Sit on the quad and shoot anything that moves," Boss Man told Juvy, explaining how the deer would come down just before dawn.

He's like, "Yeah, yeah, I got it, I got it."

I went deeper into the woods with the others. They had a nice little blind set up and I climbed in, ready for my shot.

A few minutes pass, a half hour, an hour. No deer. I heard something moving in the woods, got ready—but no deer.

More time went by. More sounds. No deer.

I was aching to get my chance. But still no deer.

Two hours passed. The sun rose. I thought to myself that Curt was wrong. There were no deer anywhere.

Then I heard something crunching. I spun around, ready—and nearly nailed Boss Man.

"There was no deer," he said. "I can't believe it. Not one."

Curt and the others came around and we headed over to get Juventud. They were really puzzled. There were always deer here, and with us spread out so well, one of us should have seen *something*.

Sure enough, we come up to the trail Juventud was watching, and there were fresh deer tracks everywhere. Dozens of tracks, just dozens. It looked like they held a deer convention there.

But Juvy was nowhere to be seen.

We started shouting: "Juvy! What happened? Where are you?"

Maybe the deer ran him over, right? The tracks ran right up to where we'd left him.

Had the deer mugged him?

Not quite. It turned out that Juventud had gotten bored a few minutes after we left and gone back to camp . . . where he went to sleep.

If he'd stayed a little longer, he could have hopped onto one of the deer and rode his way back.

We drove back to the road show, all geared up like rednecks ourselves. Muddy Mexican rednecks, that is.

Real Problems at WCW

THE STORYLINES WCW favored had a lot of conflict in them. Tempers would flare, people would turn on each other, nothing was ever straightforward. They paralleled real life in the promotion.

WCW's television ratings had come down to earth. World Wrestling Federation with its Monday night show, *Raw*, was now regularly beating us in the ratings. At the same time, WCW wasn't making new superstars. The shows started to feel stale, and you could tell we were in a ditch.

Rumors began to spread about what might happen. We heard all sorts of things, including word that WCW was going to fold.

I'd heard those rumors before. When I first came in, people were wondering if WCW was going to last. But then the ratings went through the roof and the company was as successful as any. So I didn't pay too much attention to what I heard this time around, not at first anyway.

Enter Vince Russo

THE RUMORS KEPT coming. I heard we were losing a lot of money. I figured that Eric, since he was head of WCW, would be blamed. I wasn't involved in any front office things, so I had no idea what was going on behind the scenes. But I figured that sooner or later the shit was going to go down. How much could Time Warner spend on the company without realizing that things weren't happening? Sooner or later, I thought, something would happen.

In September of 1999, Eric was sent home. I don't think they ever formally fired him, because he had a contract. By that time it wasn't much of a surprise. Bringing in Vince Russo to take his place, though—that was a surprise.

Russo was the head writer of our main rival, WWE. I wasn't in much of a position to judge how good a job he could do. But I did think that the new administration might give us a chance to get more time on camera. At the worst, the new boss might let us get a good angle going.

That angle became Filthy Animals, a heel stable that was somewhat similar to DX.

Filthy Animals

THE NAME FILTHY Animals came from Disco Inferno.

His way of calling to me and Konnan when were backstage or just hanging out would be, "Oh, you filthy animals." Whenever we were talking with him, he'd say that.

How are you, Disco?

"Fine, you filthy animals."

Time to go?

"Oh, you filthy animals."

That was Disco.

We used to kid around and tell him, "Hey, we should be in a musical group together. We'll call it the Filthy Animals."

"Oh yeah, yeah," he'd say. "That'd be nice . . . you filthy animals."

I'd met Disco during my earliest days at WCW. He was always very cool. To me, he was like the goof of the locker room, keeping things light, joking around. He had a stupid comment for everything. His offbeat humor kept things cool, and Konnan and I would hang with him quite a lot.

As a wrestler, he was nothing special. But he was a great guy, down to earth, and his character kept the fans entertained.

Disco had been with the company for a few years, wrestling and having some success in the cruiserweight division. Besides the cruiserweight title, he held the WCW Television Championship at one time. But by the fall of 1999 he had fallen from favor, and they weren't doing much with him.

Around this time we were all talking about what we might do. Konnan came up with the idea of a storyline based loosely around the idea of a disrespectful group of young wrestlers called the Filthy Animals. He may have been thinking partly of DX and other things Russo had been involved with at World Wrestling Federation. But mostly the idea followed the outlines of how we used to fool around outside of the ring.

"They're not doing anything with us anyway," Konnan said. "So let's try it. We'll all do it together, and either we'll all succeed or we'll all be shot down as a group."

Either Disco or Konnan, or maybe both, went in and pitched the idea to the new man in the executive seat.

TYGRESS.

"You're going to bury us anyway," Konnan told him. "So at least let us have fun while we're getting buried."

He was only half joking.

Maybe less than half.

Russo liked the idea, and so we ran with it. The result was probably the most fun I had in the ring without a mask.

We were really a bunch of clowns, playing pranks on the other wrestlers, teasing them, putting them down. We ribbed back and forth. Some commentators have compared us to tweens or early teenagers, disrespectful, obnoxious, disruptive. In one stretch we beat up Ric Flair, stole his watch, and buried him in the sand near Las Vegas.

That's the boys, right?

Besides Konnan and Disco—who at this point was spelling his name Disqo—Eddie, Juventud, and Billy Kidman were all involved with us. We also had two managers: Torrie Wilson and Tygress.

Mama.

As in *hot mama*, times two.

Adding them was Vince Russo's idea. It was a good one. Torrie and Tygress, I can't describe their looks with words. Both women are knockouts. I'm surprised I didn't catch flak at home with Tygress hanging all over me some nights.

It was all business, though—wrestling business. No pleasure, if you know what I mean.

I would come out with overalls, a hat—and sometimes a lollipop. Why a lollipop?

Just me being me, having a little fun and doing something different. I was switching things around, looking for a pop here or there—just a pun.

New Phase

WE GOT KIND of a bite off DX, modeling ourselves as rebellious pranksters, with our own little spins based on our personalities.

This new phase in my career was a challenge, in a very good way. I was doing things with my character that I'd never done before. I wasn't a babyface or a heel. It was more a third way, my own way. I was exploring my character.

Every now and then I'd mess with the fans, try to provoke them a little, get a reaction. I'd insult them or do something to piss them off.

It was hard at first. I don't like to hurt people, and in a way egging them on was kind of hurting them. But they took it in a fun way. They'd yell back at me, "Come on, you fucking kid. I'm going to whip your ass."

I became kind of a fun heel, almost a clown. The idea was to take the way we were out on the street—just joking around, cutting on each other, having fun, hanging out—and take it to the ring.

"Go out there and be you," we'd tell each other. "No gimmick. Just be you."

Just be one of the boys. Not hard to do.

Flair's All Wet

DESPITE THE RAP on me as a small guy, I was good enough to manage a shot at the WCW Heavyweight Title in March 1999. I'd just won the Cruiserweight title, and if I'd been successful, I would have united them for I believe the first time in history.

My opponent was one of the all-time greats, Ric Flair.

The ring was set up in the middle of a pool, with an apron circling the ring and a small railing separating us from the water. You just knew someone was going to get very wet by the end of the night.

At the time, the Nature Boy had worn the championship belt fourteen times. He had the weight, height, and experience advantage big-time; I had the dogs.

He swerved me when I gave him my hand to shake. I got a couple of drops on him in revenge, then slapped him sick. Arn Anderson, stooging for Ric, took me out on the apron. Flair started taking move, getting me down with a vertical suplex. But I kicked out of a few pin attempts, and started flying around the ring in a comeback attempt. I had Flair down, with the ref counting one-two-

He never reached three. Anderson blindsided the ref, who called a disqualification, ending the match—and my bid at the heavyweight title. (Championships can't change hands on a DQ.) In frustration, I reared back and kicked Ric into the pool.

He made a good-looking fish. A whooo-oooo fish.

It was an awesome night, going at it with one of my longtime heroes and a future Hall of Famer.

I have to say, Ric's chops hurt. Really hurt. Stiff? Getting hit by him was like getting clipped by a nuclear-powered hedge trimmer, full force. But it was an honor, a matter of pride, to get chopped by the best.

Ready to Rumble

IT WAS SOMEWHERE around here during 1999 that I got involved in making a movie. It was called *Ready to Rumble,* and so far it's the only movie I've acted in, though I'd love to do more.

The movie stars David Arquette and centers around a wrestler who is screwed out of his title by an evil promotion owner and fellow wrestlers. A pair of wrestling fans take up his cause and help him get his title back. Arquette plays one of the fans; Oliver Platt is the wrestler. The company in the movie is loosely based on WCW and features a lot of the guys from our shows. The studio that came out with the movie was Warner Bros. Pictures; they were part of Time Warner, WCW's owner at the time.

WCW arranged for a bunch of us to have parts in the movie. I didn't know what my role was until I got to the set in L.A. I ended up in a Tag Team match with Billy Kidman against Juventud and Prince Iaukea. They just kind of gave us a rundown: Do a two- or three-minute match, we'll shoot it, and then edit it down for the movie. Then they told us to go for it.

It wasn't until the director saw the stuff we were doing that he figured out what he wanted to use and began concentrating on it. One of the things he liked was my popup frankensteiner. Prince Iaukea was sitting on the top turnbuckle. Billy Kidman launched me over, and I landed on Iaukea and gave him the frankensteiner.

I did it three or four times, nailing it each time.

Including the very last.

Third Time for Knee

"CUT!" THE DIRECTOR yelled.

Cut was exactly what I thought.

When I came down that last time, Prince didn't let me go. It was a slight mistake with big consequences. I landed on my knee, and my knee rotated inward. It gave way, and I felt a surge of pain.

Familiar pain. Too familiar.

You trash your ACL a couple of times, and you know exactly what's wrong. The noise that came with it was exactly the same as the first time: a ripping sound that took the life out of me, or at least out of my knee.

Luckily, the take was a good one. I couldn't have done another.

A doctor examined my knee in L.A. For some reason the MRI didn't detect the problem, and they had to stick this needle in to find out what exactly was going on. This needle looked like it was three feet long—and it felt like it was several feet wide once they started moving it around. With a barbed hook.

I'm exaggerating about the size and the hook, but not the pain. It was part of a camera system to look inside, and they had to move it around. I swear I've never felt such pain in my life. Finally, they were done.

Not. They'd been going in the wrong direction.

"We have to pull it out and do it in the other direction."

"Do what you have to do," I told them, gritting my teeth.

The test confirmed what my body had already told me: I'd torn my knee again. Once more I headed for Dr. Andrews.

"Didn't you give me a lifetime guarantee on this knee?" I joked.

I think he may have offered to throw in an extra tendon for free.

Fortunately, he was able to do the repair arthroscopically. No knee surgery is minor, but compared to the other two, this one was a breeze. Rehab was a little easier this time. Practice makes perfect, I guess.

Standing By

EXCEPT FOR THE injury, the experience on *Ready to Rumble* was a lot of fun. Before I got hurt, I'd done a little bit of work in some of the scenes. But the best part was just being on the set, soaking up the Hollywood atmosphere. It was definitely exciting. The role was small, but at least I had the chance to say I'd been in a movie.

Being on standby, you realize how much time Hollywood actors spend making a movie. A lot of it is just waiting around. Sometimes we'd spend twelve hours a day just waiting to film for twenty-five or thirty minutes—and then maybe thirty seconds of that actually makes it into the movie.

There's downtime in wrestling, but nothing like that. You need an enormous amount of patience in the movies. Not one of my favorite qualities, though, like I said, I'd like to give it a try again.

Vince Russo

I **WAS OUT** of action for several months, from the beginning of November 1999 to the early summer of 2000. It was a chaotic and confusing time for the company. I watched things unravel from the sidelines.

Vince Russo's hiring had been controversial, and he was at WCW for only a short time before running into his own problems. I think the higher-ups were expecting much higher ratings when he came in, and that just didn't happen. Whether he had the time to do it or whatever else he might have needed, I'm not in a position to say.

Eventually Vince left, only to come back for a few months with Eric in a kind of power-sharing thing that didn't really work for anyone, or for the company.

As far as my relationship with Vince, I never had any problems with him. We weren't very close and personal, but from a business standpoint I never had a problem with him. He was always straight with me.

Always a Struggle

THE CRUISERWEIGHTS HAD always been treated on a much different level than the others at WCW. There was a big gulf between what cruiserweights, even someone like Eddie Guerrero, were paid and what people who wrestled in the heavyweight division were paid. I don't want to single anyone out, but the gap was immense.

That wouldn't have been so bad, maybe, but the company didn't seem to know what to do with us. They'd tell us to have a good match. That was it.

We were often pushed aside, even on the shows. If you go back and watch some of the shows, you can hear the commentators spending more time talking about Hogan and the others coming up at the end of the show than the match the cruiserweights were actually having in the ring.

Storylines had become very important for advancing careers and making big stars—as well as for getting fans to watch the shows. The company didn't come up with many for cruiserweights. The few that were done were invented by the cruiserweights themselves, and they were not always pushed with much enthusiasm.

Chris Jericho had this fantastic bit where he ambushed Goldberg and taunted him, setting himself up to be squashed. That was around the same time when he was starting to get serious heat with his Jeriholics. He even worked his own security guard into the show, and the kid developed a cult following all his own.

I loved Jericho's bits, especially the angle he had with Goldberg. They were always very entertaining. What I didn't know at the time, though, is that not only had Chris come up with all the ideas himself, but he had to fight to use them. He argued with Goldberg and Bischoff about how great the angle would be. And eventually it got shut down because Goldberg didn't like it for some reason.

That was the way it was for the cruiserweights: Everything was a struggle. After a while it got to a lot of guys.

Coming from Mexico, where our angles were two weeks long or even nonexistent, I guess the lack of stories didn't bother me as much as it might have. Promos had never really been my focus anyway. Most nights I'd go out, wrestle, and come back. Management would blow smoke up my ass about what a great match I'd had, and that was that.

I knew that I was putting on a good show every night, so, with that said, I really never took much of an interest in going to Eric or whoever and saying, "How about you do something more with me?" I had gotten into the Filthy Animals mix, and that felt good. At the time, I didn't see the need to do something more involved.

Honestly, I thought the wrestling was enough. It was an old-school attitude, maybe.

And, in fairness, they gave me my own little niche at WCW. Any foreign wrestler would usually find himself working with me: Justin "Thunder" Liger, for example, who came in around this time and who I still remember wrestling with. He was one of the best wrestlers in Japan, and the opportunity to work with him was an honor. It put me in a great spot. So I can't say that I was treated all that poorly, compared to the others.

Politics

EDDIE AND KONNAN would smarten me up, telling me how hard they had to fight to get their angles in and share some of the spotlight. They gave me advice too. They weren't causing dissension, which some people have since charged. It was just the opposite. They always told me to go out and tear the house down. Their argument was always this: Show them what we can do. So I would. I'd go out and try to steal the night.

Eddie, though, kept feeling as if he was being treated like secondhand talent. And Konnan was having all sorts of conflicts with Eric. Konnan was convinced that Eric wanted to fire him, or at least get him to quit. But Konnan never gave him the satisfaction.

I think Konnan may have stuck around partly because of our friendship. I always really felt as if he was looking out for me, like the big brother he'd always been. He still had my back.

Eric wasn't all that shy about firing people—ask Steve Austin, among others—so I'm sure that if he really wanted to get rid of Konnan, he would have. Maybe part of him recognized that he had a very talented wrestler in his stable, and personality clashes weren't as important as entertainment value.

Anyway, Eddie and some of the others—Chris Benoit, Dean Malenko—eventually decided it was time to go. So in January 2000, they went to upper management and got their releases. They headed straight over to WWE, where they became instant stars, even bigger than they had been at WCW. Vince McMahon saw their potential and gave them the chance to fulfill it.

"Stay Here"

THE WWE OPTION wasn't open to Konnan.

He'd already done work there. Unfortunately, he'd missed a show for them back in the early 1990s when he was working as Max Moon, and there were still some bad feelings about it. There'd been some conflict between him and the company, but the disagreements didn't justify missing a show. I know it's something he regrets to this day— "I was young and stupid" is how he puts it—but it was too late to undo.

As for me, I was in the middle of my contract, and I felt I had to honor it. And I wasn't quite on the level the others were; there was no guarantee that WWE would take me. When Eddie came to smarten me up about the fact that he was leaving, he gave me a word of advice: "Stay here. Do what you got to do. I'm going to test the waters somewhere else. We'll keep in touch."

On My Own

WHEN THE OTHERS left, it felt like I'd lost some of my best friends. Even though I'd known they were having problems, it was a shock when they actually left.

I still had some good friends at WCW: Billy Kidman and Jamie Noble, among others. And there was a bright side to Eddie and the others leaving: We got their spots. The management started pushing the rest of us. We got teased in matches with the heavyweights, increasing our own profiles.

I'd been wrestling as a professional for more than a decade, all over the world, but I still had to prove a few things in the industry. It was the same story I'd faced from the beginning.

New Blood

IN APRIL OF 2000, Eric Bischoff and Vince Russo began working together as the creative heads of WCW in a partnership that was doomed from the beginning. Behind the scenes, upper management at Time Warner began looking to sell the wrestling operation. They had a lot of things on their minds, including a merger with AOL, and wrestling was no longer seen as an asset.

Bischoff and Russo tried to make things work, shaking up the company's shows. The wrestlers were divided into two groups: the New Blood and the Millionaire's Club. Hulk Hogan was the head of the Millionaire's Club, which basically consisted of the established stars who were still in the company.

The Filthy Animals were part of the New Blood. We did our own thing and generally didn't take on Hogan directly. There wasn't a chance to: The whole idea was dropped after a month or two because it wasn't going anywhere.

When I came back from my injury that May, we got into a feud with the Natural Born Thrillers, a stable of seven wrestlers, all pretty new to the business. If I'm remembering right, they were Mike Sanders, Chuck Palumbo, Sean O'Haire, Shawn Stasiak, Reno, Mark Jindrak, and Johnny "The Bull" Stamboli.

I was still going out and giving a hell of a show every night. Most of the guys were. But we could feel the company coming apart around us. Things were hollow.

The company just felt dead.

Johnny Ace

THERE WERE SOME bright spots during this period. One was meeting John Laurinaitis, who joined the company in 2000 to work on the storylines as booker. As a wrestler under the name Johnny Ace, he'd spent a lot of his career with the All-Japan Pro Wrestling promotion, and he brought his understanding of Japanese- and Mexican-style wrestling to the company, something I really appreciated.

He came over to WWE later on, and as of right now he is head of talent relations here. He's the guy I go to if I need something. He's always taken good care of me.

Johnny has always been very creative. He's a real ring storyteller: The match in the ring has to mean something when he's involved.

Backstage, we tease him every so often about his skateboard, which, back in the day, was one of his signature props. He's got an excellent head for wrestling—but I'll stop talking about him now before it sounds *too* much like brownnosing.

Weird Stuff

AND THEN THERE were things at that time that were just weird . . . or maybe evil. Like the time Juventud went crazy.

We were in Melbourne, Australia. Juventud was there, Konnan, myself, and a whole bunch of other wrestlers. We got to town the day before the shows were supposed to start and went to see the city and enjoy ourselves a little.

Right before that, Juventud and I had had a falling out. We'd been horsing around and suddenly he took something I did as a joke way too seriously. He got really hot. I don't know if he was in a bad mood or what. But we got into a pretty hot argument. I told him he could dish it out but then couldn't take the heat when the tables were turned. The truth hurt, I guess, and things were rocky between us after that.

So in Melbourne, Juventud ran into Konnan and me in a club a few blocks from our hotel. He said he wanted to squash things between us. Eventually we cleared everything and it was all cool.

The night went on. We ended up at this after-hours club. Finally one of us said, "Hey, let's get back to hotel. It's getting late."

Actually, it was getting *early*—the sun was just coming up.

What we didn't know was that somewhere during the night, someone gave Juventud something to drink or maybe smoke that must have been laced with something. Whatever it was, by the time we got outside, he started acting pretty strange.

Juventud Goes Crazy

WE WALKED A block up the street and realized we were being followed by someone. We didn't know exactly what that was about. Was he just curious? Was he thinking of robbing us?

Maybe he'd slipped whatever it was into Juventud and wanted to see what would happen.

Whatever. We crossed the street and took a turn, trying to duck away.

We lost him by the time we got to the park next to the hotel. Now it was just Konnan, myself, and Juventud, who said he felt like hanging out some more.

All of a sudden, Juvy started wigging out. He started going off on us, first on me, then on Konnan.

"You know what?" he said. "You guys are fucking dicks. You haven't treated me with respect. You've always pointed the finger at me."

It got worse from there. His rants against us became more intense. Then he started telling us that we were all going to die.

Konnan tried to calm him down.

"No, no, you don't get it," said Juventud. "I'm a messenger. I'm God. And you don't understand. We're all going to die. Here."

It just got stranger and stranger. Later on, we realized that he had a lot of hatred, and that something evil had gotten into his spirit.

Konnan kept trying to calm him down and pull him into the hotel. Juvy came a little ways with us, then stopped near a wall overlooking the river.

He started yelling at Konnan, then grabbed Konnan's glasses and crunched them in half. Then he got in my face and did the same, breaking my sunglasses.

"We got to get in the water," he said. He started taking off his clothes and trying to climb the wall.

By now people were passing by, going to work or whatever.

"You see those people?" he said. "They know. They're with me. They know."

Some other wrestlers came down from the hotel and tried to help us. We now had a major commotion going on, and hotel security came out to see what was happening.

They asked us to calm him down or they would call the police. But there was just no way to get him calm. He looked like a total madman—with his long hair, and no shirt—and he was certainly acting like one.

Before we knew it, he was butt naked.

The cops came and arrested him. He was charged with a bunch of crimes, including assault and drug possession. I think it took six to eight cops with Mace to arrest him.

The Evil Inside

I REMEMBER WALKING back to my room thinking how crazy that was. Never in my life would I have expected Juventud to do something like that. We'd had our problems, but there was nothing anywhere near as crazy as that. He'd lived with Psicosis and me back in AAA; he was part of our family. At some point in his life, he got steered the wrong way and ended up with a lot of evil and hatred inside him.

At least that night.

I got back to my room and started praying for him—or tried to.

I couldn't focus to pray because I kept seeing his face in my mind. His eyes were white. He was just the picture of the devil.

Juventud was fined and deported out of Australia. WCW released him right after that.

One more member of the posse was gone.

Chaos and More

ALL THE CHAOS of that final year is hard to sort out. Though it played out over months and even years, thinking back on it, everything kind of blurs together.

At some point, Konnan told *USA Today* that the company had gotten stale because the " . . . old guys on top won't let the younger guys come through."

That brought him some heat with the older guys, including Kevin Nash, who was close with Bischoff and booking at the time. Konnan probably didn't care too much about pissing Nash off at that point: He once told Nash that the idea of him as "creative" was an oxymoron.

After *USA Today* printed his remarks, someone—I'm not clear who it was—went to Bill Busch to complain. Busch had been installed as top WCW exec after Eric left. The person told Busch that Konnan had a lot of bad heat in the locker room. Supposedly, wrestlers were so angry they were going to beat him up. He suggested Konnan be suspended "for his own good."

"A crock," as Konnan puts it. Konnan may have had enemies in the locker room, but no one was waiting for him with a tire iron. Busch followed through on the suspension anyway.

In the end, Konnan was out three months. And then after that, he got hurt, which took him out of the ring for a while more. It was almost a symbol of everything else that was going on around us.

The End Was Here

THE COMPANY REMAINED on life support for several months after the Russo-Bischoff experiment imploded. Then everything changed one day in Panama City, Florida.

I remember getting in, anxious for my match. Billy Kidman and I were going to pair up against Elix Skipper & Kid Romeo for the Cruiserweight Tag Team Title.

I was barely in the building when I heard that Vince McMahon was going to buy us.

It had been no secret that WCW was up for sale. Eric Bischoff had been working with a group to take over the company. But the deal fell apart in early 2001. According to Eric, Time Warner had decided that they no longer wanted to air wrestling on its networks. That decision killed the sale, because without prime-time television slots, the company was worth very little.

In the end, the executives decided to sell the company to World Wrestling Federation and Vince McMahon—the archenemy during the height of the Monday Night Wars. For them, it was a decision to not just get out of wrestling, but to get about as far away from it as they could.

They shot it in the head.

A lot of people would say they had killed it long before then.

When some World Wrestling Federation execs walked into the locker room that afternoon, the wrestlers stood up and applauded. They saw the takeover as a good thing—that adults were finally in charge.

I had all sorts of questions, mostly about my own future: Is my contract going to be bought out? Am I going to wrestle in the States again? Is WCW going to survive?

There was a lot of speculation everywhere—in the locker room, in the media. I was nervous. I didn't know what was going to happen.

That night, Billy Kidman and I wrestled for the Tag Team Title. We won—and I have the title belt to this day, framed in my house.

Lack of Unity Meant Downfall

THERE SHOULD HAVE been more unity in WCW. We had tremendous talent there, fantastic talent. Creative wrestlers. We were together at a time when the profession was at the top. When the competition with WWE increased, we should have worked even harder to get together.

You can't tap people's talents by being at war with them. Everyone has to pull together, wrestlers and management.

I think that was one of the reasons for WWE's success. When they were down—when WCW was top dog—I think the spirit was more like: "We have to stick together and make this shit work." They held together when a lot of wrestlers were leaving, when things were at their worst.

Contrast that with WCW. The attitude of the star cliques and management that kept people from escalating, the cliques themselves, politics, whatever—it all worked against us.

Maybe at the beginning there were just too many stars to handle properly, with Ric Flair, Hogan, Nash. But they should have been preparing for the day when people got tired of the others. It happens so fast. One minute you're on top, then the next second you're Dinosaur World.

That was Chris Jericho's term for WCW: *Dinosaur World*. And you know what happened to the dinosaurs.

Sitting Out

THE PURCHASE BY WWE threw everything up in the air. Some wrestlers went over immediately, but a lot of us were suddenly without a job. There was simply too much talent for too few slots.

The WCW collapse hurt a lot of Mexican wrestlers. Because of the company rule that they couldn't wrestle anywhere else, they had been out of Mexico for a couple of years and therefore weren't really known there anymore. It was tough for them to go back; it meant starting almost from scratch.

Konnan's earlier problems with WWE probably helped keep him from getting a job there, even though he was still popular in the States. Some of the other stars had contracts that the company simply didn't want, and it was difficult for them to work out deals. I believe that in a lot of cases, the contracts had been guaranteed and were paid by Time Warner, which meant the wrestler got paid whether he wrestled or not.

Unless he joined a rival. In which case the payments stopped, since the contract was broken.

That was the deal in my case. I was going to be paid *not* to wrestle.

Johnny Ace and J.R.—Jim Ross, who was the head of talent relations and in effect my new boss—told me to stop wrestling, relax, go home, and wait out my contract. That's what I decided to do. My contract had over a year to run.

Sitting Out
... and Not

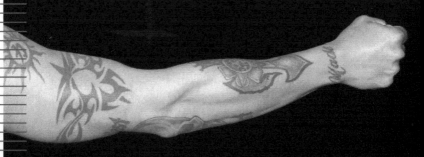

I went home to San Diego and my family. It was good to spend time with my wife and my daughter, Aalyah, who'd been born on August 20, 2001, at 7:29 p.m.

I was very fortunate to have been there for the birth of both my son and my daughter, and to get the chance to spend time with them when they were very little. We all say how God works in mysterious ways, and maybe that was true here. In each case I was out of action right after my babies were born, so that has worked out very well for me.

A Great Little Girl

DOMINIK CAUGHT US by surprise, but Aalyah we planned. My wife did all these things that are supposed to make it possible for your child to be a girl, because we wanted one of each, and when we found out she was pregnant with a girl, we were very excited. We hit it.

My daughter has so much of me. She loves attention, and is very polite, and is very smart—that she got from her mom.

I was so young when we had Dominik, and so young when we had Aalyah, that I'd like another child. I'll know what to watch for, how to act, and how to treat my wife and family so much better. I think that's my next goal in life.

Restless

BUT AS MUCH as I love my kids, I felt something important was missing. It didn't take long before I started getting restless. I'd been wrestling all my life, and except for injuries, this was the longest vacation I'd ever had.

At the same time, I was a little skeptical and worried about getting picked up. After all, there was no guarantee that WWE would hire me. And I'd always heard that they preferred very big guys on their shows.

Under the terms of my contract, I was still being paid by WCW's old parent company, Time Warner. That would have stopped, of course, if WWE signed me. But the terms of the contract didn't seem to prevent me from wrestling outside of the country and for certain other promotions.

I wanted to be positive, so I tried to get a clarification of this by calling the WCW numbers, but no one answered the telephones at the numbers. There was no voice mail, nothing—the offices probably weren't even there anymore.

It was nice to collect money, but I wanted to work. I wanted to wrestle.

I talked with my wife, and finally I went ahead and made a few phone calls to Mexico.

CMLL

I'D ALWAYS HAD a dream of wrestling for CMLL in Mexico City and appearing in Arena México.

CMLL, of course, was one of the two large wrestling franchises in Mexico. It began in 1933, founded by Salvador Lutteroth Gonzales, who's called the father of *lucha libre*. First known as EMLL—Empresa Mexicana de la Lucha Libre—it not only featured El Santo but had a whole constellation of stars throughout its long history, with wrestlers like Bobby Bonales, Tarzán López, Cavernario Galindo, and Gory Guerrero filling the cards. The names of all of the stars who wrestled there would easily fill a book this size.

Arena México is to Mexican sports entertainment what Madison Square Garden is to the U.S. Opened in 1933, it's often called the "cathedral of *lucha libre*." Fairly plain on the outside, the building hasn't changed much since it was first built. Kind of old school.

The architecture takes a backseat to the atmosphere. Just as in Madison Square Garden, the 16,500 fans who fill the seats are reputed to be among the best and most knowledgeable in the world. The fans know the history, and they bring that history to the place.

CMLL wrestlers travel to other cities just as they do in other franchises, but Arena México is their home.

The Boys Are Back in Town

ONCE AGAIN, I went to Mexico with my boys. Psicosis, Halloween, Damián 666, Juventud, and I headed to Mexico City and began wrestling with CMLL.

I didn't have any beef with AAA at the time. They weren't in a position to give me a commitment. We were going our separate ways, with no hard feelings. On my side, I knew or at least hoped that my days in Mexico were going to be very few.

We went back and started packing arenas. I wasn't wearing my mask: Once you lose your mask in Mexico, you don't remask under the same name. That's part of the tradition. And really, why would you? The fans know who you are already, so what's the sense of putting on a mask? The mask is all about the mystery and the wrestler's identity in the ring.

What is allowed—and this has been done a lot through history—is to come back with a new name and a mask. Usually a wrestler will wrestle without his mask for a year or so before doing that. Again, it's part of the tradition, honoring the way of the mask and underlining how important the mask and Mask versus Mask matches are.

But I saw no reason to wrestle as anyone other than Rey Mysterio Jr. I'd been wrestling without a mask for a while. It no longer felt strange.

My outfit at the time was inspired by the medieval knights and the chainmail armor they used to wear. I had a chainmail helmet similar to what Big Papa Pump used to wear and a chain vest as well. I also had white contact lenses, which gave me white eyes. It was a cool look.

History Calls

I REMEMBER WALKING down to the ring. I was thinking of El Santo, Blue Demon, and more recent wrestlers, the ones I grew up watching, like Jerry Estrada, La Fiera, Super Astro, Kung Fu, Negro Casas. They had all walked down this same path.

I was still considered a babyface in Mexico. I had left Mexico City as a babyface. I'd done well in the States as a babyface. Even though I no longer had my mask, people still had that original image of my character in their minds. While I had been a heel as a member of the Filthy Animals, I was not a vicious one; my image was softer—not a *heel* heel. So people took me as a good guy.

Even though I'd been wrestling for years, I was very nervous. I knew that the fans at Arena México either accepted you or they hated you. They made up their minds at the very first show, and you had to win them over.

It was torture. I had more than butterflies going around in my stomach. Bats, maybe. Huge. It was one of the worst cases of nerves I ever had.

Yes, I said the same thing about ECW, about WCW. Again and again, I've gone through this, proving myself—if not to the fans, to me.

Our contest was a Tag Team match with four wrestlers on each team. Damián, Halloween, Psicosis & Juventud were one side; with me were Negro Casas, El Hijo del Santo—and unfortunately I can't remember the fourth member of the team.

We were a semi-main event, and we rocked the house.

Paco

WE CONTINUED TO do that over the next few weeks, building a good following. We brought in a different, younger audience to the CMLL shows. We attracted a lot of teenagers, younger fans who liked our high-energy, freer style.

CMLL had always been known as the more conservative wrestling franchise—they wouldn't show blood on TV, for instance—but all of a sudden they had younger wrestlers bringing new energy to the game. People knew too that we had been wrestling in the U.S., and they wanted to see if we were as good as the reports said.

The crowds had been down for a while, but all of a sudden the promotion had full arenas. It was strictly because of us.

I decided to try and negotiate a guarantee with the owner of CMLL, Paco Alonso. An agreement would have given me security—and more money—but it also would have given CMLL some sort of commitment on my part. We made an appointment to talk and I came by.

I waited for an hour, an hour and a half. Eventually, after two hours, someone came over and said, "I'm sorry, Mysterio. Mr. Alonso had to leave for a meeting."

Naïvely, I believed him. I was thinking, *Alonso is busy. He has a lot to do and worry about. Things just got away from him.* I set up another appointment with him to come back.

The company had just started doing Pay-Per-Views and, at least as far as I could see, was making a good amount of money. So were a lot of people there—except for us. Maybe because we were newcomers, or had once been part of AAA, we seemed to be held to the lowest possible fees and cuts. I got paychecks in the area of $150 for packing the arena.

It really wasn't about the money for me. I was already being paid by WCW. I just wanted to get my respect.

That was harder to come by than money.

Alonso blew off another appointment. He was acting like the stereotypical promoter you hear about in Mexico all the time. It's cheesy: Duck the talent, and keep as much as you can for yourself.

I spent roughly three months in Mexico wrestling for him, and he never managed to find the time for me. I soon realized he was just going to duck me for as long as he could—maybe forever. I realized that's what he was all about: no respect for the wrestlers, no respect for me.

I wasn't there for the money, and not even for respect from people like Paco Alonso. I was there to fulfill a dream. I stepped inside Arena México and I performed for those fans. I gave them great shows.

For a *luchador*, that's what's important. If you never get a chance to do that, if you don't appear at Arena México and bring the fans to their feet, you'll never be considered a great wrestler. And I did it. I accomplished that, and no one is taking it away from me.

I put money and fame aside and gave the fans the best show I could, performing in front of them. And they repaid me with applause.

That's real respect. That's real *honor*, in this business.

"I Don't Need This"

WHEN ALONSO KEPT ducking me, I decided that I wasn't going to stay there very long. I talked with other people in the company— the booking team especially, who were always very polite—but without talking to the boss I wasn't getting any guarantees or a contract.

I could have been a top talent. We could have started a good friendship and possibly found a way to assist CMLL in the future. Today I still have good relations with AAA. If AAA needs a favor from my end, I'm more than happy to help out. If I can be part of a promotion or help them in some other way, I do.

AAA inducted me into their hall of fame, which is something I'm very proud of. I received the award at a *TripleMania*, and I'm sure it helped bring a little something extra to the event. Fans have made it a point to come to AAA events when I'm there. We've helped each other.

Apparently Mr. Alonso didn't have the need for Rey Mysterio at the time. From my standpoint, he was a very bad businessman, and he made a very bad decision.

But no hard feelings.

Puerto Rico

AFTER WCW DIED, Konnan wrestled in Europe. Mexico was basically closed to him at the time. There were a lot of bad feelings in both major promotions because he had managed to drain off a lot of their talent when he was running Promo Azteca. And besides, he was having pretty good success in Europe.

Then he got a chance to wrestle in Puerto Rico for the World Wrestling Council. Konnan had always wanted to wrestle in Puerto Rico because his father had come from there; it was a way to reach back to his roots.

Where Konnan goes, I'm never far behind. He asked them if they'd like to bring me in. Next thing I knew, he was calling me up and telling me how great Puerto Rico was.

They booked a few dates for me to wrestle in January 2002, and I went over to check things out.

World Wrestling Council

ANY TIME I open up a new market for myself, it's fun. There's a sense that I'm going into uncharted territory, exploring. Everything is new and fresh again. Puerto Rico was just that.

Carlos Colón, Victor Jovica, and Gorilla Monsoon got together in Puerto Rico in 1973 and started Capitol Sports Promotions. They worked their way up in the early days by touring in small Puerto Rican towns, bringing wrestling to the masses—the hundreds and thousands in rural areas who'd never had a chance to see it live before. The company, under the direction of Colón and Jovica, changed its name to World Wrestling Council during the 1990s and continues today as one of Puerto Rico's top two promotions.

During some of the hard times for the company, Carlos Colón sat down with his family and told them, "Boys, I need your help. We're going to make this company work."

He told his sons—they were still pretty young—that he needed their help to be successful. I don't think they were thinking about being wrestlers at the time, but they both decided that they were going to be wrestlers because their father needed their help.

They worked their asses off. They helped set it up and tear it down in the ring. They learned how to train and how to wrestle.

That early training paid off. Carlos's older son is Carly Colón, who now wrestles in WWE. And his brother is Primo Colón, also a WWE Superstar.

True Legends

AN ASIDE ABOUT Gorilla Monsoon: Gorilla—his full name was Robert James "Gino" Marella—had a very successful career inside and outside the ring, wrestling, announcing, and eventually promoting. He was the voice of World Wrestling Federation in the 1980s and 1990s, and if I'm not mistaken, at one time he even owned part of the company. Today we call the backstage spot right near the curtain the gorilla position in his honor.

Carlos Colón is a legend in his own right. He wrestled for a number of years in the U.S., with a short stint in World Wrestling Federation, but most of his career inside the ropes came in Puerto Rico, where he was known for his toughness and ability to withstand bruising matches. He's so famous there that his injuries were front-page news on the island.

Carlos had seen my work and had faith in me. It was totally different than working with Paco Alonso. We sat down and talked about what we could do. Carlos said he'd give me the Junior Heavyweight Title right away.

That was flattering and it made me feel very welcome, but I had to be honest with him. I told him that there was a possibility I'd be leaving in a few months, when my contract with WCW expired.

"Well, let's do what we can, while we can," he said. "If that day comes, I won't stop you."

It was a tremendous and generous response.

The Title

I WON THE Junior Heavyweight Championship the very first day I was there, defeating Eddie Colón—known now in the States as Primo Colón.

When you work with people like Primo, who have wrestling in the blood, it makes your work so much more fun. He's very charismatic. He definitely had the crowd on his side during our match. You could see he was his father's son, just from the way the crowd responded to him. Being a Colón in Puerto Rico, he was the hometown hero. I got my applause from the fans after I won the title but I don't think they ever lost their love for Primo.

I would go over for weekends—Friday, Saturday, and Sunday—and fly back home during the week. It turned out pretty well. I'd never been in Puerto Rico before, and I really came to like the island.

But I was still hoping to leave. Finally, in April 2002, I got the phone call that changed the course of my career.

Re-Masked

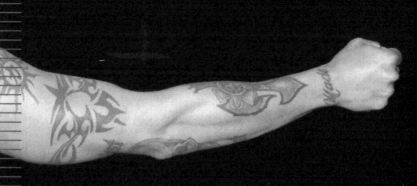

The call was from WWE, asking if I could meet

Johnny Ace and J.R. at the Staples Center

in Los Angeles when WWE appeared there.

I went in, sat down, heard what they had to

say—and by the end of our conversation I was

back in prime time as a member of WWE.

It really was that easy and quick.

J.R.

JIM ROSS—J.R.—is known to the world as the best wrestling commentator ever. There's no one better or more famous when it comes to calling a wrestling match.

J.R. has a lot of other talents. He's a chef—check out his barbecue sauce—and a restaurant owner. Besides calling wrestling matches, he's done play-by-play for the NFL and college football.

What most fans don't realize is that J.R. has also played an important role in the wrestling business behind the scenes. When I came in during 2002, he was the head of talent relations at WWE. As far as wrestlers were concerned, he was just a step below Vince McMahon and his family, the CEO and owners of the promotion. J.R. was the person responsible for taking care of all the business necessary to get us in the ring.

J.R. is a great guy, very upfront and honest with me, a guy whose word you could trust.

He laid everything out straight. The offer—it was the guarantee of a minimum in a complicated system of payments—was less than I had made at WCW. Still, it was a fair deal.

"You know what, Rey?" he told me. "Maybe what we're offering you right now isn't the biggest amount you've ever made, but I will assure you this: With the type of talent you have, you're going to be making more than what we're offering you very soon."

"As long as I have a job," I told him. "Thank you. And thank you to the McMahon family."

Ohio Valley

MY FIRST STOP back was at Ohio Valley Wrestling, also known as OVW. Ohio Valley was like our farm division, a place where new wrestlers could learn their craft. Even though I'd been doing a steady stream of shows, I asked to work for two weeks there so I could get used to the ring used by WWE, which is twenty by twenty. The rings I'd used in WCW and internationally were several feet shorter on each side.

The difference may seem small, but it's huge to a wrestler, especially someone like me who is doing a lot of high-flying spots. I had to add two or three steps when setting up some of my moves. Another huge difference is in the ropes: In WWE we use real rope around the ring, while at WCW and some other promotions the ring is bounded by plastic-covered cable. You get a much different spring from rope than cable—something that's very important when you're jumping from it.

The first time I stepped into one, the ring seemed huge. But I adapted pretty quickly. I think I get better bounce off the real ropes. They also hurt a lot less than the wire cables when you hit them.

Not that they don't hurt at all.

Since a lot of my arsenal comes from springing off the top rope, the switch to the new ring helped my work. I got some mad hops off the rope, adding even more height to my moves.

When I got to OVW, I had my costume all set: chainlink helmet, a new armor vest. I even had a sword being made. I'd found special contact lenses to turn my eyes white, giving me a real special look. (They didn't affect my sight, though they were hard to put in.)

Right after my first match, someone—I think it was probably Jim Cornette, who was running OVW at the time—pulled me aside and asked why I wasn't wearing my mask. I explained that I'd been unmasked in WCW and hadn't worn one for quite a while.

He gave me the word that Vince himself had asked that I wrestle with my mask on.

Oh shit. There went my whole getup.

A New Hood

THE MASK BROUGHT back another dimension to my character. To the top people at WWE, that character was very closely connected to my wrestling skills, and they wanted the entire package. They felt that fans wanted it as well.

"We need you with the mask," J.R. explained. "That's who Rey Mysterio is."

It felt a little odd, but it wasn't too hard to convince me. They were my bosses now, and my idea was that I would do what they wanted. And in the back of my mind, I knew that WCW had never marketed the mask the way they should have. I knew WWE would market the hell out of it, pushing it, selling it.

It soon became obvious they were right. Kids just love the masks. Everywhere I go, I see them wearing different versions. It's a nice tribute to me, and it makes me proud.

I think my signing with WWE and coming back to wrestle with my hood may have started a little trend back in Mexico. After I did it in WWE, it opened up a lot of eyes in Mexico. Tradition could still be served by bringing back the mask, at least in some instances. Among the Mexican wrestlers who took up the mask again was my uncle, who'd been wrestling without a mask for years. Another wrestler who did the same was Super Astro, an idol of mine from way back.

Eventually WWE and I did some shows in Mexico, where I wrestled in my mask. I was a little nervous about that aspect: Would the fans go for it, having seen me without it? But they completely accepted it. And so have I.

No More "Junior"

I REGAINED MY mask when I came back, but I lost something else that had been with me since practically the start of my career: the "Junior" at the end of my name.

Actually, I didn't realize that it was gone until a few matches had gone by. At first I thought it was some sort of typo or an oversight somewhere. But it was also part of the plan.

My uncle wasn't a member of the company, so as far as WWE was concerned, there was no reason to have "Junior" as part of my name. Just as many sons eventually grow out of the "Junior," stepping from their father's shadow to become mature men, I had too.

Future Stars

OVW HAD A lot of talent at that time. I remember wrestling Nova— Mike Bucci, who later came to WWE as Simon Dean. The Prototype did a run-in on the match.

You know The Prototype better as John Cena.

That was the first time I got to meet Cena. He was looking good, as always. I didn't really have a chance to talk to him much that night, but it turned out that our paths would run together during my early days at WWE.

He was a jacked kid, looking pretty good. He came down from Rick Bassman's training ground. Rick later became one of my agents, so there was another connection between us.

I could tell Cena was good, but I don't think I or anyone else could have predicted that he'd end up holding the company in his hands, like an Austin or a Rock. It just goes to show that when you've got it, you've got it. He definitely had that special something that propels a superstar beyond superstardom. It's an internal drive as much as anything.

At Ohio Valley, he was mostly a power guy, but he kept developing his craft in a phenomenal way. For a guy his size, he gets up big.

There were other stars in the making. Randy Orton, I think, was coming in around then. Batista—"The Animal"—was around at that time as well. I saw a lot of other guys with big talent.

Two Weeks Became One

THE ORIGINAL PLAN was for me to work two weeks at OVW before coming up to WWE, but I progressed pretty quickly, and after only a week I was booked on a house show in L.A. against Chavo Guerrero.

We had a great match. Chavo and I had worked together in WCW. He's part of the famous Guerrero family—Eddie's nephew—and was very familiar with the Mexican style as well as the American. He knew how to base for me, and he made me look really, really good.

Ironically, I had trouble with one spot in our first match—the move that became one of my signature spots in WWE, the 619. I remember setting up Chavo and hitting the ropes. Somehow I got tangled up, missing it. We covered up and I set him up again. The second time, I hit him.

I usually hit nine out of ten of my moves, and if there's one I'm going to miss, it's not the 619. I've done it so much. But I missed that one. Maybe a moment of excitement and a little nervousness threw me off.

The 619

I HAD BEEN doing that move, with different variations, for years. You have to see it to get a full understanding of how it works, but basically it goes like this: With my victim hanging on the lower ropes, I run to the ropes alongside him. I look like I'm going to dive out of the ring. Instead of diving out, I grab on and swing my legs around in

DAMIÁN 666.

a quick spin, bringing them back between the top and second ropes. The move lets me kick my opponent, who's slumped against the ropes, in the face or upper body.

Some other names have been used to describe the move. One is the Tiger Feint Kick. I believe that Tiger Mask came up with the move, though without setting up his opponent on the ropes; he used it as a fake or feint. (There have been several Tiger Masks; the one I'm thinking of was Mitsuharu Misawa, who had many memorable matches with Dynamite Kid when I was growing up. The character actually began as a successful manga and anime series in Japan before being adopted by All-Japan Pro Wrestling in the 1980s.)

Super Astro also did the move. He was a short, stocky wrestler. He would literally jump into the ropes, then swing around hard. Tiger Mask may have invented it; Super Astro perfected it.

I copied the move, but it was my good friend (and son's godfather) Damián 666 who told me how to change it to make it my own.

"Hey, *compadre*?" he said one day. "You know that move where you spin around? Why don't you set the guy up on the ropes and hit him with your feet?"

Until then, I and everyone else had used it as a feint. The addition turned it into a weapon.

I'm not sure whether Damián had seen someone do it, or he merely envisioned it in his mind. I tried it. Sure enough, it was a great move, and it became an instant crowd pleaser.

Names for Moves

WHEN I CAME into WWE, everyone was naming their moves, especially their finish. It helped them get over with the crowd. So I had to come up with some names of my own.

I came up with 619 by thinking about Stone Cold Steve Austin and how he had popularized 3:16. It seemed like the right set of numbers could stand out with fans, giving them something easy to remember.

I didn't just pull 619 out of the air. I grew up in San Diego, and the area code there—for the one person out of a million who doesn't know or hasn't guessed by now—is 619.

The area code would be part of a sequence, the commentary that would go with my move.

Rey is dialing it up, he's going home . . .

See? I dial it up and go home, dialing 619 and smashing my opponent to the canvas as I set up for the victory.

I smartened up Tazz and Michael Cole at the time—they were doing the announcing on *SmackDown!*—and we baptized the 619.

West Coast Pop

MOST OF MY names came from my hometown area, where I'd grown up and first wrestled: the West Coast Pop, the TJ Drop in honor of Tijuana. (The move later turned into Droppin' Da Dime, another phone reference. In the old days a phone call cost ten cents; "dropping a dime" on someone was slang for calling the police and having him taken to jail.)

The West Coast Pop is basically a springboard frankensteiner. It's the move that's probably been responsible for all my knee injuries. The TJ Drop was a springboard legdrop to the back of my opponent's head.

My idea with the names was to put over my city and my region. I wanted to represent who I am, where I came from. San Diego and Tijuana, the West Coast: The area is so much a part of me. I wanted my fans to be able to relate to me.

At first, not that many people seemed to know about San Diego. A lot asked what 619 meant, not really connecting it to an area code, let alone San Diego. I'm happy to think that maybe I had a tiny part in raising their awareness.

I also remember around that time, Ludacris had a song called "Area Codes"—which does *not* include 619. He's got 916, 409—it seems like every number except ours. I was really pissed off. What's up with that? Why not San Diego? San Diego is a bomb-ass city, and it deserves its props.

SmackDown!

RIGHT AFTER I signed my deal, Kevin Dunn and his staff put some videos together and started airing them on *SmackDown!* They were little vignettes of me wrestling in WCW. At first the action flew by so quickly you couldn't tell who the wrestler was. All you saw were the words "He's coming . . ." filling the screen.

Who is he? Fans wanted to know.

As the weeks went by and my debut on television came closer, the wrestler came more into view.

Rey Mysterio.

The promos really built me up. I had no idea they were going to do this. One day I was watching *SmackDown!* at home and I saw the vignette. It was really cool.

He's coming . . .
He's coming . . .
He's here!

Under Stage

MY FIRST SHOW was the July 25, 2002, edition of *SmackDown!* We taped in Indianapolis. While the video promotion was playing on the big screen, I was hunkered down beneath the stage, standing on a small platform, starting to sweat.

Dean Malenko came up with the idea of having me pop up onto the stage. Not only was it the best entrance I've ever had, but I want to say it was one of the best that *SmackDown!* ever had.

They had a bigger stage back then, and I was able to walk underneath without ducking my head. I got on top of a small platform. I squatted down and took hold of a lever at the center of the platform. On one side of me, two guys were ready to push weights that would help propel me into the air. On the other side, a production guy was counting down.

"Three . . . two . . . one!"

I pulled the lever and shot up as my pyro was going off. I must have flown seven, eight, ten feet into the air. The crowd went crazy.

It was an awesome entrance. I'm still working with Kevin to get another as good.

I've Made It!

AS USUAL, I was nervous as hell that first match. I remember going out there in front of the crowd, not really sure how they were going to react.

But in spite of all that nervousness and whatever jitters were rattling through my stomach, I thought one thing: It doesn't get any better than this. This is the number-one wrestling promotion in the world, and I'm here. I've made it.

I had on red pants and a red mask. There were signs for me throughout the crowd, and the people were just roaring.

Chavo stood in the corner, pouting. How come I was getting all the applause? He'd show them.

He really put me over.

We started with a handlock. I flipped over as Chavo held my arm.

He caught me in the gut with a kick, then flipped me over his head. But I managed to spin over and get on his shoulders, and I nearly took him out with a quick pin after he fell to the mat.

Chavo turned things around, slamming me on the ropes so hard the crowd probably thought I'd split in two. He tossed me around for a while, even sliding me out of the ring.

As the beating continued, the crowd began chanting my name.

Instant energy. The momentum began to turn. I did a corkscrew off the ropes, out of the ring, and onto Chavo, taking him down in front of the runway. We did a fancy bridge but I couldn't get a pin. Then a Gory Bomb from Chavo almost took me out.

Chavo came at me in the corner. I got him in a toehold and slammed him against the ropes. While he hung there, dazed, I ran back, then flew into a 619. A springboard hurricanrana—the West Coast Pop—and Chavo was pinned.

The crowd exploded, welcoming me to my new home.

"That's You, Dog"

VERY FEW PEOPLE asked about the mask. And the people who gave me feedback, most of them liked the mask.

"Love the mask, Rey."

"That's you, Dog."

"Rey Mysterio without the mask ain't Rey Mysterio."

It was a good vibe and a real plus for me.

I took the positive comments and fed off them. WWE started marketing replicas of my masks to fans, which brought me a little extra income and helped spread my name. So overall I had a very positive feeling. Not only was I back in the ring in the States, back in prime time, but I was with a top organization that treated me right and showed how sharp they were from the start.

I was in the shit.

Eric Was Back, Too

I WASN'T THE only one from WCW returning at that time. Eric Bischoff returned to the air that year as well. His return shocked the audiences and generated a lot of heat for him as he became the man fans loved to hate.

Eric had a bit of heat in the locker room as well. He had a lot of beef with some of the WCW guys, Flair and Jericho especially. Some other guys were just angry that he hadn't taken them to the next level, and that wasn't really personal.

We had pretty much squashed the beef between us by then. Of course, it still pisses me off that he dicked me around about my mask, and he didn't have a vision of what Rey Mysterio and *lucha libre* could be, but I've said all that. The bad feelings are in the past.

We were on different shows, so our paths didn't cross that much. There wasn't much interaction between us at all, and whatever there was was polite and professional.

I was kind of glad that he came back, though, because I had a feeling that they were going to make him pay for everything he'd done to WWE back at WCW. They did, and it was funny to watch.

A Save and a Near Fall

MY FIRST NIGHT on *SmackDown!* could have been my last—ever.

After my match, I did a thing with Test where he bumped into me and gave me a look, like, *Come on, kid, walk away.* I eyed him down.

That was the first hint that there was going to be some big guy–little guy action in the future. But emotions really started ramping at the very end of the show, at a Cage match between Edge and Chris Jericho. Edge beat Jericho in the match, but then he started getting beat on by Jericho's allies, The Un-Americans. Test was a member of that group, along with Christian, Lance Storm, and William Regal.

I had climbed a cage only during a match, never at WWE. But when they asked if I could do it, I said sure.

"Can you do something off it?" they asked. I forget exactly who "they" were, which is probably a good thing.

"Sure, sure," I answered.

"How about a dive off it?"

"Sure, sure," I said.

But deep down inside, I was scared shitless.

Doing the dive meant I had to climb the cage, stand on top of it, and then throw myself down into the middle.

That had to be, what, a thousand feet up?

Don't bother correcting me. That's how far it felt.

"Do a cross-body and jump onto Christian and Test," they added.

"Yeah, yeah. I'm good."

Ha!

When the time came, I was down the ramp and up the cage in less than two seconds flat. If I'd done it any slower my heart would have stopped. My eyes weren't closed, but they could have been.

Zip, zip, up to the top, and off. If I'd thought about what I was doing, let's just say my debut would have been memorable for all the wrong reasons.

The dive itself was easy, though, because I'd have been scared to go back. Landing, of course, is always a different story.

I came down, they got me, and I felt the most enormous sense of relief possible.

Whoosh, I'd made it.

Billy Kidman and Other WCW Alumni

THOSE FIRST FEW weeks with *SmackDown!* passed pretty quickly, turning into months without me noticing.

I remember wrestling with Billy Kidman in those early days. Billy was always very creative, coming up with different moves. He always wanted to bring something new. The fans were really behind us, and they loved to see us working together. We had some awesome matches, including one with Shelton Benjamin & Charlie Hass that was one of the greatest Tag Team matches I've ever been in, or seen.

It was almost like Billy and I picked up where we'd left off in WCW, where we could feed off each other's energy and creativity to get a good match going. We told each other that we had to work even harder here.

When we teamed up during a tag match, Billy had a thing where he would pick up the opponent in an electric chair. I'd spring to the top rope and jump off, hitting him at the same time. We'd do a popup frankensteiner where he would launch me into the air and I'd land sitting on our opponent on the ropes, then bring him in with a frankensteiner. That was probably one of our favorite moves as tag team partners.

There were a lot of WCW alumni there. Besides Billy and Chavo, Eddie Guerrero, Chris Jericho, and Chris Benoit were all WWE Superstars. Paul Heyman came on *SmackDown!* at some point this year as well, so the promotion bloodlines ran thick through sports entertainment's top shows.

But my most memorable storyline after coming back to the U.S. was probably my clash with Kurt Angle.

Kurt

KURT WAS A tremendous amateur wrestler, taking a gold medal at the 1996 Summer Olympics in Atlanta. He accomplished that despite two broken cervical vertebrae: As he puts it, he had a "freakin' broken neck" and still ranked as the best amateur wrestler in the world.

Kurt joined WWE a short time later. By the time I came in, he'd been both U.S. Champion and WWE Champion. Just before I came in, he was feuding with Steve Austin; he'd soon get into storylines with The Rock and then Hulk Hogan.

I've always had a lot of respect for the guys I've worked with in WWE. They're at the top of our profession. In Kurt's case, I think there was a little extra respect, because I knew what he'd done as an amateur in the Olympics, and how hard he had worked overcoming his injuries.

Our action came about totally because of him. Kurt was a badass in the ring, a real shooter. But behind the scenes, he was very humble, a true gentleman—and a fan.

He called me one day before *SummerSlam* in 2002 and told me that Vince had given him three options of who he could work with at the show: Ric Flair, Cena, or Rey Mysterio.

"I picked you," he said.

"Wow, thank you very much," I told him. "You didn't have to."

"No, I think you and I can really go at it. You and me can make some money for this company."

And he was right.

A Twelve-Year-Old

KURT STARTED OUR conflict with the classic big guy–little guy insult, calling me nothing but a twelve-year-old and making all the requisite jokes about my height. Naturally, I had to stand up for myself—and I think that's something all shorter guys know and can relate to. The only way to deal with a bully is to be ten times as ferocious as they are.

I don't know who came up with all his vignettes—I suspect Kurt did all or most of them himself—but, damn, were they silly and fun. Good, natural moments. Kurt was saying all sorts of things that I would have heard in real life from people who didn't know me.

Onscreen, I was getting angry, but behind the mask I was smiling and sometimes even laughing. The insults were just so good I was cracking up.

"Am I really going to beat up a twelve-year-old kid?" he asked at one point.

This twelve-year-old kid was ready to rumble.

The Equalizers

BIG GUY-LITTLE guy matches can be fun for the audience, but only if they believe that the little guy can somehow defeat the odds and win. It's a tricky proposition, because, let's face it, size usually does matter in the ring. If it didn't, there wouldn't be different weight classes.

In my case, speed, agility, and wrestling knowledge can be a great equalizer. But I wasn't just wrestling a big man here. Kurt Angle was known as a great mat wrestler, strong on technique—he was an Olympic champion, after all. So my athleticism was only going to go so far.

Of course, there's also heart, the greatest equalizer of them all: The size of your body says nothing about the size of your heart. But Kurt had a big one himself.

I got a win against him leading up to *SummerSlam*. I forget the circumstances now—I believe it was in a Tag Team match a few weeks before the Pay-Per-View, when I caught him offguard—but I can still see the West Coast Pop putting him down.

That made him furious, stoking the storyline. And it put the idea in the back of fans' heads: *You know, maybe Rey will just pull this off.*

Tearing Him Open

IN THOSE DAYS, the rules were a little easier on how matches went, in terms of what the endings could be. I believe I got the win even though I wasn't technically the legal wrestler in the ring. Nowadays the legal guy has to win, and they're pretty strict about that. We have all kinds of rules that have to be followed, and there's usually no way around them.

A week after the surprise pin, we had another confrontation, this time after a match he'd had with Brock Lesnar. I did a headscissors and he ended up taking a bump to the floor. He came up bleeding.

The blood wasn't planned.

Oh shit, I thought to myself. *I cracked him open.*

You don't hurt someone in the ring—or on the floor, for that matter. Shit happens, of course, but the other man is your responsibility when you're wrestling. You have to take very good care of him, whether he's bigger than you or not.

When we got backstage, I checked up on him. It turned out that my knee brace had caught him and slashed his head, slicing him open. He ended up having to get a couple of stitches.

I was bummed that I had busted him. You don't know how many times I apologized.

"Oh, please, no," he kept saying. "Stop. Rey, I'm okay."

Fortunately, he was okay. But I still felt like shit.

SummerSlam

I THINK OUR match at Nassau Coliseum in New York may have been one of the best of my career. Without a doubt.

Kurt wanted to throw everything on the grill. I was pleased. It was a chance to use my whole arsenal. I wanted to prove myself.

Kurt's entrance came first. He was waiting for me in the ring, expecting me to come down the ramp. But when you fight Rey Mysterio, you have to expect the unexpected.

And so do I.

Before he came down, I'd snuck through the audience in a jumpsuit and hidden beneath the ring. I watched everything through a monitor. It was dark down there, and a little claustrophobic, but I figured I could handle it. We were the first match, so it didn't look to be a long wait. I pitched everything to the side, got ready—then realized I'd left my mask with my jumpsuit.

Where had I tossed it?

I started looking around on my hands and knees. While thousands of fans in the arena and another few million at home were watching Kurt make his entrance to hot music and pyro, I was scrambling around trying to find my mask. After a while I realized I could use the monitor as a flashlight. Luckily, I found it a few seconds before I had to go on. I slipped it on and jumped out. I didn't even have time to tie it.

Surprise

I CAME UP from under the ring, sprang to the top rope, and hit Kurt with a knees-on-top-of-the-shoulders headscissors. I tucked in and gave him a forward roll.

Boom, down we went.

Kurt sprawled across the ring, and we were moving. Scissors, dives, flying kicks—we had the fans on their feet for the start of the Pay-Per-View. I pulled out moves I hadn't done in years. That first move was something I'd done when I was fifteen—and hadn't done since.

Watch the match, and you'll see that Kurt did a good amount of flying himself. For a big guy, he was incredibly light on his feet. We had a few spots where we could slow down the match, letting the crowd catch their breath before we took them right back into the fury.

Kurt, of course, couldn't just settle for the pin. He'd promised to make me tap out, to cry uncle, to admit he was the better man. He'd been so frustrated by my standing up to him—not to mention my attacks inside and outside the ring—that he didn't just want to win. He needed to humiliate me. So I took a lot of punishment; withstanding it all was a victory in itself.

Around and around we went. I used the ref as a stepladder to vault out of the ring, dashing Kurt to the floor.

The crowd smelled upset. I smelled upset.

But size does matter, or it did that night . . .

About nine minutes in, Kurt sat on the turnbuckle, seemingly out of gas. I came up to give him a frankensteiner. He gathered his strength and pushed me off. I landed on my feet, then sprang up to the second rope and went for another frankensteiner. This time he hooked my ankle. We slipped slightly, but he came back and got me in the Angle Lock.

Then he started walking me around the ring, like I was a broom and my ankle was a handle he wanted to twist off.

I nearly grabbed the rope to escape, but Kurt was too big and strong to let me get away with that. He waltzed me to middle of the ring, where eventually I had to tap out.

He'd won, but I'd put up such a strong show that I'd won the respect of the crowd. Kurt had really done the job for me.

USING KURT'S SIZE AGAINST HIM, I SET HIM UP FOR THE 619.

Tag Team Title

NOT TOO LONG after that I hooked up with Edge and we started competing for the new WWE Tag Team Championship.

At the time, *SmackDown!* did not have tag team champions. Stephanie McMahon, who was the on-air manager of the promotion at the time, instituted a special competition for a new title, to be called the WWE Tag Team Championship.

Edge & I lost to Kurt & Chris Benoit at *No Mercy* that October. We came back a few weeks later and beat them on *SmackDown!* in a Two-Out-of-Three-Falls match—a rarity for WWE. But our reign was very short-lived: Eddie & Chavo Guerrero, wrestling as Los Guerreros, beat us less than two weeks later at *Survivor Series*.

The Knee Again

THAT FALL AND early winter were difficult for me personally, because I was hurting once more. My knee was giving me problems. Finally, I got it examined by Dr. Andrews, and it turned out that I needed to have arthroscopic surgery—to get it "scoped."

I've had so many surgeries now, I don't remember that one specifically except that it was done by Dr. David Chow in San Diego. The exam is recorded, or at least some of it is, on my *619* video. You'll see me crutch my way into the examining area, get a tour of some of my scars, and hear Dr. Andrews pronounce "wrasslers."

I remember the doc being impressed that I was still moving. He said my knee was pretty busted. He didn't understand how I'd been able to do most of my ring work without being in pain.

In reality, I was always in pain. I just worked through it.

DVD

THE KNEE ASIDE, making the DVD during that time was a lot of fun. We went back to Tijuana and shot video of my old wrestling school and some of the other landmarks. The DVD includes some of my best American matches, including my first match with Dean Malenko at WCW and my debut on *SmackDown!*

We also got my wife and my parents on for a bit, along with Dominik. It was a family production.

My Toughest Critic

IT WAS A lot of fun to watch Angie being taped. She's always been one of my toughest critics, giving me comments and suggestions for everything I do on TV.

"You say the same things over and over," she'll tell me. "Try this."

Her advice is usually pretty good. And no matter what, she's very confident when she delivers it, very authoritative, like she knows exactly what she's talking about.

Of course, when it came time to film the DVD, she found out that things weren't as easy as they looked. They were shooting one day in my house—just her, the camera people, and the interviewer.

She couldn't get a lick out of her mouth.

Nothing.

She got nervous and completely froze.

"See how it feels?" I told her.

They kicked me off the set. As a matter of fact, they kicked the crew off too. She sat there with just the interviewer—and she still couldn't get it. Not at first, anyway.

So maybe that's a lesson for critics: It's never as easy at it looks.

The Rock,
the Title, and
WrestleMania

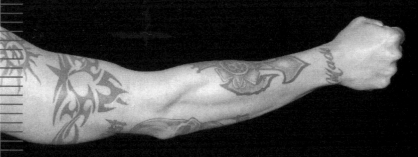

I came back from the injury in January and

wrestled at *Royal Rumble*. I was quickly in the

flow of things, working with different people:

Jamie Noble, Matt Hardy, Kidman again,

Shannon Moore.

But the highlight of that year had to be my

first *WrestleMania* ever.

WrestleMania XIX

I WAS WRESTLING Matt Hardy, with Shannon Moore in his corner. The Cruiserweight Championship was at stake. Matt had worn the championship belt since taking the title from Billy Kidman back in November; I thought it was my turn to slip it around my waist.

Just being in *WrestleMania*, at Safeco Field, was huge. There were over fifty thousand people, and the emotion and energy were overwhelming. Anyone who is a wrestling fan knows what *WrestleMania* is all about. Being part of it and knowing that you're being watched by millions of people around the world is awesome. Even the music was hot. Limp Bizkit performed at that *'Mania*, and Ashanti sang the National Anthem.

I wasn't nervous at all. A few butterflies, but otherwise I was totally jacked. I wanted to rock the show.

We were the first match. It's always said that if the show starts off right, it will end right. So it was an honor to get the slot.

I wore a costume inspired by Daredevil, the action hero character who stars in comic books and movies. A movie with Ben Affleck came out that year, and I'd always been a big fan.

Matt and I turned out to have really good chemistry together. We started fast. Shannon Moore tried distracting me, but I got him out of the ring quickly. Within minutes, I had Hardy on the ropes, set up for the 619—only to have Moore interfere. Taking the upper hand, Matt tried to

end the match with his patented Twist of Fate. (It begins with a front facelock and ends with a cutter; you could say it begins and ends with pain, and the middle ain't too much fun either.) I spun out of it to stay alive.

Shannon Moore remained a thorn in my side, helping Matt grab a rope when I was about to claim the championship. Then Matt grabbed the bottom rope for leverage and got the pin, needing to cheat to keep the championship.

"Rocky"

Thinking about Seattle makes me think about The Rock: Dwayne "The Rock" Johnson, wrestler and movie star. What a good dude.

I forget where I *first* met him—maybe in L.A. or someplace on the road. But I remember that the first time I really got a chance to spend some time with him was in Seattle.

Chavo and I were there talking with him one night, and he suggested we go back to California with him on his chartered plane. He was shooting a movie—it may have been *Scorpion King*—and the plane was scheduled to take him into L.A.

I thanked him and everything, but I told him I already had a ticket on a regular flight the company had paid for.

"Don't worry. I'll take care of it," he told me. "What do you like to drink?"

"Anything."

"No. What do you like to drink?"

"Uh, beer."

"That's it?" asked The Rock.

"Whatever you got." I felt a little weird because I didn't know him all that well and I didn't want to impose. Not to mention that I had been watching him on *Raw* for a long time and was impressed by his work.

"All right," he told me. "I'll order some beers for the plane, a couple of martinis, this and that."

We were heading toward the plane when I realized that we were going to Los Angeles—and I had no way to get down to San Diego.

"Don't worry about it, Rey," he told me. "I have it all set. A limo's going to pick you up and take you home."

Sure enough, there would be one waiting when we landed at the airport in Los Angeles, and one for Chavo as well. The Rock took care of everything.

The Rock Was a *Fan*

WE JUMPED ON his plane, just the three of us, and flew back. He told me he'd love to work with me if he ever had the chance. Which was really flattering. Here was a guy I admired as a star in Hollywood as well as in the ring, saying he wanted to work with me.

He confessed to me that he had watched me back during my WCW days. And that was the only thing he watched on the show.

Since then, he's been kind enough to include me as one of the three people he mentions when asked who he'd like to wrestle if he ever comes back. He even spoke about it when he was at the induction ceremonies for his grandfather, High Chief Pete Maivia.

Unfortunately, we never had the chance to work together in the ring. It's a shame, because me and him—it would be a classic big man–little man match. A dream match.

I think we all look up to and admire The Rock on different levels. Who wouldn't want to be a professional wrestler, take the company to the high level he took it to, and then jump over to Hollywood?

My respect goes to Hogan. But The Rock took it all to another level.

Tough Enough

I KEPT GETTING little tastes of what it would be like. There was *Ready to Rumble*. And not too long ago I was on *WWE Tough Enough*, which was a joint WWE-MTV reality television program. The show followed would-be wrestlers through training and some of the trials and tribulations involved in starting a career in our business.

I flew into L.A., and the next morning I went up to the camp where it was being held. Every week they had another Superstar appear. I gave them the scoop on what I had been through as a professional wrestler, the ladder I had to climb. My message was simple: As often as I tripped, I got up and climbed again.

To show my respect for them and their efforts, I spoke to them as fellow professionals. I took off my mask for them as the cameras were shooting me from behind.

Main Event

MATT HARDY BEAT me at *WrestleMania XIX*, but the way he won cried out for a rematch.

I knew it. He knew it. Best of all, the fans knew it.

It came in historic fashion on *SmackDown!* that June. We were the main event, the first time ever that the Cruiserweight Championship had been given that honor.

The order of matches is not as important in the U.S. as it is in Mexico. There, promotions keep their cards in very strict order. A main eventer never starts a show. The big draws are always on last. But even if the hierarchy is not so strict in WWE, it was still a great honor to close out the night. It was a sign that the cruiserweight division was getting the respect it deserved from fans and everyone in the company.

No Repeat

SHANNON MOORE WAS once more in Matt's corner. Crash was there too. They stayed out of the ring at the beginning of the match, but once Matt got me outside the ropes, they went to town, kicking and stomping until the ref chased them out of the arena.

Matt tried for a splash bomb; I reversed it, but he went to work on my leg and groin, which had been injured a few weeks earlier. We exchanged a series of moonsaults, throws, and near pins. Matt took me down in a side effect from the top rope, but after he failed to get the pin, I turned the tables on him with a Twist of Fate—Matt's own move. He kicked out at the last moment.

But that only set him up for a 619.

We ended up outside the ring—a problem for me, since the title could not change hands on a disqualification.

I jumped back in, but while the referee was distracted, Crash and Shannon ambushed me, leaving me on the mat while their leader climbed to the top rope, preparing to cover—I should say smother—me for the pin.

I shocked him when I escaped. The crowd got to their feet. And they stayed there.

Matt set me up for the Twist of Fate. But as he hooked me, I clipped his legs and jackknifed him backward. His shoulders were down. I covered him for the pin.

The crowd went crazy. The title was mine.

A Perfect Match

WE WORKED OUT that match perfectly. There's nothing I would change in it. We had it from beginning to end. Matt hit everything on me, and vice versa. It was a real feel-good moment.

The fans were so alive. I don't know what it was. Anaheim has a big Hispanic population, and that may have played a part. Or maybe they were tired of seeing bad guys win, and it was time for the good guys to take control. Whatever. They wanted to see me win, and I was happy to oblige.

I go back now and I can see my son and daughter standing near the barrier, watching, all excited. It makes me smile all over again. Dominik came into the ring with me. I gave him the title and held him up on my shoulder. The show ended with a shot of Angie, tears of happiness streaming down her face as she held Aalyah in her arms.

We Had the Talent

THE CRUISERWEIGHTS GOT a real push from WWE in the early 2000s. We had the talent. We had Matt, we had Billy Kidman, Shannon Moore, Jamie Noble. We had Yoshihiro Tajiri, the Japanese wrestler who had wrestled in Mexico as well as in ECW before joining WWE.

I had some good matches with Tajiri. He got a rap for being lazy, but I never saw it. He was never lazy with me. He always wanted to work.

Ultimate Dragon, Chavo Guerrero, Shoichi Funaki—Funaki was another member of the cruiserweight division at the time. I'm probably leaving out a bunch. It was an all-star lineup.

Battle Royal and Team Angle

THE DIVISION WAS so stacked we were able to have a Cruiserweight Battle Royal at *WrestleMania XX*. There were ten of us in the show. Ultimate Dragon started us off, pinning Shannon Moore. Jamie Noble took care of him, and Funaki, and Nunzio, who was

eliminated on disqualification. Billy Kidman pinned him. I pinned Billy and Tajiri. Finally Chavo came in and pinned me—with a little help from his dad. The win allowed him to retain the cruiser-weight title.

We were doing a lot of tag teams at the time. I remember when Kurt Angle had his Team Angle thing going. It was him, Shelton Benjamin & Charlie Haas. They called themselves the World's Greatest Tag Team.

I don't know if they were the greatest—I think I was on some pretty good teams myself—but they were great opponents. Kidman and I lost to Shelton and Charlie Haas at *Vengeance* in a great match. We all put our heads together and came up with some great moves. Any time you have four guys with each one really thinking and working hard, it seems to work out.

There was another thing. We were all up-and-coming stars, hungry to prove ourselves and move up in the company. If you go back and watch the match, you can see us inventing things—teasing finishes and taking them away. There was just great chemistry between us all.

The Dead Man

BIG MAN-LITTLE man contests are one of my specialties. I think the fans get a real kick out of seeing me go up against a bigger opponent and, hopefully, cutting him down to size.

But all bets are off when it's a big *dead* man versus a little man, like the time I took on Undertaker in 2003.

We were doing a tournament elimination contest to decide who was going to be the number-one contender for the WWE Championship against Brock Lesnar. I may have been an underdog, but I was still in the mix, pushing for my turn against the bigger guys.

Undertaker rode his motorcycle into the arena and got a good pop from the crowd. Then I popped out from under the stage, and we were on.

You have to remember, I grew up watching Undertaker. I love watching his entrances. Later on in my career we had another one-on-one matchup, and I was in the ring first. I stood in the corner and watched him come in, totally lost in his show. I almost forgot we were having a match.

In our first encounter, I scrambled around a bit before he finally caught me and flicked me into the corner. He threw a couple of swings. I got a kick in. He came after me. I ended up dropkicking him to the floor.

He was my size now.

But not for long. He came back in, slid, and gave me the big boot to my face.

Boom!

What a boot.

I crawled to the ropes and got to my feet. I got a number of my moves in, including an awesome variation of the DDT. When he picked me up for a powerbomb, I spun around and hooked him into a DDT to bring him down. It was an awesome move, and it was his idea. We looked like a human avalanche.

Undertaker was down, perfect fodder for a 619. But as he always seems to do, he came back from the dead, slamming me off as I tried to cover for the pin. I got on the ropes and tried a West Coast Pop; he caught me and brought me down with a Last Ride, an elevated powerbomb that left me sprawled lifeless on the canvas. He covered, and that was the end of the match.

Working with 'Taker was an honor. When you face your best opponents, the real Superstars, you always learn something. With Undertaker, I learned how to pace myself, and how to get my spots into the best places in the match. I go back and watch that match a lot. Any time I have to work a bigger guy, I check it out.

Cruising Along

I SPENT MOST of 2003 and 2004 facing other cruiserweights. I lost the championship belt to Tajiri in September before a packed house in Philadelphia. I beat him the following January in Washington, D.C., to get it back. Chavo took it from me in February.

The championship is considered to include the WCW years, and so all together I've held it seven times, which is more than anyone else. You look at some of the other names on the list—Chavo, Psicosis, Billy Kidman, Chris Jericho, Dean Malenko, Eddie Guerrero—and you realize that it's a hall of fame of not just cruiserweights but wrestlers period. It's such an honor to be included in that.

But it wasn't until I stepped beyond the cruiserweight division that I found my true potential in the company. And the person who helped me take that step was my good friend, longtime wrestling partner, and sometime opponent, Eddie Guerrero.

Eddie, Dominik, and the Worst Day of My Life

Eddie Guerrero and I had been friends and wrestling opponents for my entire career, starting back in Mexico. In WCW we faced off for one of the greatest matches of my career. We worked together in the Filthy Animals before Eddie got hurt and then later left the company.

We wrestled together for a short while during my early days in WWE, but we were never opponents in an extended storyline at WWE.

Until 2005.

We started the year as allies. Then we became enemies in a storyline that has been called one of the best of the last twenty years.

Tag Team

ROB VAN DAM and I held the Tag Team Championship in 2004, going into 2005. We lost it to the Basham Brothers during a four-way competition in mid-January. Eddie and Booker T were another of the teams in competition; after RVD was hurt, Eddie and I began wrestling together as a team. We took the tag team title in February at *No Way Out*. It looked like a partnership made in heaven.

Almost. We were forced to face each other at *WrestleMania*, and our partnership unraveled. It was one of the first times that tag team champions faced each other while still wrestling as a team. But let me reminisce about Eddie as a tag team partner first.

Though we'd had some excellent matches in WCW—my first mask match with him was one of my best ever—I don't believe we'd ever teamed up for a tag team contest before 2005. But as soon as we started working together, we developed a very cool working rhythm.

I was Eddie's other half in the ring. As partners, we could talk on the side during the match, something we'd never been able to do while wrestling against each other. That made it even easier to call the match as we went.

Eddie's comments were like a master class in wrestling. I really came to understand not just how he moved in the ring but how he thought. Subtle things about how the flow of the match should go, how he picked up on the fans' energy, the strategies he used to heighten it—it was all on display.

"Just listen to me out there," he used to tell me. "Listen."

That became my motto. I got some Q-tips before I went into the ring and took all the wax out of my ears. The only thing I didn't bring was a pen and paper.

Wrestling with Eddie was always a true lesson. And not only was I learning, but I was having fun.

Those Moments

EDDIE BEING EDDIE, there were moments when working with him could be a test. Eddie had a vision for what should happen in the ring. He may not have been a perfectionist, but he worked at a very high level and had incredibly high standards. If things didn't go right—and especially if he thought he had done something wrong—his temper could flare. He was hard on other people, but he could be vicious on himself.

If something got messed up, I'd hear, "Shit, fuck, God damn it!"

"Eddie, Eddie, you okay?" I'd ask.

He'd just go on. Then after the match, we'd walk into Gorilla together. I'd turn around, and Eddie would be gone. He'd slip back through the curtain by himself.

"I don't want to deal with the yelling or the agents going off on a shitty match," he once explained.

You have to understand: It is rare, very rare, for an agent to do that—and especially in a match that Eddie was involved in. But those were the high standards he held. If some small thing went wrong, he saw that flaw and thought it had wiped out most if not all of the good that had happened.

And when something went wrong, it was rarely, if ever, his fault. But he took it personally.

Fiery Eddie

THAT WAS EDDIE. Very emotional and always one hundred percent committed.

You might find him backstage dragging his feet, run down from whatever injury he had. But once he went past the curtain, there would be a complete transformation. When he laced up his boots, he gave it his best.

I know he battled a lot of demons. He'd been injured in a car crash, which led to an addiction to painkillers so severe he had to fight his way out of rehab. It's all in the public record. What's not there is the determination and strength that carried him through. He tackled the problem like the true professional he was, wrestling with it one day at a time.

I remember a couple of times being in the ring when he would grab his lower back. You could see his pain and his agony, but he wouldn't give in.

"You okay, Eddie?" I'd ask.

"Yeah, yeah, yeah," he'd say, and we'd continue with the match.

Champions

ONE OF THE unique things about our partnership was the fact that, while I was a babyface good guy, Eddie still had the lie, cheat, and steal reputation of a heel. He was really well liked by the crowd—they chanted for him at the beginning of most matches—but he wasn't above using underhanded tactics if he thought them necessary for a victory. And the crowds loved it.

I remember the night we became tag team champions, beating the Bashams in Pittsburgh on February 20. It was at *No Way Out*, and we were the first match. Eddie had a whole bunch of bits laid out for the night—"hot dogging," as the announcers put it.

He tied the tag ropes together to make them longer. He lay down in the middle of the ring, playing possum before turning the pin attempt.

Not that the Bashams were playing fair, exactly. They were double-teaming behind the ref's back the whole match. Eddie made them pay, taking them on together for a few minutes.

Eddie went out to grab a chair, then came up with the championship belts, intending to use them as weapons.

"No, Eddie, what are you doing?" I yelled.

"I'm going bash 'em."

"No. We have to win clean."

"Let me do it."

I kept the titles and the chair out of the ring—but only for a minute. Then the Bashams brought a title in, and it was fair game. I threw the other championship belt to Eddie, he used it, and we ended with the victory.

WrestleMania

WE HELD THE tag team title, defending it for a number of weeks. Ordinarily, we would have been working toward a tag team showdown with another team, or maybe a rematch with the Bashams, at *WrestleMania 21*.

But instead, we were forced to face off against each other—a first in *WrestleMania* history.

Just a little history: Eddie had been WWE Champion the year before, having won at *No Way Out*. He lost to JBL thanks to a controversial decision by Kurt Angle, the GM at the time. Kurt kept after him for a few months, tormenting him time and again, before Eddie worked into the competition for the tag team title.

While we were champions, Chavo Guerrero began sewing dissension—and doubt—in Eddie's mind about me. That set the stage for our conflict.

Over the past year, Eddie had had a few matches against me, and I'd always found a way to frustrate him. If you looked back through his recent history, I seemed to be the kryptonite to his Superman. Even when he was on top, I beat him.

So the buildup to *WrestleMania 21* had people wondering

whether the jinx was real. Could Eddie beat me? Or was I really his kryptonite?

We were still friends and partners. But the seeds of dissension were sewn. Eddie suggested we wrestle each other, to give the fans a great show.

Or maybe to prove to himself, once and for all, that he was better than I was.

Trouble was brewing. A few days before *WrestleMania*, we accidentally interfered in the other's singles matches, costing each other the victory.

Accidental? Not everyone thought so.

At Each Other's Throats

EDDIE RODE INTO the *WrestleMania* arena at Staples Center in his Chevy convertible.

I wore a jumpsuit with American colors on the back, and Mexican green and red on the front. I have to say, there were an awful lot of "Eddie! Eddie!" chants when we stepped to the center of the ring.

At times, fans must have thought they were looking into a double-sided mirror. We traded leapfrogs, did a double bridge to avoid pins, and flew back and forth like a pair of birds. Eddie thought I was a monkey on his back; I gave him a monkey flip almost out of the arena.

The crowd was into it. What they didn't realize was that I was suffering a wardrobe malfunction. My mask had a Velcro connector at the bottom beneath my chin. It came off at the very beginning, and there was no way to fix it. I had to keep grabbing my mask every few seconds.

(I never used that mask again. Usually I just use an outfit once, then put it aside, especially something from *WrestleMania*, but I was doubly sure to do that in this case.)

THE ENERGY IN THE STAPLES CENTER FED US
AS EDDIE AND I TRADED OFF MOVES.

The mask problem was a shame, because we had a great match all planned out. Needless to say, my wardrobe malfunction made things difficult. It messed with my concentration. If I was running to the ropes, I had to grab my mask so it wouldn't fall off. I think we were able to pull off every move we planned, but the faulty mask threw off my timing and my ability to really work the match.

I managed a corkscrew off the ropes into the arena, slamming Eddie against the floor. I broke a try at the Three Amigos but almost had my body bent in two when Eddie gave me a backbreaker over his knee. Then I rolled out from under a frog splash.

My ability to hang in frustrated him. Then a 619 stunned him. Eddie turned one of my West Coast Pops into a near pin, but he let down his guard long enough for another hurricanrana that put his shoulders against the canvas just long enough for me to get the pin.

The Heat Builds

I BEAT HIM, and that really amped things up. He couldn't believe it. We shook hands after the match, but you could see the frustration and bafflement on his face.

He was thinking I was better than him.

A thought that he couldn't stand.

We wrestled together as a tag team at *SmackDown!*, facing Mercury & Nitro (MNM). They were brand-new to the show, and we were very heavy favorites—which made our loss all the more shocking.

Eddie, of course, was convinced it was all my fault. He slammed me to the mat after the pin.

The following week, we smoothed things over. Eddie even gave a great speech about how we were such good friends. But those proved to be just words once we got into the ring. I hit him accidentally; he thought it was on purpose. That led to him walking out.

The crowd—we were in England at the time—chanted his name,

bringing him back to the ring. But he came back more spectator than wrestler, and once again we lost the match. I'd been beaten to within an inch of my life.

Two weeks before, at *WrestleMania*, the crowd had chanted "Eddie! Eddie!" Now they were yelling "Eddie sucks! Eddie sucks!"

We were just beginning the storyline. Eddie had come up with an idea where turning on each other was just the start. He was planning a much more vicious reversal.

The Secret

WE CONTINUED FEUDING through spring. Then at the end of June, Eddie—completely frustrated by his failure to dominate me—started hinting that he had a secret that would destroy me.

A hint here, a threat there. At first no one knew what the secret was—no one but Eddie and myself, and our families. I pleaded with him not to reveal it. My wife, his wife—everyone started asking him to show mercy.

That only made him feel more powerful, and more diabolical.

The secret, he said, involved my son, Dominik.

We had a match at *American Bash* in July. At stake was the secret. He claimed that if I won, he'd keep it to himself.

I won. Eddie shut his mouth—but only until his next television appearance.

Dominik, he revealed, was really *his* son.

My Flesh and Blood

I'D BETTER SAY for the record that Dominik *is* my son, completely and absolutely; he wasn't adopted, as Eddie alleged on the show. He is my real son.

The reason I have to say that is because Eddie was very, very convincing.

And so was Dominik, who came on TV over the next few weeks as Eddie and I played our own cruel version of Daddy Dearest, fighting for Dominik's custody. Our showdown eventually culminated in a custody battle. Not in court—we fought in the ring, during a Ladder match at *SummerSlam*.

According to the storyline, Eddie had had Dominik during some little adventure that he had. He couldn't take care of him because he was living the wild life. So my wife and I decided to adopt him. Eddie was cool with it. Dominik was raised by my wife and me.

It was supposed to be a secret. As far as Dominik knew, we were his mother and father.

The premise was very realistic. In the not too distant past, parents of adopted children were often told not to tell their children that they were adopted, for fear that it would hurt them psychologically. The thinking has changed a lot—most parents are very up front with their adopted kids now—but the situation we laid out was still possible.

At first, Eddie used the secret to hurt me, taunting me with it. Then he grew to want custody of Dominik, trying to tear him away from me, which led to our final showdown at *SummerSlam*.

Eddie and Dominik

THE ANGLE WAS Eddie's idea. I'm not sure where exactly it came from. There was a somewhat similar storyline back in ECW with Sandman and Raven, with Sandman's son turning on him, though I never really asked if it had inspired Eddie.

My wife and I talked with Dominik about the storyline and what he would have to do—if he wanted to do it. He was on the fence about doing it, I think, until he spoke to Eddie himself.

Dominik was in third grade at the time. We wanted to make sure that he understood that he would be on TV every week, and that some people might have different reactions to the story. Of course, it would also be a lot of fun.

"You can travel with me, be on TV. What do you think?" I asked him.

"I don't know, Dad" was his first reaction. That was his natural shyness coming through; he didn't say no, just that he would think about it.

Eddie smartened him up about what it would involve. I think Eddie talked to him longer than I did. He wanted to make sure Dominik was cool with it.

We had to clear everything with his school and teachers, arranging to get his schoolwork and make sure he could do his work when he was on the road.

My wife and I kept saying to him, "You know this isn't real, right? It's just made up."

"Oh, yeah, Dad, I know. It's not real."

But you'd never know that by looking at his face when the cameras rolled.

Not Camera Shy

DOMINIK HAS BECOME a bit shy as he's grown, but he was a great actor during these vignettes, even though he'd never had a chance to act before. He seemed to know what to do even before anyone gave him direction.

When we did the first vignette—it was somewhere in California—we were at a park. Dominik was playing. Eddie was there, and so was I.

"Come on, Uncle Eddie," he said. "Push me, push me."

Behind him, Eddie gave me a look that meant *I know a secret that will deeply hurt you if I tell.*

In the middle of the scene I started worrying that I was pushing Dominik a little too hard, treating him like an eighteen- or nineteen-year-old instead of a boy who was seven. But his performance calmed my fears. I tried to relax and enjoy the moment.

One of the things that really impressed me was the fact that he never once looked at the camera when he wasn't supposed to. He was completely natural with Eddie, and with myself. And when it came time for him to show fear and everything else later on in the storyline, he did it like a seasoned pro.

Pressure? He didn't seem to have any. As soon as he was finished shooting, he grabbed his PSP and went back to whatever video game he was playing. He was a kid having fun, and working on the set was just part of the fun.

Family Time

WE SPENT ABOUT four months or more on the storyline. If you add in our tag team time and then the conflict before Dominik comes in, we're talking about eight months. It was the longest story I'd ever been part of. Bruce Prichard, my road agent, really helped us keep it interesting and on edge. It took my work with Eddie to a different level, and it pushed me in ways I'd never been pushed before.

It also brought me closer to my family. Not just Dominik—eventually my wife and even my daughter got involved.

Angie was nowhere near as nervous as she had been during the DVD shoot. We laid it on her: Go with this as if it's real. How would you feel if someone was going to take your child away?

Maybe that was the hook, because she carried it off beautifully. Her role was a lot harder than on the DVD—she had to walk out in front of a huge audience during our custody battle—but she did a great job.

She was shaking. Her jaw was going back and forth.

When they told us that they were going to put Dominik in foster care while the custody thing was decided, she broke down and cried. They got it on tape. It was awesome.

The Ladder Match.

DOMINIK'S CUSTODY WAS decided at a Ladder match at *SummerSlam*. Pins were unimportant: The idea was to set up a ladder in the middle of the ring, climb to the rafters, and then retrieve a briefcase where Dominik's custody papers were. Whoever came down with the papers won Dominik.

Dominik was in the audience near the ring as we were introduced. I went up to him and told him everything was going to be okay, that we were going home today.

He said, "Yeah, Dad. I know."

I kissed him on the head. He never looked over at the camera. Then later, when Eddie came over to try and one-up me, Dominik just stared with his big eyes, looking very scared.

We had a great match. We had fun with it, calling some of the moves as we went.

There was one spot we messed up. Eddie was going to do a sunset flip over the ladder, bringing me down so we'd set up a powerbomb. When he pulled me, I didn't let go right away. We missed the bump at the bottom—he hit and then I hit about a second later. But everything else went the way we planned.

Almost.

"Learn to Love Me"

TOWARD THE END of the match, Eddie tossed me across one of the ladders and sent me to the mat. He began climbing toward the briefcase.

Dominik vaulted over the barrier and slid into the ring. He grabbed

DOMINIK WAS
A NATURAL,
PLAYING OFF
EDDIE AND ME.

the ladder and started shaking—a little too softly at first. But even that worked out well, as Eddie came down and confronted him.

"Give me a hug!" yelled Eddie.

Dominik backed away, shaking his head.

"Give me a hug!" added Eddie. "You're going to love me now."

Dominik wouldn't do it. Eddie threatened him.

"You're going to learn to love me the hard way," he said, then reared back to smack him.

I interfered just in time.

The Missed Cue

DOMINIK SLID OUT of the ring while Eddie and I continued to go at it. Finally Eddie was able to trap me under the legs of the ladder. He taunted me, then climbed to the top, but he couldn't get the briefcase undone before I managed to knock him off. We wrestled some more, and Eddie finally managed to knock me into the corner. Then he started for the ladder.

His wife, Vickie, was supposed to come out to try and stop him. But our improvisation had put me into a different spot on the canvas, and we missed the cue.

"Where's Vickie?" Eddie growled as he climbed. "Where the fuck is Vickie?"

I knocked him off the ladder. After he finished yelling to the ref—he was outside the ring at this point—to bring Vickie down, he began his Three Amigos set on me, capping it with a suplex onto the ladder.

Once again, Eddie started climbing the ladder. This time Vickie came running out and started pleading with him not to take Dominik away from me.

And when that didn't work, she knocked him off the ladder herself.

Smiling Faces

I SCRAMBLED TO my feet, got the briefcase, and won Dominik back.

His smile could have lit up the arena. The story ended happily ever after.

Dominik was paid for the appearances. We put the money into the bank for him, and he's allowed to use it for special purchases. But the best part of it was working with Dominik and showing him what my work is really like.

When we were on the road, he was one of the boys, whether it was riding with me and Charlie Haas or going over homework in the arena before the show. It was a bonding experience. He was probably too young to understand it all, but now it's there in his memory banks.

I'd love to see him as a wrestler some day. I'd love him to continue the Mysterio dynasty. I feel like he has a shot. I don't want to push him, but if he ever asks, I'd be more than happy to train him.

One for My Girl

I HOPE WE get a chance to work up something for my daughter down the road, a storyline where she and I can work together. She loves attention, and she's really talented. She loves to dance and sing. Aalyah is so good she really scares me. And she already loves the wrestling business. Every time she comes with me she loves going backstage and hanging out with the divas.

But to be honest, I see my daughter doing something bigger than professional wrestling. I see her aspiring to Hollywood or Broadway. She has that kind of talent. I guess every father thinks the world of his children.

Then again, she might give me a curveball and be a veterinarian. Which would be great too.

The Cross

SUMMERSLAM ENDED THE storyline between Eddie and me. From there, Eddie started an angle with Batista that had him vying for the championship belt. I got into a feud with JBL. Our long-running feud had helped both of us, but it was time to move on.

Our lives outside the ring were packed as well. Eddie moved to Phoenix, and I got busy with my family.

In early November of 2005, WWE was planning a tour in Europe. We were going to meet for a big show in Minneapolis and then leave from there. It was a Sunday; I believe we were taping a special *Raw* and *SmackDown!* show that night before leaving.

Originally I was scheduled to fly into Phoenix and grab a connection there, coming up to Minneapolis with Eddie and Chavo. But I changed my plans at the last minute, deciding to fly up alone on a red-eye and arriving Sunday morning instead.

Friday before I was going to leave, I stopped at my mom's house. She brought out a little present for me: a small wooden cross with Jesus on it. She knows I like crosses and still to this day will buy me a piece if it looks unique.

"Wow, it's beautiful!" I told her.

There was a piece of paper with the cross. The words were all in English, which my mom couldn't read. She'd chosen it just because it looked nice.

The words read: *This cross is to be given to someone so that they may have a better death.*

"Did You Hear?"

SUNDAY MORNING I landed in Minneapolis around eight, eight-thirty. I got a cab and shot straight to the arena.

When we pulled up to the building—by now it was nine-thirty, ten—I got out and took my bags. One of our truck drivers ran up to help.

"Rey, did you hear what happened to Eddie?" he asked.

"No."

"He passed away."

It hit me like a bullet.

"Yeah, he passed away," repeated the driver.

"When did this happen?" I asked, not really believing.

"I don't know."

I left my bags there and ran inside the building. People were crying—and now I was too.

I ran into Tomko, who was working with us at the time. We hugged each other.

"Where is he?" I said.

"At the Marriott, I think."

"You know where it is?"

"Yeah," he said.

"Take me."

We started to walk. I couldn't believe it. I still can't.

The Room

I DIDN'T KNOW what to expect.

We went up to the floor where Eddie had been staying. Earlier that morning—just a few hours before I came into town—Chavo had gone into his room and found him passed out on the floor. He'd tried to revive him, tried to give him CPR, but Eddie had already passed. According to the doctors who examined him later, he had been killed by arteriosclerotic heart disease, a hardening and narrowing of the blood vessels that supply blood and oxygen to the heart. Heart disease in general is one of the leading causes of death in the U.S., and thousands of people as young as Eddie die each year from it.

I didn't know any of that then. My mind was running in all sorts of directions. The elevator opened up.

The medical people were inside the room, evaluating the body.

I thought to myself, *Maybe they can save him.*

Chavo told me that apparently Eddie had had a heart attack.

For twenty minutes, I stood out in that hallway. Silent. Not in peace, not even in confusion anymore, in nothing but silence.

Like He Was Sleeping

THE MEDICAL PEOPLE came out. We asked if we could go in and see him one last time.

They let us.

I'll never forget it. He was lying next to the bed, his feet where the pillow would be. A sheet had been pulled over his legs.

If I didn't know what had happened, I would have sworn he was sleeping.

We stood over him, looking. Finally I kneeled down, kissed him on the forehead, and told him I loved him.

When I got up, they put his body on a stretcher and walked him out.

Doing the show that night was hard for everyone. But we knew that Eddie would have wanted us to. He would have done it in our place. He'd have balled out his eyes for us, then gone into the ring and given the best performance he could.

I taped a short tribute to him. The words just tumbled out. As I spoke, my mask became claustrophobic. I undid it and pushed it up on my head while the cameras rolled.

The audience couldn't see my face, but Eddie could.

At his funeral, I took the cross my mother had given me and placed it in his hands in the casket.

That's what it was for: a better death.

I pray he left us in peace.

A Gift from God

God gifted me by allowing me to work with Eddie all those months, letting me get to know him a lot better.

A lot of people say that when you feel your death coming close, you start doing things that you wouldn't normally do.

Did that happen here? Did Eddie choose to work with me because he felt his death coming close?

I don't know. This is our profession; we have storylines beginning and ending, opponents changing all the time. All I know is that I thank God I had a chance to work with him so closely before he died.

Goodbye, Wiwito

We used to call each other Wiwito. It was a little joke between us. The word came partly from the nickname his family had for him when he was little, Edwiese. Out of nowhere we flipped that into Wiwito.

Wiwito.

I called him that; he called me that. It was just one of those silly, goofy things friends do.

Eddie would call me that, Chavo would call me that.

The last time I saw Eddie alive, he and Big Show were sitting in a hotel room, rapping about the Bible. I came in to say goodbye.

Every time I said goodbye, I would give him a kiss on the cheek. He would do the same.

"Goodbye, Wiwito," he said.

"Goodbye, Wiwito."

Goodbye.

Champion

When I came into WWE, I told myself, "This is as good as it gets." I thought things couldn't get any better.

But I was wrong. There was one thing beyond joining WWE, beyond holding the tag team titles, even better than winning the cruiserweight title.

It was slipping the World Heavyweight Championship belt around my waist.

All championships are important, but the

heavyweight title is the pinnacle. It's the top *SmackDown!* title, one of the three top titles in WWE. The champion becomes the face of the company and, by extension, our entire profession. It's the most prestigious title in the most prestigious wrestling company in the world.

As you would expect from its name, the big men have had a monopoly on the title.

Until I got my chance in 2006.

After Eddie

FOLLOWING MY SERIES with Eddie, I worked into some big man–little man matches. After he died, many of my shows were dedicated to Eddie. The fans responded really well, honoring our friendship. They would chant Eddie's name at different points in the matches. They felt I was carrying his torch.

Heavyweight Champion Dave Batista and I teamed up as a tag team. We were a big man–little man team—I come up to Dave's chin—but we were all heart. We eventually became Tag Team Champions by defeating MNM—Mercury, Nitro, & Melina—in a *SmackDown!* match on December 19, 2005. MNM took the Tag Team Championship back a few weeks later, but my partnership with Dave extended through the first part of the year.

Our conflict with MNM in the ring was spiced up behind the scenes with some hot stuff between Batista and Melina. She tried to persuade him to not show for the match. She was very persuasive—and physical—about it.

Dave ate the apple, but in the end he stayed true to me and the sport. When it was clear he wasn't going to throw the match, Melina accused him of sexual harassment. (All storyline.) We ended up giving up the title, thanks to interference from Mark Henry, who became Melina's misguided defender.

Build Up

I HAD OTHER things on my mind besides Melina. Even the tag team title paled compared to my new goal: the heavyweight title.

At the time, Randy Orton was considered one of the top heavyweights in the company—the likely challenger to Batista when *Royal Rumble* was held that January. The winner of the *Rumble* was promised a shot at the heavyweight title. Whoever won would also have recent history on his side: Batista, like several other champions in the past, had used a victory at the *Rumble* to springboard into top contention for the title the year before.

Anyone who said they thought I might get a shot at the title would have been laughed at. Not just because of my size, either. I drew a very unlucky two when the entry order was announced. There were thirty entrants. Numbers one and two went in first, and so on down to thirty. Since the winner is the last man standing at the end, the odds were very heavy against me.

Randy drew thirty.

Rumble

I STARTED OFF with Triple H. After he'd pounded me awhile, Simon Dean came in and tried to toss me from the ring to eliminate me. But I turned the tables and sent him from the ring.

This match brought me together with Psicosis, and we brought back some of our old moves. But when he tried to flip me out of the ring, I pulled off a scissors and reversed him right into elimination.

Ric Flair, Big Show, Chris Benoit, Rob Van Dam, Carlito, Chavo, Shawn Michaels—they all came and went. Triple H hung around for more than an hour, until it came down to Randy Orton, Triple H, and myself.

The two big men ganged up on me. Triple H picked me up in

UNLUCKY NUMBER 2, ME, TAKING ON NUMBER 30, RANDY ORTON, IN THE *ROYAL RUMBLE.*

his arms and went to the ropes, aiming to toss me over so he could concentrate on Orton. But I grabbed the top rope and spun, using his momentum to send him out of the ring.

Leaving me to face Randy Orton by myself.

Contender

ANGRY AT BEING disqualified, Triple H reached back in and pulled me out, throwing me against the stairs before the referees could stop him.

The crowd was going crazy. They were completely on my side.

And I was completely on my back, flattened by Triple H's attack. I lay on the mat while the refs chased off Triple H.

Randy picked me up like a rag doll. Then he twisted me around, looking to launch me out of the ring the way Kevin Hall had thrown me like a lawn dart back in my early WCW days.

What he didn't know, though, was that I was playing possum. He took me to the ropes, aimed—and suddenly found himself in midair as I grabbed the ropes and tumbled back through them, tossing him to the ground in the process.

I was the new number-one contender.

Latino Heat

NEVER HAD A big man–little man match gone so well for a little man. Not only did I win, I set a record for the longest *Rumble* turn, clocking in at 1:02:12.

I raised my hands to the sky, dedicating my match to Eddie.

Many things helped me in my run for the belt. The crowd and the push that I'd gotten from Eddie were certainly on my side. And I really have to give credit to Pat Patterson, who played a big role behind the scenes pushing for me, vouching that I would make a good champion.

At the time, Pat was a producer and consultant to WWE, working behind the scenes. Older fans will remember that he was a longtime Superstar as a wrestler, then an onscreen personality and commentator. He actually began wrestling in 1958, and while he officially retired from the ring in 1984, he was in combat between the ropes as late as 2000. Among his many memorable matches was an Alley Fight contest in 1981 with Sgt. Slaughter that old-timers still remember as one of the best ever.

I don't know what Pat saw in me. Maybe it was my professionalism. Maybe it was my love for this business, and the passion inside me. Maybe he liked my style or thought I'd be able to bring something new and unexpected to the company. Whatever it was, he made the case to the top people at WWE, including Vince. I didn't know anything about it until right after the *Rumble*, when I was called into a meeting with the top execs.

"You're Going to Be Champ"

"**YOU'RE GOING TO** be Heavyweight Champion," they told me.

"Oh, shit," I answered.

I'd broken the size barrier. But could I carry the company?

I remember seeing Eddie when he was champ, exhausted and pulled in a thousand different directions.

"Eddie, come on to the pretape over here."

"Eddie, come on, you got to get your match ready."

"Eddie, there's an interview next."

It's a heavy load.

It hit me at the moment: I was overwhelmed. But then it kind of faded away. The impact, I mean. There was so much to do in the leadup to *WrestleMania* that I didn't have time to think about it.

In the back of my mind, I thought it might not happen. They always say, "This is what we're going to do . . ." But it can all change.

Kayfabe aside, I'd never gunned for the heavyweight title before. It wasn't just because of my size. The title was so prestigious and important, I never saw myself in that role. Maybe I was too humble.

Out—Then Back

OR MAYBE NOT. Because I soon lost my chance in a match to Randy Orton at *No Way Out*. Randy had used insults about Eddie to goad me into the contest, then he won by using the ropes for a pin.

It looked like my chance was over, at least for the near future. Then Teddy Long decided to square things up by adding me back into the match, arranging for a three-way, Triple-Threat match for the title at *WrestleMania*.

Three Times the Fun

WHEN *WRESTLEMANIA* CAME, I made sure I had the right wardrobe, and the right buildup. I had the handmade Aztec hood designed and personally delivered to me backstage at the Allstate Arena in Chicago. I wore special black contact lenses that gave my eyes a hawklike look.

I brought in P.O.D. for my music, along with my boy Mad One— aka Thomas Lopez—who created my "Booyaka 619" song. When I went out, I climbed up the tower and put on my headgear while Mad Dog One and P.O.D. played my song live. It was a feel-good moment. Definitely a feel-good moment.

I went down to the ring. The high point of my professional career was just moments away.

The Match

TO THAT POINT, I was unusually calm. Then, in an instant, I was really nervous. I wanted to make sure that everything that night was to the T. But I had to overcome two opponents—and my usual butterflies.

Randy Orton started off the match by attacking Kurt Angle before the bell. Randy and I tapped feet with flying kicks as we scrambled together. The way the match worked, the first wrestler to get a pin or submission would win. Angle was the champ, but he didn't have to be pinned to lose the title.

He fought fearlessly. He gave both Randy and myself a suplex in the early going, throwing me against the turnbuckle.

Kurt got me in an Angle Lock after breaking a 619. Then Randy tried to join the party by bringing a chair into the ring. The ref was distracted, and he missed me tapping out.

A few moments later, I returned the favor for Randy, grabbing the ref when Kurt squeezed another Angle Lock on Randy.

It's Here

I MISSED ONE spot. Kurt was on the second rope, selling, with half of his body inside the ring. He was very close to the turnbuckle. I was on the ground. I had to run down, grab the post, and hit him with the 619. When I gripped the post, I slipped and caught him with only one foot.

When I mess something up, my natural instinct is to think fast and make it work somehow. I jumped back up on the apron, and I double dropkicked him and bounced him back. It worked; it all went so quickly that there wasn't a chance for anyone to notice or think about the slip.

"THAT THING I DO."

Before the match, I'd been talking about it with Randy. He suggested I do the West Coast Pop.

He called it "that thing you do."

I told him how to base for me, and we set it up for the finish. Now in the ring, he was battling hard with Kurt. Kurt flew to the apron, while Randy staggered to the ropes.

It was 619 time.

I flew across the ring, hit the ropes, and kicked him in the face. Then I climbed to the top and executed a West Coast Pop.

He caught me beautifully. I covered him for the pin.

Inside, I was thinking, *Oh, shit, it's here.*

The Moment

THE REFEREE PUT the championship belt in my hands. I went to the corner and hung over the turnbuckle, calling out to my wife and kids. Then I knelt and prayed in the ring.

The moment was incredible. There was no acting. It was all emotion, all real.

Without a doubt it was one of the best feel-good moments in my career. At the end of the runway, Chavo and Eddie's wife, Vickie, met me and congratulated me. The Guerreros had given me tremendous support through my whole run. I thought about Eddie, and I was overwhelmed with tears.

Just about everyone who was close to me was there that night: wife, kids, friends, fans. My parents and uncle couldn't make it, but I spoke to them all when it was over.

And then it was time to carry *SmackDown!* on my shoulders for a little while.

Losing

THE MONTHS THAT followed were hard work, inside and mostly outside the ring. There were media interviews, appearances, a tour in Europe—it was grueling, but it was an honor and a pleasure. I'm proud to have been able to help the company and our business.

The irony was that even though I was Heavyweight Champion, I actually lost most of my matches during that time.

I wish I could have done better, gotten maybe a little more mileage out of it, but they put me against all bigger guys, like Big Show, the Great Khali—tremendously big guys who had huge size advantages. No one would have believed it if I won most of those matches. I got squashed several times.

But I was the champion, and I managed to hold on to the title against Orton, Angle, JBL—he had to leave *SmackDown!* because of my win—and Sabu. Fans across the world had a chance to see Rey Mysterio as World Heavyweight Champion.

But all good things come to an end. Booker T—he was calling himself King Booker at the time, acting as if he really *was* the king—began angling for the championship. He gathered a "court" of supporters around him, aiming for a showdown with me at the *Great American Bash*.

Boogeyman Got My Eyes

HERE'S A *WRESTLEMANIA* footnote. After the match, I decided I didn't need the special black contact lenses anymore. So I passed them on to Boogeyman.

He makes a joke out of it now:

Rey Mysterio is the only wrestler to give the Boogeyman two black eyes.

Great American Bash

I **WORE THE** title through the spring and into early summer, managing to fend off any challenge. As the dog days of summer began, my feud with King Booker and his court began to sizzle.

Behind the scenes, Booker always gave me a lot of advice and was always on my side. In front of the cameras, it was different. He was on me like stink on a mule.

They were calling me the underdog champion when I came into the ring at Conseco Fieldhouse in Indianapolis for the *Great American Bash*. (The annual July Pay-Per-View is now known as *The Bash*.) JBL—who was sitting at the announcer's table, still angry at my victory over him—did everything he could to put me down as I was announced. But the biggest putdown, and surprise, came later in the match.

Booker had won five championship belts in WCW, but he heard a lot of boos from the fans that night. He had a lot of heat from the crowd, amplified by his kingly conceit. He mugged for them, laughing and egging them on as we got under way.

He kicked and stomped me against the ropes for a minute or so before I turned the tables and got a near pin. The crowd began chanting, "Eddie! Eddie!" the chant that had both commemorated Eddie Guerrero and urged me on in my run for the title.

This was another big man–little man matchup, with King Booker relying on his superior size to pummel me, while I tried to fly around and outmaneuver him. A flying leg scissors put him into the corner around midmatch, but he reversed the momentum by thumbing me in the eye.

Booker's "queen" (and real-life wife) Sharmell attacked me while I was on the ropes. That was just the beginning for her. A few minutes later, Booker ducked out of a 619, then barely escaped a pin before I set him up again. Just as I was about to take off, Queen Sharmell

TRYING TO BRING DOWN
KING BOOKER.

reached in and tripped me, sending me to the mat and once more giving Booker the advantage.

A foot to Booker's face, a flying headscissors, a cross-body from the second rope, a flying DDT—we wore each other down, then knocked the ref out of the ring. By this time the crowd was completely absorbed in the match. They were behind me, chanting, "619! Eddie!" standing and urging me to pin Booker.

I stunned him with my third 619 of the match, then did a frog splash in honor of Eddie to cover him for the pin.

But there was no ref in the ring.

The crowd chanted one-two-three.

Without a referee, there was no end to the match. Booker got up, stunned me with a shot below the belt, then went out into the audience for a chair.

A dropkick took the chair from Booker's hands.

Then Chavo ran in. He slid into the ring, grabbed the chair, and made like he was going to hit Booker.

Instead, he caught me across the head, giving King Booker the crown.

Stunned

THE CROWD WAS stunned. Until that moment, I'm sure they thought Chavo was on my side.

Chavo claimed that he turned on me because I had been living off the Guerrero family name, taking glory from the Guerreros. Chavo's turn set up a storyline feud between him and me that continued into the fall, with a match at *No Mercy* that sent us brawling into the audience. The rules of the match stipulated that a pin *anywhere* would count, and I won with a cross-body off a stairway barrier, pinning him against the concrete.

The climax of our conflict aired on the October 20, 2006, edition of *SmackDown!*, billed as an I Quit match.

I Quit matches can only end when one person gives up, which usually means that there's a lot of pain involved.

And there was that night.

"I Quit"

FOR YEARS, CHAVO had put me over. This night, it was my turn to repay the favor. We went off the hook.

We ended up outside the ring, up the ramp, and ended up in a backstage area near the lighting tower. We fought on the steel structure until I ended up tangled upside down, hanging several feet from the floor. At that point I was an easy target, and Chavo went to town on my knee, breaking a chair over my left knee as he hit it again and again.

Until the only thing I could do was say, "I quit."

SmackDown! versus Raw

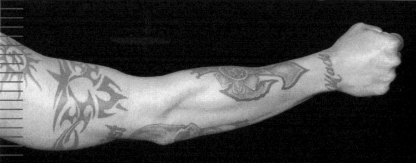

I was out for several months with a legitimate rupture to my anterior cruciate ligament (ACL) and a tear in my patella tendon. It was a change of pace having my left knee out, but I'd rather have skipped the experience entirely. It meant surgery and months of rehab.

Traveling from the East Coast back home right after surgery took a lot out of me, so I started working with Dr. David Chow. He may not be quite as famous as Dr. Andrews, but he's an excellent doctor. He takes care of the NFL Chargers and is well known in San Diego.

Revenge

I DIDN'T MAKE it back into competition in time to get a match at *WrestleMania* that year, but I did return to action in San Diego, appearing at the end of February 2007 and immediately working into a little storyline with Vince McMahon and Umaga.

I spent the next few months in different angles that featured big man–little man matches, but everyone knew I was angling toward Chavo and a measure of revenge for my knee. We hooked up at *Summer Slam*, where I beat him. Then in September of 2007, we did a rerun of our I Quit match.

Requested by Chavo, by the way.

It was another high-flying contest. I dipped into my *lucha libre* roots, throwing myself around the ring.

After the action took us beyond the ropes, Chavo grabbed a chair and began pounding on my leg and the rest of my body. The chair became another character in the match, squashing under our weight after I dove into Chavo from the turnbuckle. With him tangled on the ropes, I took revenge on *his* knee—and this time it was Chavo who quit.

Climbing a Mountain

THE NEXT FEW months saw me in more big man–little man matchups, including one with the Great Khali. Khali makes everyone look small, even Dave Batista, and fighting him was like climbing a mountain.

With the big guys, it's hard to keep nonstop action going. It's more chop, chop, chop the tree down. I work from the legs up, cutting them down to size. Or I wear them down.

Khali, being so tall, made for a great contrast. I looked and felt like Jack in Jack and the Beanstalk. Khali wasn't just the Giant—he was the beanstalk, the cloud, and the castle.

Tattoos

WHILE I'M BEST known for my masks, I've also developed a reputation for my body art over the years.

Myself, Pscicosis, Konnan, and Juventud met this guy after the show and started talking. It turned out he did tattoos in his house. Within a few hours . . . maybe a drink or two . . . we were all sitting in his living room, waiting to get tatted up. Then one by one we realized: hey, we don't know this guy. How good a tattoo artist is he?

None of us wanted to be the first to find out. Eventually we ganged up on Juvy and volunteered him to the head of the line. The tattoo artist went right to work, totally freehand, not drawing on his arm or anything.

But damned if it didn't come out looking pretty good. I sat down and had myself inked up: that's where my Angie tattoo was created.

The letters are pretty small compared to what I've had done since. Sometimes I joke

that's because I was just married and wasn't sure the marriage would last. I usually don't say that when she's around, though; I don't like taking my life in my hands outside the ring.

After that, I started to get addicted to tattoos. From the first to the second to the third, the time between them shrank. I never thought I would have so much ink on my body.

I have the names of my kids, Dominik and Aalyah, embroidered on my arms. I have my rosary around my neck. I have "619" on my forearm—you can see me getting it on my *619* DVD.

My back is tatted up. My back takes a lot of shots, and the inked spinal cord there helps out my chiropractor when he goes to work on me.

That's a joke.

The doctors tell me, though, that the inking is accurate and perfectly aligned. So it is there for reference.

I have a cross and a tombstone in memory of Eddie, and a remembrance of my brother-in-law. Across my wrists, front, and back, is a saying: "Made man by God." That's a reminder to me of who I am.

I have a skeleton with my mask. As I mentioned earlier, I'm a big fan of the Day of the Dead and its religious significance.

On my right back shoulder I have a Japanese symbol that means "king." On my left, "mystery." Put it together and you have my name, King Mystery—Rey Mysterio.

On my neck I have a cross that I got back in WCW. A group of us decided to get tattooed together to show our friendship: Konnan, Psicosis, myself, Halloween, and Lizmark.

We copied a cross worn by Tupac Shakur, the rapper. Ours are a little smaller, but the style is the same. Then we added the year that we were born.

On my left ring finger, I have my wife's name. (In case I forget my wedding ring.)

I have a cross that was created by one of my great friends, Ed

Camarse. He's the head director of my Website and Team Mysterio. He's always been there when I need him—his wife and son too. Ed designed the cross using different elements from the Aztec calendar, a crown, and graphic images of falcons.

I have falcon wings on my chest and the word "Mexican" on my stomach. On my calf, there's a tattoo of my wife and me kissing that says "Love till Death." It's a heart formed from our skeletons. It means we're going to be together until the end of our days on earth.

I still have a lot more to go. I have a piece that I want to get done. It's a body of a skeleton kneeling down and praying at an altar. The face will be half skull, half mask. A buddy of mine has a similar tattoo, and I like it. It seems to sum up who I am.

One guy does all my tattoos: Jason Salinaz at Avalon Tattoo in Pacific Beach, California. You can watch him work on my *619* DVD. He's done a couple of pieces on Edge and Umaga too. We all have a different style, but he's able to do a great job for all of us.

There's a surprising amount of prep work that goes into deciding how the tattoo should look and how it should be done. There's a little bit of a sting or pain as it's done, but if you're into the art, it's a small price to pay.

Usually. The big pieces can be tough. I almost didn't make it through the tattoo on my back. Jason had me sitting there for so long I started getting numb. He saw it was getting to me, but I told him to keep going. I didn't want to have to come back and go through the same experience again.

A Family Thing

MY MOM WAS against piercings at a young age, and tattoos were just out of the question. I remember when I got the first one, she told my wife, "I can't believe you let him have a tattoo. You have to make him stop."

My wife said, "He's a grown man."

My mom started accepting, slowly. There's nothing moms can do at that stage.

My dad's old school too, but he's a little more accepting, at least of tattoos. We happened to be talking about this the other day, all three of us. "Hey, it looks good," he said. "What the hell."

Tattoos have become a family thing. My wife has my mask, my name, and the kids' names on her neck. She also has a sun tattoo on her shoulder, a star on her foot, and a bracelet on her ankle. There's also a bracelet that says "Oscar" on her wrist.

I think she got the first tat because she wanted to blend in with my lifestyle and maybe see what tattoos are all about. But after that, she liked it and got the others. She's working on a big piece right now, trying to get the design just right.

If my son wants a tattoo, when he's eighteen—and if he has good grades—then I'll take him myself. I'd love to get some ink down with him.

Bad grades, no tattoo.

My daughter, same way.

Piercings: sixteen. A piercing isn't necessarily permanent, unlike a tat. Tattoos are there for life.

My Biceps Roll Up

IN 2008, WHILE I was working my way into a challenge for the U.S. Championship, I hurt my arm.

We were on tour in South America. We had done Panama and Costa Rica and were ending in Santiago, Chile. We had two dates there in February 2008. I was in the ring with Hawkins & Ryder—Edge's team. Kane was in my corner.

We were doing well. I remember the date, though: February 13. Not a Friday, but maybe an omen.

I grabbed one of the guys—I can't remember now if it was Hawkins or Ryder—and got ready to run him into the turnbuckle. I was a step forward and he was a step behind me. I pulled him, gently, just enough for him to feel the force and go with me.

As soon as I did that, I felt my biceps pull. As he went into the turnbuckle, I tried to extend my arm. It wouldn't go.

I tried again. It curled up on me.

I looked at my arm. There was a big hole where my biceps used to be.

Torn

I HAD A big old ball up on top of my arm. I looked at it, then tried to straighten my arm, flex my muscles.

I'd never had a biceps tear, so I didn't know what was going on. It felt more like a cramp.

I told the ref, "I think I'm hurt. It just feels weird."

After tagging out, I rolled to the floor. My arm wouldn't give, no matter how hard I tried straightening it out. Finally I realized something was really wrong.

We had a couple of minutes left in the match. I got back in, did a pulldown spring, did a 619, and got a pin.

Back in the locker room, the trainer and the doctor looked at it.

"Oh shit, man," said one of them. "You tore it. It's gone."

"Don't say that," I answered.

"Yeah, it's torn."

Like Superman

THE NEXT THING you know, I was on a flight going back to Florida to see Dr. Andrews. (Dr. Andrews has offices in Florida as well as Georgia.) I met up with my wife and cousin Art Morales in L.A. on the way.

At least I got to spend Valentine's Day with my wife.

God, I was in a lot of pain.

My arm turned all black and blue. I got to Florida and saw Dr. Andrews the next morning.

The doc eventually said the biceps was torn, but I still needed an MRI, or magnetic resonance imaging, to verify his diagnosis. I've had plenty of MRIs, and I hate that capsule: They send you into a long tunnel where a magnetic field is used to look inside your body and show the doctors what's going on. It's considered noninvasive— they don't cut you up—but it can be uncomfortable under some circumstances. You have to hold certain poses, and the machine can be claustrophobic.

The technician didn't exactly put me at ease when I came in, though he was truthful.

"The biceps is probably the worst MRI you can have," he told me before it started, "because it's a very uncomfortable position."

He wasn't exaggerating. I had to sit in there for thirty-five minutes. I'm a little claustrophobic to begin with, and sitting like a broken pretzel for more than half an hour felt worse than taking a Tombstone Piledriver from Undertaker.

They put me in the machine arms- and headfirst, like Superman. They put a two-pound sack on my hand to help rotate my arm and hold my hand upward. Half of my body was in, half out.

For thirty-five minutes.

I kept telling myself to relax. And not to move. As bad as it was, it would be much worse to screw it up somehow and go through it all again.

Luckily, I made it through.

"What do you know," said the doc. "It *is* torn."

Duh.

No *WrestleMania*

AT THAT POINT, we were only a few weeks away from *Mania*. I didn't want to miss it. I'd missed it the year before because of my knee.

"How long can I go on wrestling like this?" I asked the doctor.

"Anywhere from two to three weeks," he said. "Then we'll never be able to fix it."

I managed to do *No Way Out* against Edge in Las Vegas, did a *SmackDown!* in San Diego, and went to see Dr. Chow to get my arm put back together. That wasn't a knock on Dr. Andrews. I just figured it would be easier to get it done near home.

Dr. Chow was able to use a new procedure that calls for small cuts in the front of the biceps and the back of the elbow. He promised the recovery time would be much shorter—four weeks—than with the older style procedure, which called for a much larger and more invasive incision.

It sounded good.

Milk and Blood

THAT WAS THE plan. But my arm had other ideas.

A week after the surgery, I was getting ready to go on a promotional tour in Italy. My wife and I had packed, and we were a few hours away from leaving for LAX—the big Los Angeles International Airport— to board a flight to Milan. It was Saturday evening.

I had gone to see Dr. Chow, to make sure I was okay for the trip. He checked me out, said I was good to go, and sent me on my way. I swung by the store to pick up some milk, then headed home.

As I put the bags down on the kitchen table, a bunch of liquid ran down my arm.

Damn, I thought. *The gallon has a hole in it.*

But I couldn't find a hole.

I took off my jacket and looked at my arm. Water, blood, and puss were flowing from my incisions.

I canceled the trip and called the doctor.

Fixing It, Times Three

THE DOCTOR EXAMINED it the next morning, Sunday, and scheduled me for surgery first thing Monday. He went in and took another shot at patching me up.

I walked out of there thinking I was done. But a week later, it was leaking again, the wounds unhealed. The doctor took a look at it and set me up for my third surgery.

This time I had to wear a catheter in my arm with a bag of antibiotics for eleven days to beat the infection that was threatening my body.

With the tube finally gone, I began feeling a lot better, but my arm was still immobile. While waiting to heal well enough for rehab to begin, I planned to go to Florida on vacation with my family.

My son and I went to *WrestleMania* together in Orlando. We planned to leave from there, meet my wife and daughter, and then go on to Hawaii. I was in the hotel bathroom the night before we were to leave, looking at the wound.

There was a little purple puff near the incision.

It didn't feel good.

I put some pressure on it.

Spitttttt . . . blood and puss came out.

No!

Visions of another operation, another catheter, more weeks immobile . . . true scenes of horror flew through my head.

I told myself, *Not this time!*

I squeezed out the puss really well and willed myself to be better. I kept at it until my arm was flat.

Whether it was willpower, God, or just my finger pressure flushing it out, the wound remained clean after that.

Fortunately, the surgery took. I did my rehab and managed to get back to full strength over the next several months.

No one was really sure why it took such a complicated series of procedures to fix my arm. My theory is that ink from one of my tattoos somehow interfered with the healing of the wound on the first two operations. But that's just my theory.

Kids on the Road

SOMETIMES I TRAVEL with my kids when I'm performing at shows on the road. It gives my wife a little break at home, and it gives me some good daddy time with them. I've traveled with just Dominik, just Aalyah, and both of them together. They're really good kids, very respectful and polite, which as a father makes me very proud.

Aalyah loves kicking back with the Divas. Dominik's very cool backstage. Occasionally another wrestler's son will be on the road, and they hang out together. They'll play ribs on the wrestlers, and the wrestlers rib them back.

It's great seeing second- and third-generation children mixing in. Going back, things were a little more private backstage, and kids weren't always as welcome, at least not before a show. Now, though, there's a little more openness, and maybe a little more of an attitude that says families are very important. It's a very healthy thing for the kids, I think.

Can you imagine, ten years from now, if some of these kids become wrestlers and are able to face off against each other? Maybe we'll see some footage of them running around backstage in the promos before their matches.

But I don't just travel with the kids. Every so often my wife and I leave them with their grandparents and travel together. It's a little break for her, almost a minivacation, where she gets to relax a little and not worry about all the day-to-day things at home you have to watch.

Because I spend so much time on the road—at least four or five days out of just about every week—my wife has to shoulder a heavy load at home. Taking care of the kids and the house, doing things for me—it's a 24/7 job with a lot of demands and responsibilities, as I'm sure every wife and mother knows. And then when I get home, she has to deal with me spoiling the kids. So giving her a little break now and then is the very least I can do. I give her a lot of credit.

Quake

I WAS IN China in May 2008 when the Great Sichuan Earthquake hit.

It was a promotional tour, meeting and greeting people there, introducing them to WWE and our brand of professional wrestling. My wife was with me and we were very excited. We flew into the country and then over to Xi'an. Xi'an is one of the oldest cities in China, an ancient capital. It's located in Shaanxi province, just to the east of the geographic center of the country. It's about five hundred and seventy miles southwest of Beijing, the country's capital.

We arrived at Xi'an the day after coming to China, still jetlagged. My wife was kind of tired, so she stayed at the hotel while I went to catch up with the media. They took me to a building about twenty minutes away. It was an older building, and we went up to a large, open lobby, on the third floor or so. There was a TV station in the building, and we were going to go up when they were ready for us.

The skin on my hands was so dried out that it was cracking, so I took off my wedding ring and started to rub some lotion on. All of a sudden, I felt the floor shake.

"You feel that?" I asked.

"No," said the translator and the others with me.

All right, maybe I imagined it.

All of a sudden, the building began to rumble.

Boom.

Everyone ran to the door. But rather than continuing out, they pulled me into a room, thinking they were protecting me.

"No, no," I told them. "We have to get out."

I'm from California—I know earthquakes.

Finally, I took off. They came right behind me. The stairs were shaking, almost rolling like on a ship. I made it to the door, then outside. There was a building in front of me—and then there wasn't. It was replaced by a huge cloud of dust.

It was chaos. Sirens, people screaming, things falling. I have never seen anything like that.

Our building, fortunately, never collapsed.

I grabbed my cell phone and tried to call my wife, but the towers had been wiped out and I couldn't reach her. The people with me finally agreed to take me to her hotel.

As we drove, we saw people carrying their children, crying, stunned. Little houses and stores had been crushed. There was debris all over the place. I prayed that the hotel was still standing. It took only forty-five minutes to get back, but it was the longest ride of my life.

The hotel, thank God, was still standing. There were crowds outside.

I jumped out of the car and began looking for my wife. I found her on the corner, wearing a coat one of the security people had given her. We hugged for the longest time.

Angie had been sleeping in our room on the sixteenth or so floor when the quake hit. She went out without her shoes, let alone her passport or rings. It was dark in the hall and she didn't know where to go. An older Chinese woman saw her and grabbed her. She pulled her into her room with her, where other people had gathered. The old lady hid under a sink. My wife finally persuaded her and the others to get out of the hotel. My wife found the stairs and helped the others out. It was amazingly orderly, she told me later; the hotel security people did an excellent job.

Many weren't as lucky as we were. Centered in Sichuan province, the disaster killed at least 69,000 people. Some estimates put the toll closer to 90,000 and higher.

Following the earthquake, WWE helped AmeriCares, a U.S.–based international aid group, raise money to build a pair of field hospitals for quake victims. I donated myself, thankful for the care and concern the Chinese people had shown us.

I continued the promotional tour, talking to kids and others at different schools around the country. At every stop I was impressed by the inner strength of the people. I was glad to get a chance to do what little I could to help them and maybe take their minds off their problems.

I've always believed that when disasters strike, it's important that we put aside any differences—language, culture, religion, race—and come together as human beings. Now that I've lived through it, I know how true—and critical—this is. It makes a difference.

Different Brands

AFTER REHABBING MY arm injury, I came back to work and found myself drafted to *Raw*.

While we were all part of the same overall corporate family, there's a bit of competition between *Raw* and *SmackDown!* A lot of people think that *Raw* is the A team and *SmackDown!* is the B team. That feeling may come from the fact that *Raw* is live, and *SmackDown!* is usually taped. But in reality, each brand has its own set of Superstars, and those of us on *SmackDown!* don't feel inferior to anyone.

And neither do the people on ECW.

In some areas, *SmackDown!* is *measurably* better than *Raw*. The Hispanic market was conquered by the *SmackDown!* team, which has featured a lot of Latino wrestlers ever since Eddie went over from WCW. So that's one place where *SmackDown!* has an advantage.

I think my becoming Heavyweight Champion helped the ratings among Hispanics. They were loyal to their champion. They wanted to see Rey Mysterio defend the title.

Drafted

MY FIRST NIGHT back to work was the night of the draft, in June 2008. I think most fans know that the selection happens live, with each wrestler's fate decided by a massive roulette wheel. Of course, the lineups have already been worked out in advance; what happens on the broadcast is just for show. But most of us don't know what's going to happen until it does.

Or at least I don't.

That night I walked out as they spun the wheel. Since I'd been on *SmackDown!* so long I just assumed that's where I was going. Then the roulette wheel stopped and popped up *Raw*.

I was completely surprised. Stunned. So much so that I continued down the ramp and hopped into the ring, kind of in a fog.

Triple H looked at me like I was an alien. I wasn't supposed to do that at all.

"What are you doing?" he asked.

"I don't know," I told him—and everyone watching at home. "This is a big surprise."

"Well, welcome to *Raw*," he said, adlibbing as he shook my hand.

Of course, then he got drafted to *SmackDown!*, which was pretty funny.

Cues

RAW WAS A big change, since I'd been in *SmackDown!* since joining the company. But it was exciting, and not just because I found myself working with a new set of wrestlers.

Since it's a live show, you don't get time to second-guess yourself. You pull the match off in the heat of the moment. I had to learn to work a little differently, since there is no chance to cover things up. I had to hit my times just right, because the match can't go over its allotted time.

Fortunately, I've been pretty good over the years at hitting my marks and holding my time.

The ref gives us cues, which ultimately come from the gorilla position. The show has to make way for commercials, so when they say you gotta go, *you gotta go.* If you had something else planned out, you just have to block that out and get on with it.

Painkillers

I LIKED BEING on *Raw*, but 2008 wasn't a great time for me. I spent a month that summer in a medical clinic—I hate to call it rehab, though others will—to fight my abuse of painkillers. I was in for thirty days, exactly.

After all my operations, I had a lot of pain. The doctors prescribed painkillers, including mild narcotics, to help me deal with it. Unfortunately, I developed a dependency on the drugs and continued to take them long after the operations.

These were legal drugs, which help millions of people every year. The pain from operations—whether they have to do with wrestling injuries or just everyday life—shouldn't be underestimated. Painkilling drugs, when prescribed by doctors, are an important way to get better.

But like anything, too much of them can be a very bad thing. In the summer of 2008, following the three operations on my biceps and my recovery, I realized I had developed an addiction.

I was abusing my body, taking too many pills for a longer period than I should have. I'd crossed some sort of line. I couldn't function without the medications. I was worried that my kidneys would be affected by the medications, and I felt that my head was in a fog at times. I was never to the point where I didn't know where I was or what I was doing, but I knew I had a problem.

I also realized that the drugs were hurting my relationship at home, making my head less than clear and making me feel exhausted. I wanted to get myself on a better path.

I talked with my wife and kids. I was very straight with my children. I told them that Daddy needed to care for himself. And I confessed that sometimes when I had been tired at home or in a bad mood, it was because I had been taking medications I wasn't supposed to take.

My wife gave me her total support and love.

"It's time to move on," she told me. "Do something good for yourself."

I went to WWE and told Johnny Ace that I wanted to check myself in and stop taking painkillers. Then I went to see Vince McMahon.

"You're not aware of this," I told him, "but I've been abusing my pain medications. I don't want to continue taking them. It's time for a change. I want to go in and get myself sorted out."

He was very cool about it. I remember his exact words:

"Rey, it takes a man to really accept what you just told me. I'm proud that you're doing this. We'll be here waiting for you."

WWE was incredibly supportive.

The Clinic

ART MORALES, MY cousin, found the clinic for me. He even took me there, along with his wife and Angie. I thank them all for their support.

I was nervous, but I knew I was doing something positive. And once I decide on a goal, I don't rest until I accomplish it. That's what I did there.

At the clinic, the patients all supported each other. A few were wrestling fans, but whether they knew who I was or not wasn't very important. We were all working together.

The staff and other patients were fantastic. It was difficult work, but every day I felt a little stronger. Maybe I was able to help others as well. The counselors told me I brought a lot of peace and tranquillity to the clinic. They told me they would really miss me when I left.

You know what? I miss them too, but I hope I won't see them soon. At least not there.

With Our Troops

ONE OF THE high points of 2008 was our visit in December to Iraq, where we entertained the troops. It was my third visit; I'd gone in 2004 and 2007 as well.

I've been humbled by the reaction of the men and women I've met every time. Especially the Hispanic troops. They're all so grateful for us coming out. But really, we're the ones who are grateful. They put their lives on the line for us, for our freedom, for our children. They're real heroes.

We go over on C-17s. The C-17 is really a cargo plane with a huge hold—they can put tanks in it. But when the military wants to move a lot of people around, they put these special seats in. I've always sat on the far end, near our gear. Once the plane takes off, I can get up and go lie on the bags or mats and get some sleep.

The trip is long and usually runs in two legs. This past year we flew from Washington to Germany, which was ten or eleven hours. We got some grub while the plane was filled up with fuel, then from there it was another five or six hours to Baghdad, Iraq.

No One Shoots at Vince

THE FIRST TIME I went, I was a little nervous. I told Johnny Ace that I wanted to be in Vince's group, because I knew nothing would happen to him.

Seriously, though, you do have a little fear going into a war zone. No matter how calm it may be, it's still a combat area. In 2004, things were volatile on the ground, but the military took very good care of us.

An hour and a half before we landed, they dimmed all the lights, making it harder for anyone to spot the airplane. Inside, everything was shaded red by the special night-flying lights in the cargo area.

Then they gave everybody bulletproof vests and helmets.

We landed fine, then went right to work meeting troops. One of the biggest kicks of my life was being transported in a Black Hawk helicopter. I was like a little kid when I jumped in. I've seen my military movies—*Platoon* and *Black Hawk Down* are two of my favorites—and to be part of that and actually living it, it was incredible.

The Machine Gun and I

EVEN COOLER THAN riding in the Black Hawk was the time I got to fire a machine gun in 2007.

We went to a forward-operating base in the north somewhere. Things were calm; violence had dropped considerably in the country, even compared to the last time I'd been there. Still, troops were on guard with live ammunition, and the security around the base, not just for our visit but all the time, was heavy.

I went up to one of the lookout towers after our show to thank the soldier there for his service. He was in a space, oh, say, about six by six, and he had a fifty-caliber machine gun. I asked if I could fire

it—I've always been curious about those weapons—and he called his commanding officer and got clearance.

His watchtower overlooked an empty area; there were acres and acres of clear terrain ahead. After some basic instruction, the soldier stepped back to let me try the gun.

I slid over and got into position. It was kind of chilly, and I had gloves on.

"Just one burst, all right?" said the soldier. "Just a burst or two, and that's enough, okay?"

"Sure, sure," I said. I just wanted to see what it felt like; I didn't want to start a war or anything.

I squeezed the trigger. I let go almost immediately, but as I went to pull my finger away, my glove got caught. Bullets poured from the barrel of the gun.

"Stop! Stop!" yelled the soldier.

"I can't," I told him, desperately trying pull my hand out.

I don't know if he thought I wasn't listening to him or what. He reached in and tried to pull my hand away from the trigger, but the gun came with my glove.

The barrel swung left and right as bullets flew. Finally we managed to get my glove out, and the firing stopped.

"No worries," he told me, after making sure I hadn't done any damage. "No worries."

Maybe not, but I'm guessing they won't draft me any time soon. Or let me near another machine gun.

Intercontinental Champ

JBL and I have had our moments inside and outside the ring. Back in 2004, he tossed me around the ring en route to his WWE Championship showdown with Eddie Guerrero. Then came his bad-mouthing during my championship reign. Our matches are a study in contrasts. He's a

DARING TO DO THE POSSIBLE, I SQUASH JBL.

natural heel; I'm an old-school babyface. He's a big man; I'm short. My style is speed and flight; he's a brawler.

In 2009, leading up to *WrestleMania XXV*, JBL won the Intercontinental Championship from CM Punk. The next month, he and I faced off at *WrestleMania* for the title.

Anyone who didn't know much about wrestling could take one look at our sizes and predict that the result would be a squash. They would've been right—but about the length of the match, not the outcome.

JBL kicked me during the referee's instructions, sending me to the mat. I got up for the bell, launching myself in a fury. He grabbed my leg, which only set me up for a kick that took him by surprise and left him hanging on the ropes.

One 619, and he was history.

I'd won my third different championship in WWE. And my first at *Raw*—though that was about to change as well.

Back to *SmackDown!*

I'D BEEN ON *Raw* for a little less than a year, though I missed a lot of that time due to my injuries and personal difficulty recovering. During that time, the ratings for *SmackDown!* suffered. One theory was that the decrease was caused by a drop in Hispanic viewers.

A lot of Hispanic viewers don't happen to get *Raw*, since it's on cable, but they will follow *SmackDown!* because it's a local channel. A lot of Hispanic viewers seemed to have stopped watching our shows in 2008, maybe because we had lost a lot of Hispanic wrestlers over the years. So the front office decided to draft me back to *SmackDown!* With me on the show, it may be possible to target that audience again.

I don't have a say in that, but I was happy to not just help the company but also get a chance to reconnect with my fans. My

Hispanic followers have always given me a big boost, and it's a good feeling to be able to entertain them. I think it's a good move from a business standpoint. We want to have more viewers, more Hispanic viewers, and it was a good call.

Once again, I didn't know I was going back until the day of the draft. This time, though, I managed to avoid embarrassing myself and stuck completely to the script.

Steroids

BEING A PUBLIC person, your name gets connected with a lot of so-called news: good, bad, false, and true.

At one point over the past year or two, there were rumors about me taking steroids.

Here's my answer: *I've never touched a syringe or cranked it up to get bigger.*

Steroids never played a role in my life. They were never big in Mexico or in *lucha libre* when I got my start. My uncle never used steroids.

I've always been a small cat. I never had the physique of a bodybuilder. My physique doesn't play a role in the ring, so I really don't have a need to do that. And steroids were never around me, so I wasn't tempted. If they had been around in my teenage days, I don't know what I might have done. But they weren't.

They're not good for you. Eventually they catch up with you. But I can't judge anybody.

If I was speaking to kids today, I would say that steroids are not the way to go.

"You have so many natural enhancements now that can take you to the next level," I'd tell them. "Vitamins, amino acids, proper nutrition. Good training programs are easy to find. Work out, sleep right, eat right. You'll have natural growth right there."

Staying in Shape

YOU HAVE TO be in great shape to wrestle, and that means a lot of work outside the ring. I try to get a good workout every day: If there's time, that means about two hours in the gym. Cardio is thirty minutes or so, with the rest on weights and various exercises. I have to adapt if there isn't enough time—there are days when the schedule is so hectic, all I have is thirty minutes, very concentrated—but two hours is my base workout.

When I first started wrestling, I didn't work out with weights. My workouts included a lot of exercises that I could do without any extra equipment: squats, pushups, et cetera.

I started lifting weights while I was in Mexico, looking to add a little more strength and bulk to my body. I picked up the exercises and techniques on my own, partly by talking to people, and partly by looking at magazines and books. I would work on a body part a day: chest one day, back another, and so on.

Right before I came into WWE, I had to rehab my knee. And I worked with a trainer for three months. I ended up in the best shape of my life. The trainer would meet up with me every day at my house. He even wrote out a diet for me. Maybe the most radical thing about it was that it had me eating every three hours. They'd be small portions, designed to give my body the fuel and nutrients it needed to grow. I ate a lot of protein—two protein shakes a day, on top of things like egg whites and fish.

My trainer was pretty good. He'd stop by in the afternoon when we were going to work and he'd take one look and say, "Hey, you cheated! You had bread today."

"No, I didn't."

"Yeah, bro, I can see it."

He was wrong: I had tortillas.

Hah.

He was good, on my case all the time, whipping me into shape.

He was intense during workouts. The first few days, it was hard to adapt. My butt was on the floor—along with the rest of me. But once I started eating right and then getting into the exercise routine, I began digging it. I could see the results.

One of the things he emphasized was technique. A press was not a press unless it was done exactly right. A curl—you get the idea. When you work out right, your muscles respond according to plan.

We worked together for three months. At the end of that time, my body was transformed. I looked incredible. Even better, I knew how to work out. He gave me a blueprint to follow. And he showed me what I could do if I kept my discipline.

The 300

RECENTLY, I'VE STARTED altering my workouts a bit, adapting a plan Charlie Haas taught me. Charlie and I had a chance to work out together in Texas a little while back, while we were on the road together. He had just opened up his nutrition store and started doing something called the 300 workout.

It gets its name from the total number of reps. You begin with 25 pull ups—a good, basic exercise that starts you pumping. Then you do 50 deadlifts—in my case with 135 pounds. You do 50 pushups, then 50 box jumps on a two-foot platform: jump up, jump down, and by the time you're done with that, you're going to be a little loaded. Then you grab a bar, lie down on the ground, and do 50 windshield wipers. Those are done with the bar extended over your face and your legs up in the air. You move the bar back and forth to touch your legs, swinging like you were a car windshield wiper.

When I do them, I have 135 pounds on the bar.

When you're done, you do 50 clean presses, 25 on each arm, with 35-pound dumbbells. To finish up, you go back to the pull-up machine and do 25.

It's a bitch getting through it—especially the first few times—

but once you finish, you're full of energy. You're pumped and excited.

The 300 works out all the little muscles in your body. You don't rest too long between the sets, so it helps build your cardio system as well as your other muscles.

Cardio workouts—running or working on an elliptical—are a big part of my personal routine. I run or use the elliptical for thirty minutes every day. I've had a lot of trouble with my knees, so I monitor them pretty closely. Normally it's pretty good; I wear a knee brace when I'm working to protect the knee from any twists. There are times where they hurt and I switch to a power walk, but otherwise I haven't had too many problems.

Stretching and Warming Up

When it comes to talking about nutrition or exercise routines, I'm very bad at telling people what to do. I'm an expert on *my* body, no one else's. But I do believe that the key is discipline. That's really what's worked for me. You have to find what works for you and stick to it, on a schedule, day to day, week to week, month to month. It has to become part of your life.

I've been lucky there: I've always had good discipline when it came down to preparing myself for something, whether it was inside the ring or outside the ring.

One thing I would say to other people, especially kids who are starting out: Learn to warm up and stretch. Make that part of your routine.

Back in Mexico, we never warmed up or stretched much. Some of the old timers' prematch routines consisted of smoking a few cigarettes and downing a couple of beers in the locker room. The funny thing is, they wouldn't blow up. I'd never see them in the gym, though I guess they must have worked out *somewhere*. They were thick and rugged, though not as big as you see these days in WWE.

But no matter what their physiques looked like, they'd never stretch. Our way was just to get a pump on: a couple of sets of pushups, then grab an elastic workout band and flex up the biceps and shoulders. That was it.

That was the way I was raised. But then I started getting hurt. I blame a lot of those early injuries on the fact that I didn't know how to warm up and properly get my muscles ready for the work they had to do.

It wasn't until I got to WCW that I learned about stretching. I started seeing guys doing long routines before the show. Dean Malenko was one. He would sit down and stretch for literally forty-five minutes. He'd start with his hamstrings, move to his quads—every muscle in his body would be ready by the time the show started.

Then we'd hit the ring and he'd stretch me.

Another person who helped me learn about stretching out was RVD—Rob Van Dam—who would spend maybe thirty or forty minutes just stretching his legs.

Even with these examples, I didn't adopt a stretching routine at first. In fact, it took three knee operations before I really saw the light. The doctors had been telling me all along. After the first surgery, the doctor gave me a long lecture on how important it was for me to stretch my body out. Well, it took me two more surgeries before it sank in. I regret it. Maybe I would have had to have only one operation instead of three.

Now I'll stretch out every day before a workout and just before hitting the ring.

Teenage fans sometimes ask me to recommend a workout. My first piece of advice is for them to find and work with a coach or trainer who will be able to take the time and really get to know them. They can also study up on their own, reading books or articles on the Web, and watching videos to get a good understanding of technique and what is possible. Magazines like *Muscle Fitness* and *Flex* are also good sources of information.

A lot of teens want to start out with very heavy weights, because they think that's the way to gain strength quickly. I understand that; I was that way myself in the beginning. I wanted to push heavy weights. But I know from experience that pushing heavy weights can hurt your joints. So I try to suggest a more balanced workout, with lighter weights that are easier to manage. I've seen a lot of kids at the gym who pick up the heaviest weight they can, and their bodies are all out of whack. Their posture is terrible and they're just swinging the weights around. You can tell they're going to get hurt—that they're training their bodies for an injury. Too much weight puts pressure on your body beyond what you can use to train. The lower back is very vulnerable. I can't tell you how many injuries I've seen because of that.

If I were starting over at fifteen or seventeen, I'd begin at a very slow pace and make getting the right form down my first priority.

Do your research, whether with an experienced trainer or a book or magazine. Learn the proper posture. And be open to new things. You see something good, steal it and make it your own. Apply it to your own workout and health. Make sure you have good form, then go.

Another thing I tell younger fans is not to forget about their diet. It's so important if they want to look good. They need to get a balance of different foods. You can work out, bust your ass—but if you eat like shit, it's going to show.

I understand, it's not easy. At this point in my life, I like to enjoy life. I go to the movies and I'll eat my popcorn or candy, whatever. But when I remind myself that I want to look good, I get motivated again. *WrestleMania*'s coming up—I tighten up my food and I'm taking care of myself again.

I like to kick off my day with four egg whites and maybe a piece of bacon, along with a dry piece of toast. Two or three hours later, I have a protein shake. Lunch might be salad with some protein: chicken-Caesar salad is one of my favorites. Dinner will be a nice steak or a piece of fish—anything but salmon, which I don't like. And a shake after I wrestle.

A Hero Unmasked

EVEN WHEN YOU reach a point in your career when you think you've had all the highlights you can possibly have, new ones come along to humble you.

Recently I was with WWE doing a show in Mexico. While I was there, a magazine called me to arrange for a photo shoot with Mil Máscaras. I mentioned Máscaras earlier; he's a wrestler for whom I have a great respect, a legend in our business who still has many faithful fans after decades of wrestling. He's also still very careful about his identity. And in fact, even though we had wrestled together when I was younger, I had never seen his face when the magazine called.

We set an appointment at my hotel for 10:00 A.M. I went about my business the day before. That morning I got up, worked out, and was just about to hit the shower when someone knocked on the door. Thinking it was the management or maybe one of the boys checking in on me, I grabbed a towel and ran to the door, leaving the water running.

I opened it, and there in front of me was Mil Máscaras. Without his mask.

And I'm without a lot more than my mask.

I forgot to be embarrassed, though. This was Mil Máscaras in front of me. To see him without a mask was a deep honor.

I took a cowboy shower—as soon as the water hits you, you're done—got dressed, and hurried out to talk with him. He was full of advice and old stories, and the time just flew away from us as I listened to him speak. Finally, the photographer herded us toward the camera. With both got our masks on and went to work.

Making It Look Easy

A FAN WAS complimenting me the other day on how easy some of my moves look. Then he asked me, "How do you do it?"

I wish I had an answer.

It just comes naturally. I've trained to do it all my life. I've trained for years. As long as the guy is positioned the right way, I'm going to hit him the right way.

I've been doing it for so long that it's part of me. I can't stand back and analyze it any more.

Even though I'm a perfectionist, I'm not perfect. Sometimes the move goes wrong—even the 619.

I've been doing the 619 for a long time now, and it's become a real favorite with the fans. But it hasn't gotten easier, and recently I had an incident in Texas that reminded me how dangerous it can be, for me as well as my opponents.

I went to hit it on Chris Jericho and missed the rope completely. I had so much momentum that I flew out of the ring onto the floor.

The crowd just went silent. I've been to motorcross shows like that, where the guy goes up on the jump, and instead of coming down right, he goes one way, the bike another, and the crowd just goes silent.

That exact thing happened to me. I went down hard. Everybody went *Whooooo!* and stood up. They knew instantly that it wasn't part of the show.

I landed on my knees. The pain was so intense I couldn't get up. I lay there, completely stunned and paralyzed.

Fortunately, it was a Tag Team match. My partner, Shawn Michaels, came in and Superkicked Chris and then his partner Kane, and he rolled up the end of the match. Then he helped me back to the locker room.

I wrestled the next night, of course. It hurt, but it wasn't as bad as it could have been.

I remember another time when I missed the move and found myself in a world of pain. It was with Charlie Haas. He was draped over the ropes and I tried to do something a little different, starting with a backflip off his back. I hit the top rope as I came down, which started it shaking. It bounced so much that when I swung around to grab it and do the 619, I missed it completely.

Bam, out to the floor.

Ow.

Which just goes to show: It may look easy, but every step is a delicate balance between success and failure. You can never take anything for granted.

Looking Ahead

WRITING THIS BOOK has made me stop and think about my career. It's amazing to me how many things I've done.

I guess it's amazing to others as well. In 2007, I was inducted into the AAA Hall of Fame. It was a great honor, especially considering that I went in with Antonio Peña, the founder of the promotion.

But I don't really spend my time thinking about the past. I'm still moving forward. Just this year, in 2009, I signed a new contract with WWE that will have me wrestling for some time. That means five more years, at least, of pushing myself and inventing new things. Five more years of Pay-Per-Views, championships—I hope—and, best of all, high-flying wrestling.

Sleep?

Sleep is very hard for me to catch up on. It's hard being on the road.

My old boss, Antonio Peña, would never sleep. He was always working.

"Boss, when are you going to sleep?" someone would ask him.

"When I die," he'd say, "I'll sleep a long time."

Looking back over my career and everything I've done, all I can think of is what I still want to do. As for sleep, I'll think about that when I retire.

ACKNOWLEDGMENTS

WRITING THIS BOOK has shown me how blessed I've been in life. I have so many people to thank that I am afraid to start, for I'm sure to leave someone out. But I must name a few people who made my career and this book possible.

I would like to thank God; my wife and kids; my parents; my brothers; my mother-in-law for dealing with me and letting me sweep her daughter away; my father-in-law, whom I'm sure I would have loved had I been fortunate enough to meet him while he was still with us; my grandmothers, Leonor Diaz and Esparanza Gutierrez; my uncle Rey Misterio; Konnan; all my trainers; Felipe Castellanos; AAA, and especially Antonio Peña, God rest his soul; Octagon; Emilia Escalera; Arturo Morales; WWE and the McMahon family; ECW; Paul Heyman; Shamu II; Damián 666; Psicosis; Mad One; Pat Patterson; WWE Universe; my uncle and one my biggest fans, Ampelio Rubio; all my fans around the world; and last but not least, all my Latino people.

I would also like to take a moment to remember all my fallen friends and family members, who are now resting in heaven, especially Eddie Guerrero, Love Machine, Wild Pegasus, Antonio Peña, my brother-in-law Teto Contreras, and my father-in-law, Adalberto Contreras.

My coauthor and I would also like to thank editor Margaret Clark and Simon & Schuster; my copyeditor, Bob Castillo; and designer Richard Oriolo. And thanks, Jim, for taking the heat without burning up.

I hope that I have remembered things correctly and not left too many people out. So much has happened so quickly that names and faces, events and places, have occasionally jumbled together. I apologize for any omissions and confusions—I'll straighten them out when I write the book about the second half of my career—in another twenty or thirty years!